LIVES ON THE LINE

LIVES ON THE LINE

The Testimony of Contemporary
Latin American Authors

Edited and with an Introduction by
DORIS MEYER

UNIVERSITY OF CALIFORNIA PRESS
Berkeley   Los Angeles   London

University of California Press
Berkeley and Los Angeles, California

University of California Press, Ltd.
London, England

Copyright © 1988 by The Regents of the University of California

Library of Congress Cataloging in Publication Data

Lives on the line.

    Bibliography: p.
    1. Latin American literature—20th century—History
and criticism. 2. Literature and society—Latin
America. 3. Authors, Latin American—Biography.
I. Meyer, Doris
PQ7081.A1L58   1988   860'.9'98   87–25522
ISBN 0–520–06002–4   (alk. paper)

Printed in the United States of America

1   2   3   4   5   6   7   8   9

CONTENTS

ACKNOWLEDGMENTS

Excerpt from "Autobiographical Essay" from *The Aleph and Other Stories (1933–1969)*, by Jorge Luis Borges, edited and translated by Norman Thomas di Giovanni in collaboration with the author. English translations copyright © 1968, 1969, 1970 by Emecé Editores, S.A., and Norman Thomas di Giovanni; copyright © 1970 by Jorge Luis Borges, Adolfo Bioy-Casares and Norman Thomas di Giovanni. Reprinted by permission of the publisher, E. P. Dutton, a division of NAL Penguin Inc.

"Literature and Political Awareness in Latin America," from *Literatura y conciencia política en América Latina* by Alejo Carpentier. Copyright © 1969 by Alejo Carpentier. Translated by José Piedra and published by permission of the estate of Alejo Carpentier and Harold Matson Company.

"Woman's Past and Present" from *Testimonios*, 7a serie (1962–1967) by Victoria Ocampo. Copyright © 1967 by Editorial Sur, S.A. Translated by Doris Meyer and published by permission of Editorial Sur, S.A. English translation copyright © 1986 by Doris Meyer.

Excerpt from *Memoirs* by Pablo Neruda, translated by Hardie St. Martin. English translation copyright © 1976, 1977 by Farrar, Straus and Giroux, Inc. Reprinted by permission of Farrar, Straus and Giroux, Inc.

"Questions and Realities" from *Latinoamérica y otros ensayos* by Miguel Angel Asturias, published in 1968 by Guadiana de Publicaciones, Madrid. Translated by Doris Meyer. English translation copyright © 1986 by Doris Meyer.

Excerpts from *The Foreign Legion* by Clarice Lispector, translated by Giovanni Pontiero. Translation copyright © 1986 by Giovanni Pontiero. Reprinted by permission of Giovanni Pontiero and Carcanet Press Ltd.

"Letter to Roberto Fernández Retamar," by Julio Cortázar, published in *Casa de las Américas* 45 (Sept.–Dic. 1967). Translated by Jo Anne Engelbert. Copyright Julio Cortázar and heirs of Julio Cortázar. Published by permission of Carmen Balcells Agencia, S.A.

"Early Writings" from *Mujer que sabe latín . . .* by Rosario Castellanos. Copyright © 1973 by SepSetentas. Translated by Maureen Ahern.

"English Profanities" from *O* by Guillermo Cabrera Infante, copyright © 1975 by Guillermo Cabrera Infante. Translated by Peggy Boyers and published by permission of the author.

"Central and Eccentric Writing" by Carlos Fuentes. Copyright © 1974 by Carlos Fuentes. Reprinted by permission of Brandt & Brandt Literary Agents, Inc.

"Social Commitment and the Latin American Writer" by Mario Vargas Llosa. Copyright © 1978 by the University of Oklahoma (*World Literature Today*). Reprinted by permission of the University of Oklahoma.

"And Here's to You, Jesusa" by Elena Poniatowska, published in *Vuelta* 24 (Nov. 1978). Translated by Gregory Kolovakos and Ronald Christ and published by permission of Elena Poniatowska. English translation copyright © 1987 by Gregory Kolovakos and Ronald Christ.

"Words of Greeting" from *Prosa de prisa (1929–1972)*, tomo III, by Nicolás Guillén, published in 1976 by Editorial Arte y Literatura, La Habana. Translated by Cynthia Ventura.

"The Telltale Mirror" by Octavio Paz in *One Earth, Four or Five Worlds*, translated by Helen Lane. Copyright © 1984 by Borsenverein des Deutchen; English translation copyright © 1985 by Harcourt Brace Jovanovich, Inc. Reprinted by permission of Harcourt Brace Jovanovich, Inc.

"The Myth of Creation" by Nélida Piñon. Translated by Giovanni Pontiero and published by permission of Nélida Piñon.

"The Solitude of Latin America" by Gabriel García Márquez, translated by Marina Castañeda. English translation copyright © 1982 by The Nobel Foundation, Stockholm, Sweden. Reprinted by permission of The Nobel Foundation.

"Ithaca: The Impossible Return" by José Donoso. Reprinted from *The City College Papers*, no. 18 (New York: City College, 1982).

"List of Errata" by Manuel Scorza, published in *El País* (Madrid), December 1983. Translated by Doris Meyer. English translation copyright © 1987 by Doris Meyer.

"Afterword" by Heberto Padilla in *Heroes Are Grazing in My Garden*, translated by Andrew Hurley. English translation copyright © 1984 by Farrar, Straus and Giroux, Inc. Reprinted by permission of Farrar, Straus and Giroux, Inc.

"The Writer's Kitchen" by Rosario Ferré. Translated by Diana L. Vélez and published by permission of Rosario Ferré.

"A Generation on the Move" by Antonio Skármeta, published in *Nueva Sociedad* 56–57 (Sept.–Dic. 1981)). Translated by Lori Carlson and published by permission of Antonio Skármeta.

"Closing Address" by Ernesto Cardenal, published in *Casa de las Américas* 129 (Nov.–Dic. 1981). Translated by Cynthia Ventura and published by permission of Ernesto Cardenal.

"The Truth of Invention" by Lygia Fagundes Telles, translated by Giovanni Pontiero and published by permission of Lygia Fagundes Telles.

"On Being a Writer in Peru and Other Places" by Isaac Goldemberg, published in *Hispamérica* 42 (1985). Translated by David Unger and published by permission of Isaac Goldemberg.

"The Spirits Were Willing" by Isabel Allende, published in *Discurso Literario* 2 (1984). Translated by Jo Anne Engelbert and published by permission of Isabel Allende.

"Poetry and the Temptations of Power" by Pablo Antonio Cuadra. Translated by Steven White and published by permission of Pablo Antonio Cuadra.

"Writing: A Metaphor for Exile" by Augusto Roa Bastos, published in *El País* (Madrid), July 1985. Translated by Helen Lane and published by permission of Augusto Roa Bastos.

"A Legacy of Poets and Cannibals: Literature Revives in Argentina" by Luisa Valenzuela and translated by Lori Carlson. Copyright © 1985 and reprinted by permission of Luisa Valenzuela.

"To Write is Not to Live" from *Confissões de um poeta* (Cap. VI) by Lêdo Ivo, translated by Giovanni Pontiero and published by permission of Lêdo Ivo.

"The Writer's Commitment" by Claribel Alegría. Published by permission of Claribel Alegría.

Permissions outstanding among the above selections have been requested. (Ed.)

INTRODUCTION

We can say without irony or lack of respect that in order to speak solely of Latin American literature today one has to create an environment similar to that of an operating room with specialists who only look at the patient lying on the stretcher and the patient can be called novel or short story or poem. In all honesty I can say that the few times I have been in those operating theaters of literary criticism I have gone out into the street with a burning desire to drink wine in a bar and to look at girls in the buses. And each day that passes it seems more logical and necessary to approach literature—whether we are writers or readers—as one approaches the most basic encounters of one's existence, such as love or death, knowing that they form an inseparable part of the whole, and that a book begins and ends much before and much after its first and last word.[1]

—JULIO CORTÁZAR

The integral relationship between life and literature in Latin America would seem to be an obvious fact. Yet, all too often, the well-intentioned reader—especially the non–Latin American reader—lacks the information to make this relationship meaningful. To read Latin American literature today without a sense of the reality lived by its writers is to miss what makes it most vibrant and stimulating. And also to miss what Carlos Fuentes has called "an urgent literature."[2]

Before the first word and after the last comes the writer's experience as a self in a vivid, personal circumstance. This is the informing substance of literature, the subjective drama of human life. It is made up of incidents large and small, which are transposed by the imagination into creative texts. What differentiates contemporary Latin American literature from other world literatures is the nature of the relationship between the writer and the environment: the context in which he or she prepares for a literary calling, the milieu (cultural, political, socioeconomic) in which

1

that vocation is exercised, and the awareness of self-as-writer in a given place and time. The purpose of this anthology is to capture a sense of this intimate personal experience of intellectual life in Latin America through the first-person testimony of writers themselves.

The essays presented here were written between 1960 and 1986, a period of exceptional richness in Latin American literature and of equally exceptional turbulence in Latin American daily life. This correlation is no coincidence. By their own testimony, Latin American writers, with few exceptions, confess to an engagement with reality that is *entrañable* or visceral, and it would seem that the vitality of their writing is connected to the urgency with which they perceive and experience that reality. According to Carlos Fuentes, the act of writing in Latin America is an act of faith:

> The paradox of writing on a continent where the majority is illiterate isn't so great; perhaps the writer knows he's writing to keep alive the connection with that prodigious cultural past that only rarely found correspondence in politics. Not to do it would be a way of admitting defeat, and one need only walk along the streets of Bogotá, Mexico City, or Lima to know that the quota of Latin American defeats is already filled.[3]

More than anywhere else in the so-called Third World, writers from Latin America have proven their willingness to put their lives on the line, both in the literary and the physical sense of the expression.

Today more than ever, the writer in Mexico, Central America, the Caribbean, and South America feels the critical nature of his role in society both as witness and social conscience—his "double responsibility," in the words of Uruguayan author Mario Benedetti, "to his art and to his surroundings."[4] This attitude is not new, as excellent studies of Latin American intellectual history by Martin Stabb and Jean Franco, among others, have shown: since the nineteenth century, the writer in Latin America has not only addressed the most vital concerns of his society but has also traditionally wielded enormous influence as a man of letters in a society where men of politics were mistrusted. (My emphasis on the masculine gender is intentional here; with rare exception, women were excluded from positions of intellectual or political authority in a male-dominated Latin American culture until very recently.)

Deeply embedded in this sense of responsibility, since the last century as well, has been a desire to define a Latin American identity, both on a universal and a regional (national) level. Roberto González Echevarría has called it "the main theme of Latin American thought," with its own "mythology of writing" in the essay as well as in the novel and poetry, that has yielded ambiguous results.[5] What is not ambiguous is the intensity with which writers from Sarmiento and da Cunha to Paz and Cabrera Infante have expressed their fascination with Latin American identity. Indeed it has been an obsession born of unique historical, geographical, and cultural circumstances.

Briefly summarized, from the sixteenth to the nineteenth century, Latin America's history was that of a colonized continent ruled by a highly institutionalized and oppressive foreign empire—more so in the case of Spain than of Portugal, and thus the difference in Brazil's path to independence. Three hundred years of such occupation led to a "colonized mentality" much harder to overcome than that of the English colonies in North America. Geographical remoteness—between Latin American cities and between the continent and Europe or North America—and the hostility of the terrain produced a feeling of solitude and isolation. In addition the *mestizaje*, or mixture of Indian, European, and African races, has enriched the culture of Latin America but has made it much harder to define its values. Many essayists have pondered the sociological and psychological complexities related to these factors, particularly after the Spanish-American War of 1898, the Mexican Revolution of 1910, and the First World War served to heighten disillusionment with Eurocentric positivism, a popular philosophy at the turn of the century in Latin America.

The influence of the North American writer, Waldo Frank, and the Spanish philosopher, José Ortega y Gasset, cannot be underestimated in the increase in Latin American essays, from the 1930s on, relating to the quest for identity. In different ways, both men were persuasive in their call for self-knowledge and authenticity as a means to achieving a true Latin American destiny. Ortega, in particular, focused on the importance of individual experience in a given historical context—the interaction between self and circumstance as a basis for action. His example, interpreted on a nationally introspective level, spawned such works as Ezequiel Martínez Estrada's *X-ray of the Pampa* (1933), Gilberto Freyre's *Roots of Brazil* (1936), Octavio Paz' *The Labyrinth of Solitude* (1950), and Luis Cardozo y Aragón's *Guatemala, The Lines of Your Hand* (1955). Some of the most fertile mythology of Latin American culture was the legacy of these writers and their contemporaries to the younger generation of writers today. The problem of self and circumstance continues to feed the Latin American imagination with more urgency than ever before.

The period of the early 1960s to early 1970s (especially in reference to the novel) has come to be known as "the Boom in Latin American literature"—a popular expression that continues to resonate despite the efforts of some critics to silence it. Since most of the writers in this collection have been tagged as either pre-Boom, Boom, or post-Boom, the term's origins and significance are important. It was, without doubt, an explosive period in the history of literature in Latin America.

When the term was first used in 1966 in a Buenos Aires magazine, it was meant to highlight the success of the "new novel" in Latin America. The most remarkable aspect of this success was the international profile that certain authors and works had begun to achieve. In 1961, for example, Jorge Luis Borges (who had been publishing in Latin America for forty years prior to that) was awarded along with Samuel Beckett the prestigious Formentor Prize in Paris. The following year, Spain's Seix Barral Prize for the best novel written in Spanish went to Mario Vargas Llosa, the first Latin American recipient; thereafter, the prize was won by Latin Americans in all but two of the next seven years, making the names of Carlos Fuentes, Julio Cortázar, Gabriel García Márquez, and others, instant literary celebrities at home and abroad. In 1967, Guatemalan author Miguel Angel Asturias became the second Latin American (after Gabriela Mistral in 1945) to win the Nobel Prize for Literature, followed in 1971 by the Chilean poet Pablo Neruda. At the same time, García Márquez' *One Hundred Years of Solitude* (1967) was breaking international sales records for a Latin American work in translation.

Unquestionably, the quality of their writing justified the attention these authors received, but it is not the whole story. For the first time, a handful of Latin American writers were seen as commercially valuable and were treated as marketable commodities, with their own literary agents and publishing houses. Their works were publicized and reviewed on a scale never before accorded to Latin Americans, thus stimulating further book sales. True, this applied to less than a dozen authors— notably all male and all acquainted with one another, to the point that envious colleagues called them "the Mafia." Nonetheless, recognition from the literary elite in countries like Spain, France, and the United States—where Latin American literature had the reputation of being exotic and (since it was unknown) inferior—was a symbolic triumph for a continent of writers.

But the Boom was not just a literary phenomenon; political and economic developments gave it cohesion, and primary among them was the Cuban Revolution of 1959. More than the War of 1898 or even the Mexican Revolution, Fidel Castro's overthrow of the Batista dictatorship focused world attention on problems in Latin America and the forces in conflict there. It also raised the self-consciousness of Latin American intellectuals. Although divided in their reaction to a Marxist government in their midst, they were united in their awareness that Latin America was replacing Europe as a battleground for opposing political ideologies. In the early 1960s, many leftist writers supported the Castro regime, praising the Cuban ideal of social justice and condemning the autocratic heritage that had exploited Latin America since the Colonial period. A climate of free expression—despite known cases of government censorship—prevailed in Cuba in those years, following decades of repression. With the founding of the Casa de las Américas to promote Cuba's cultural relations with other countries in Latin America, Havana became a major center of intellectual exchange. The revolution seemed to engender a spirit of unity and optimism among many writers of the Boom generation who visited Cuba and took part in literary activities there.

After the invasion of Czechoslovakia in 1968, Castro aligned himself more closely with the Soviet Union. Communist ideology was more strictly enforced in Cuba, and the government increased its censorship of dissenting intellectuals, unequivocally reaffirming the orthodox view that art should serve the cause of the people's revolution. One incident, particularly explosive in its effect upon the Latin American intellectual community, involved the poet and journalist Heberto Padilla. Padilla had been a Castro supporter and foreign correspondent for the government newspaper, but he fell into disfavor for criticizing the regime. He was arrested, imprisoned, interrogated, and eventually forced to publicly retract his views and denounce his fellow writers (including his wife, Belkis Cuza Malé) in order to regain his freedom. This took place in 1971. That same year the Cuban Congress of Education and Culture officially defined the limits of tolerance of artistic freedom and excluded "pseudo-leftist bourgeois intellectuals" from taking part in the culture of the revolution.

The "Padilla affair" produced widespread disillusionment among Latin American writers who had openly or tacitly backed Castro. Jośe Donoso, in *The Boom in Spanish American Literature: A Personal History* (1972), suggests that the discord it engendered tolled the death knell of the Boom. Controversy about the role of literature in a revolution and the nature and extent of a writer's involvement had been brewing for years; between 1969 and 1971 the pages of the Uruguayan journal *Marcha* recorded an ideological debate between several prominent authors. Another blow to the Boom was dealt by the economic recession of the 1970s, which forced many publishing houses to close. Even more disruptive was the return of right-wing political regimes to intellectually active countries like Argentina, Brazil, Uruguay, and Chile. (The CIA's role in toppling Chilean president Salvador Allende confirmed the worst fears of many leftist writers who were also dismayed by Castro's persecution of Padilla.) The diaspora of artists and intellectuals began in earnest. As early as 1968, political intrusion put an end to the effective influence of *Mundo Nuevo*, a literary journal edited in Paris by the influential critic Emir Rodríguez Monegal. *Mundo Nuevo* had published Boom writers and brought their works to international attention. Its demise, and the general deterioration of the cultural atmosphere in Latin America in the early 1970s, signaled the advent of a new era of urgency in Latin American letters.

In 1972, Carlos Fuentes wrote the following in the journal *Triquarterly*:

> To write on Latin Ameria, from Latin America, for Latin America, to be a witness of Latin America in action or in language is now, will be more and more, a revolutionary fact. Our societies don't want witnesses. They don't want critics. And each writer, like each revolutionary, is in some way that: a man [*sic*] who sees, hears, imagines and says; a man who denies we live in the best of worlds.[6]

Male or female, the Latin American writer of the 1970s or 1980s knows both the history and reality of his society's institutional penchant for discouraging free speech or critical thinking of any kind. The Catholic Church, responsible for the spread of culture during the Colonial period, also cast a long Inquisitorial shadow across the Atlantic: it regulated the importation of books and set the tone for all future intellectual endeavors. Colonial censorship took many forms: from the burning of Mayan bark-paper "books," effectively silencing an entire indigenous culture, to the cloistering of women's minds, virtually denying female participation in the power structure. Overall, its effect was to limit the reading public to an educated few, whose literary taste was urbane and elitist; writers who weren't also statesmen or churchmen were suspect, or worse, ignored.

Over the centuries, the writer's situation has changed for the better. Yet it still remains a risky venture on many fronts. Less than twenty years ago, Mario Vargas Llosa of Peru—who, like many others, began his writing career as a journalist—observed that "a few have managed to conquer the hostility, the indifference, the scorn that exists in our countries toward literature, and they wrote, published and were even read. It is true that not all could be killed off by starvation, oblivion or ridicule. But these fortunates constituted the exception."[7] In Brazil, the situation was equally dismal, according to literary historian Afrânio Coutinho: "Brazilian literary people are scattered among heterogeneous activities or are prisoners of public administration, where everything conspires against the spirit."[8] In the face of chronic illiteracy, cultural isolation, and economic hardship so severe that even the populace who reads can rarely afford to buy books, Latin American writers have been quick to acknowledge the Quixotesque quality of trying to succeed in their profession—despite the success of the Boom. In the 1970s, in authoritarian countries, their very lives were in danger: many writers were imprisoned, tortured, and "disappeared" under regimes more brutal than the Catholic Inquisition. Violence from both the right and the left essentially fore-closed any possibility of a normal intellectual existence, and emigration to neighboring countries—to Europe or the United States—increased. For those remaining, internal exile and self-censorship could be even more damaging than voluntary or involuntary exodus.

And yet this very inhospitable climate has bred a contemporary writer—male and female—who is extraordinarily attached to his home-land, and far more inclined than his European or United States coun-terpart to discuss the writer's role in society. Whether living at home or in exile, he or she is more likely to acknowledge a basic expectation among the Latin American public: that the writer's vocation entails a moral imperative to speak out on issues of national concern—or when this is not feasible, to encode political dissent into the pages of "creative" literature. At times, the pressure to voice a commitment on the socio-political level is strongest from a writer's peers—generally those of Marx-ist persuasion. Authors who have chosen to avoid politics (rarely possible in the course of a Latin American life) have often been disparaged for their "aloofness" or "elitism." Jorge Luis Borges, whose life was com-pletely absorbed by the company of books, was one of those repeatedly criticized by leftists, some of whom suggested that by virtue of his pref-erence for European literature, he wasn't even Latin American. Nowa-days, such manifest xenophobia is the exception rather than the rule among Latin American intellectuals, who freely acknowledge their in-debtedness to American films and rock music as much as to Sartre or Kafka. But the xenophobic does represent a current of thought in Latin America, going back as far as the turn of the century when nationalists and universalists took sides against each other.

It is interesting to note that women authors have remained outside many of these literary–political debates until recent years, due in part to their marginalized status in both arenas. A woman's personal struggle to become a writer was often lonelier and fraught with more obstacles than a man's; her chances of being taken seriously as a professional, much smaller. Because of her gender experiences, she tended either to immerse herself in a private world of literature (Clarice Lispector and Victoria Ocampo, for example) with primarily male mentors (for lack of a female network of support), or she identified strongly with the oppressed (Ro-sario Castellanos and Elena Poniatowska) and devoted her works to their cause. Today, women authors are becoming more politically active and their works reflect a wider range of personal involvement.

Beyond the political sphere, the larger profile accorded women's writ-ing in Latin America has focused attention on another side of human experience and has thereby called into question certain assumptions about societal values in a historical context. Because women's voices were not heard publicly for several centuries, their role in private and public life remained obscured by patriarchal dominance, but today this is no longer the case. Women are writing about the problems of being female in Latin America, and their words have a healthy, subversive resonance. Old mythologies regarding male and female relationships are undergoing reevaluation, and many male authors have responded with new awareness on their part. As forgotten works by women authors are brought to light, the true picture of life in Latin America—both past and present—will emerge and force a *re*vision (in both senses of the word) of Latin American social and cultural history.

In the 1980s the Central American crisis has captured world attention in the way Cuba did twenty years earlier, stimulating a renewed cohesiveness among Latin American intellectuals. Most decry the Reagan administration's intervention in the regional affairs of Nicaragua, El Salvador, and Honduras. Even writers who have been skeptical or critical of Sandinista policies are calling for a Latin American solution to the conflict. At the same time, the reestablishment of elected democracies in southern-cone countries such as Argentina and Uruguay has brought a new and potentially disruptive intellectual crisis. Many expatriate writers are returning, or contemplating a return, to their homelands after years in exile. They are finding, however, that the process of *desexilio* (or "disexile"), as Mario Benedetti has named it, can be as traumatic as the original decision to flee repression;[9] the temptation toward reproach—on the part of those who left and those who stayed—must be tempered, says Benedetti, by an effort toward understanding.

Less apt to grasp at quick solutions, today's Latin American writers concentrate instead on asking questions fundamental to their continent's future. They are probing the implications of dependency and underdevelopment, and questioning the viability of inherited myths and cultural assumptions, including the notions of "modernity" and "progress." The very sense of "otherness" that brought despair to an earlier generation of Latin American writers is, in the words of Carlos Fuentes, what makes for "an eccentric culture"—indebted to the Mayan *Popul Vuh* as well as to the Judeo-Christian Bible—and thus potentially richer for its cultural *mestizaje*.

An awareness of cultural vitality is at the heart of many of the essays in this collection, despite what the authors may feel about the history or politics of their various countries. And the essence of that vitality is language itself, the writer's protean instrument, which he or she shares with a culture. Latin American writers are affirming a plurality of cultures within a larger sense of being "Latin American": Pablo Neruda's love affair with Spanish ("It's a fine language we inherited from the fierce conquistadors"); Augusto Roa Bastos's effort to ransom the Paraguayan-Guaraní "ancestral voice" ("A language without writing that in another time contained within itself the very essence of the soul-word"); and Nélida Piñon's travels through "the archipelagos of language"—before she could arrive at the conviction that "[g]uided by language and its historical process, the Brazilian writer must learn that mythologies and intrigues were created in such abundance in this country that they can never be exhausted or diminished." For despite similarities in historical background, what defines the Latin American identity is not one but many ways of being rooted in Latin American reality. And each writer, with each book, has the possibility of writing that identity based on his or her own experience or "reading" of it, through the medium of language.

This anthology was assembled to give both the general and academic reader an idea of the variety of personal experiences and perspectives among Latin American writers. It is meant to be a provocative complement to the study and enjoyment of contemporary Latin American fiction, drama, and poetry—too often read in isolation from the vital contexts in which they were created. I hope that it will lead readers familiar only with the most famous Boom authors to explore the works of other writers as well. All of the authors represented here have been published in English, even if only once or twice, and more translations are forthcoming. But the insidious cycle of supply and demand depends upon a knowledgeable readership, and Latin American authors still suffer the reputation of being marketing liabilities because they aren't well enough known among English-speaking readers.

Several guiding considerations were applied to selecting the essays in this volume: First, the date of composition was to be 1960 or later. Second, only essays informed by a certain quality of testimony were sought. And finally, considered together, it is hoped the works collected here reflect the plurality of Latin American cultural experience among authors of recognized quality. Naturally, many important voices had to be left out; the choice was not easy, given the wealth of testimony available. With the exception of a few excerpts from longer works, they are all essays and, as such, they resist facile generic description. No attempt was made to achieve uniformity of style or unity of purpose in this collection; some essays were originally speeches, others letters, and each one was conceived with different intentions and a different audience in mind. The flexibility of the essay itself—its ability to let the author mold it to suit the needs of the moment—makes it the obvious choice for autobiographical reflections. Whatever the form of discourse or rhetorical devices, which cannot be studied here, my primary concern has been the nature of the subjective content and its authenticity as testimony.

Thirty authors from twelve countries are included in this anthology; the more literarily active countries, such as Argentina, Mexico, Cuba, Brazil, and Chile, are represented by four authors each. The arrangement of essays is based as much on chronology of events described as on date of composition, with a balance of approaches and geography also taken into consideration. Many pieces are published here for the first time in English; several were written and translated at my request especially for this volume.

Preceding each selection, I have supplied a bio-bibliographic note about the author with relevant information regarding the essay to follow. In these notes I have adopted the following system of citing Latin American literary titles and their English translations: after an original title and its date of publication, I place in brackets the italicized title of a published translation and its date—for example, *El libro de arena*, 1975 [*The Book of Sand*, 1977]; *or* I put in quotations my own translation of a title as yet unavailable in English—for example, *Latinoamérica y otros ensayos*, 1968 ["Latin America and other Essays"].

This book was begun during a 1984–1985 sabbatical from Brooklyn College, where I taught for eighteen years, and was completed during my first year on the faculty of Connecticut College in New London. Most of the research was conducted at Yale University's Sterling Library, which has a superb collection of Latin American journals.

An anthology of this magnitude would be a formidable task without the generous collaboration of authors (or their representatives), translators, colleagues to whom I turned for advice, and the editorial staff of the University of California Press. In this case, it was an experience in international cooperation which was extremely gratifying.

DORIS MEYER
Essex, Connecticut
January 1987

NOTES

1. Julio Cortázar, "Reality and Literature in Latin America," (1980), ed. and trans. Gabriella de Beer and Raquel Chang-Rodríguez (New York: The Jacob C. Saposnekow Memorial Lectures, City College, April 1982), p. 13.
2. Carlos Fuentes, "Una literatura urgente," in *Latin American Fiction Today: A Symposium*, ed. Rose S. Minc (Takoma Park, Md.: Hispamérica, 1980), p. 9. [Translation mine]
3. Ibid., p. 13.
4. Mario Benedetti, "Situación del escritor en América Latina," *Casa de las Américas* 45 (nov.–dic. 1967): 34. [Translation mine]

5. Roberto González Echevarría, *The Voice of the Masters: Writing and Authority in Modern Latin American Literature* (Austin: University of Texas Press, 1985), p. 13.
6. Carlos Fuentes, "The Enemy: Words," trans. Suzanne Jill Levine, *Triquarterly* 23/24 (Winter–Spring 1972): 120.
7. Mario Vargas Llosa, "Fate and Mission of the Writer in Latin America," trans. Maureen Ahern, *Haravec* (Lima) 4 (Dec. 1967): 56–57.
8. Afrânio Coutinho, *An Introduction to Literature in Brazil* (New York: Columbia University Press, 1969), p. 36.
9. Mario Benedetti, *El desexilio y otras conjeturas* (Madrid: Ediciones El País, 1985), pp. 39–42.

Jorge Luis Borges
[1899–1986]

GENERALLY ACKNOWLEDGED as the most influential and intellectually gifted Latin American writer of his time, Jorge Luis Borges was born in Buenos Aires, of English, Spanish, Portuguese, and Jewish heritage. Both sides of his family had lived in Argentina for many generations, however, and Borges—the quintessential man of letters—was deeply attached to his native soil. He was brought up fluent in English and Spanish; in fact, English was the language of the first books he read in his father's large library, including a translation of Cervantes' *Don Quijote*, along with Stevenson, Dickens, Twain, Poe, and both Lane and Burton's editions of *One Thousand and One Arabian Nights*. "Georgie," as his family called him, was educated at home by an English governess. He understood at an early age that his father's failed vocation as a writer (due to inherited blindness that advanced with age) would become his own. (Borges would also suffer eventually from the same progressive blindness.)

Traveling in Europe when World War I erupted, Borges and his family took up residence in Switzerland where he completed secondary school. There Borges learned French and Latin and taught himself German, thus expanding his literary horizons to include works by Schopenhauer and Nietzsche, two major influences on his thinking. From 1919 to 1921, he traveled in Spain where he met avant-garde writers of the period and wrote his first poetry and prose.

Back in Buenos Aires, Borges began to publish his own volumes of poetry and essays and to contribute to literary journals,

13

among them Victoria Ocampo's *Sur* for which he did stories, reviews, and translations. In 1937—as the accompanying essay relates—he began working in the municipal library, and he also started writing his famous metaphysical stories, the first collections of which were entitled *El jardín de los senderos que se bifurcan*, 1941, republished with additional stories as *Ficciones*, 1944 [*Ficciones*, 1962]; and *El Aleph*, 1949 [*The Aleph and Other Stories*, 1970].

In the course of a long and prolific literary life, Jorge Luis Borges continued to write poetry, short stories, and essays, but he was identified primarily with the ingenious tales full of literary allusions and philosophical speculations that dazzled readers all over the world. Others of his publications include *Otras inquisiciones*, 1952 [*Other Inquisitions*, 1964]; *El hacedor*, 1960 [*Dreamtigers*, 1964]; *El informe de Brodie*, 1970 [*Dr. Brodie's Report*, 1971]; and *El libro de arena*, 1975 [*The Book of Sand*, 1977]. Borges traveled frequently to teach classes and give lectures in the United States and Europe during the last decades of his life. He died at the age of eighty-six in Geneva, Switzerland.

The following is an excerpt from the longer "Autobiographical Essay," first published as a profile in *The New Yorker* on September 19, 1970, and later included in *The Aleph and Other Stories*. Borges was not given to writing memoirs, and thus this is one of the rare first-person testimonies he has left of his life.

MATURITY

(from *Autobiographical Essay*)

Jorge Luis Borges
Translated with Norman Thomas di Giovanni

In the course of a lifetime devoted chiefly to books, I have read but few novels, and, in most cases, only a sense of duty has enabled me to find my way to their last page. At the same time, I have always been a reader and rereader of short stories. Stevenson, Kipling, James, Conrad, Poe, Chesterton, the tales of Lane's *Arabian Nights*, and certain stories by Hawthorne have been habits of mine since I can remember. The feeling that great novels like *Don Quixote* and *Huckleberry Finn* are virtually shapeless served to reinforce my taste for the short-story form, whose indispensable elements are economy and a clearly stated beginning, middle, and end. As a writer, however, I thought for years that the short story was beyond my powers, and it was only after a long and roundabout series of timid experiments in narration that I sat down to write real stories.

It took me some six years, from 1927 to 1933, to go from that all too self-conscious sketch "Hombres pelearon" to my first outright short story, "Hombre de la esquina rosada" ("Streetcorner Man"). A friend of mine, don Nicolás Paredes, a former political boss and professional gambler of the Northside, had died, and I wanted to record something of his voice, his anecdotes, and his particular way of telling them. I slaved over my every page, sounding out each sentence and striving to phrase it in his exact tones. We were living out in Adrogué at the time and, because I knew my mother would heartily disapprove of the subject matter, I composed in secret over a period of several months. Originally titled "Hombres de las orillas" ("Men from the Edge of Town"), the story appeared in the Saturday supplement, which I was editing, of a yellow-press daily called *Crítica*. But out of shyness, and perhaps a feeling that the story was a bit beneath me, I signed it with a pen name—the name of one of my great-great-grandfathers, Francisco Bustos. Although the story became popular to the point of embarrassment (today, I only find it stagy and mannered and the characters bogus), I never regarded it as a starting point. It simply stands there as a kind of freak.

The real beginning of my career as a story writer starts with the series of sketches entitled *Historia universal de la infamia* (*A Universal History of Infamy*), which I contributed to the columns of *Crítica* in 1933 and 1934. The irony of this is that "Streetcorner Man" really was a story but that these sketches and several of the fictional pieces which followed them, and which very slowly led me to legitimate stories, were in the nature of hoaxes and pseudo-essays. In my *Universal History*, I did not want to repeat what Marcel Schwob had done in his *Imaginary Lives*. He had invented biographies of real men about whom little or nothing is recorded. I, instead, read up on the lives of known persons and then deliberately varied and distorted them according to my own whims. For example, after reading Herbert Asbury's *The Gangs of New York*, I set down my free version of Monk Eastman, the Jewish gunman, in flagrant contradiction of my chosen authority. I did the same for Billy the Kid, for John Murrel (whom I rechristened Lazarus Morell), for the Veiled Prophet of Khorassan, for the Tichborne Claimant, and for several others. I never thought of book publication. The pieces were meant for popular consumption in *Crítica* and were pointedly picturesque. I suppose now the secret value of those sketches—apart from the sheer pleasure the writing gave me—lay in the fact that they were narrative exercises. Since the general plots or circumstances were all given me, I had only to embroider sets of vivid variations.

My next story, "The Approach to al-Mu'tasim," written in 1935, is both a hoax *and* a pseudo-essay. It purports to be a review of a book published originally in Bombay three years earlier. I endowed its fake second edition with a real publisher, Victor Gollancz, and a preface by a real writer, Dorothy L. Sayers. But the author and the book are entirely my own invention. I gave the plot and details of some chapters—borrowing from Kipling and working in the twelfth-century Persian mystic Farid ud-Din Attar—and then carefully pointed out its shortcomings. The story appeared the next year in a volume of my essays, *Historia de la eternidad* (*A History of Eternity*), buried at the back of the book together with an article on the "Art of Insult." Those who read "The Approach to al-Mu'tasim" took it at face value, and one of my friends even ordered a copy from London. It was not until 1942 that I openly published it as a short story in my first story collection, *El jardín de senderos que se bifurcan* (*The Garden of Branching Paths*). Perhaps I have been unfair to this story; it now seems to me to foreshadow and even to set the pattern for those tales that were somehow awaiting me, and upon which my reputation as a storyteller was to be based.

Along about 1937, I took my first regular full-time job. I had previously worked at small editing tasks. There was the *Crítica* supplement, which was a heavily and even gaudily illustrated entertainment sheet. There was *El Hogar*, a popular society weekly, to which, twice a month, I contributed a couple of literary pages on foreign books and authors. I had also written newsreel texts and had been editor of a pseudo-scientific magazine called *Urbe*, which was really a promotional organ of a privately owned Buenos Aires subway system. These had all been small-paying jobs, and I was long past the age when I should have begun contributing to our household upkeep. Now, through friends I was given a very minor position as First Assistant in the Miguel Cané branch of the Municipal Library, out in a drab and dreary part of town to the southwest. While there were Second and Third Assistants below me, there were also a Director and First, Second, and Third Officials above me. I was paid two hundred and ten pesos a month and later went up to two hundred and forty. These were sums roughly equivalent to seventy or eighty American dollars.

At the library, we did very little work. There were some fifty of us doing what fifteen could easily have done. My particular job, shared, with fifteen or twenty colleagues, was classifying and cataloguing the library's holdings, which until that time were uncatalogued. The collection, however, was so small that we knew where to find the books without the system, so the system, though laboriously carried out, was never needed or used. The first day, I worked honestly. On the next, some of my fellows took me aside to say that I couldn't do this sort of thing because it showed them up. "Besides," they argued, "as this cataloguing has been planned to give us some semblance of work, you'll put us out of our jobs." I told them I had classified four hundred titles instead of their one hundred. "Well, if you keep that up," they said, "the boss will be angry and won't know what to do with us." For the sake of realism, I was told that from then on I should do eighty-three books one day, ninety another, and one hundred and four the third.

I stuck out the library for about nine years. They were nine years of solid unhappiness. At work, the other men were interested in nothing but horse racing, soccer matches, and smutty stories. Once, a woman, one of the readers, was raped on her way to the ladies' room. Everybody said such things were bound to happen, since the men's and ladies' rooms were adjoining. One day, two rather posh and well-meaning friends—society ladies—came to see me at work. They phoned me a day or two later to say, "You may think it amusing to work in a place like that, but promise us you will find at least a nine-hundred-peso job before the month is out." I gave them my word that I would. Ironically, at the time I was a fairly well-known writer—except at the library. I remember a fellow-employee's once noting in an encyclopedia the name of a certain Jorge Luis Borges—a fact that set him wondering at the coincidence of our identical names and birth dates. Now and then during these years, we municipal workers were rewarded with gifts of a two-pound package of maté to take home. Sometimes in the evening, as I walked the ten blocks to the tramline, my eyes would be filled with tears. These small gifts from above always underlined my menial and dismal existence.

A couple of hours each day, riding back and forth on the tram, I made my way through *The Divine Comedy*, helped as far as "Purgatory" by John Aitken Carlyle's prose translation and then ascending the rest of the way on my own. I would do all my library work in the first hour and then steal away to the basement and pass the other five hours in reading or writing. I remember in this way rereading the six volumes of Gibbon's *Decline and Fall* and the many volumes of Vicente Fidel López' *History of the Argentine Republic*. I read Léon Bloy, Claudel, Groussac, and Bernard Shaw. On holidays, I translated Faulkner and Virginia Woolf. At some point, I was moved up to the dizzying height of Third Official. One morning, my mother rang me up and I asked for leave to go home, arriving just in time to see my father die. He had undergone a long agony and was very impatient for his death.

It was on Christmas Eve of 1938—the same year my father died— that I had a severe accident. I was running up a stairway and suddenly felt something brush my scalp. I had grazed a freshly painted open casement window. In spite of first-aid treatment, the wound became poisoned, and for a period of a week or so I lay sleepless every night and had hallucinations and high fever. One evening, I lost the power of speech and had to be rushed to the hospital for an immediate operation. Septicemia had set in, and for a month I hovered, all unknowingly, between life and death. (Much later, I was to write about this in my story "The South.") When I began to recover, I feared for my mental integrity. I remember that my mother wanted to read to me from a book I had just ordered, C. S. Lewis' *Out of the Silent Planet*, but for two or three nights I kept putting her off. At last, she prevailed, and after hearing a page or two I fell to crying. My mother asked me why the tears. "I'm crying because I understand," I said. A bit later, I wondered whether I could ever write again. I had previously written quite a few poems and dozens of short reviews. I thought that if I tried to write a review now and failed, I'd be all through intellectually but that if I tried something I had never really done before and failed at that it wouldn't be so bad and might even prepare me for the final revelation. I decided I would try to write a story. The result was "Pierre Menard, Author of *Don Quixote*."

"Pierre Menard," like its forerunner "The Approach to al-Mu'tasim," was still a halfway house between the essay and the true tale. But the achievement spurred me on. I next tried something more ambitious— "Tlön, Uqbar, Orbis Tertius," about the discovery of a new world that finally replaces our present world. Both were published in Victoria Ocampo's magazine *Sur*. I kept up my writing at the library. Though my colleagues thought of me as a traitor for not sharing their boisterous fun, I went on with work of my own in the basement or, when the weather was warm, up on the flat roof. My Kafkian story "The Library of Babel" was meant as a nightmare version or magnification of that municipal library, and certain details in the text have no particular meaning. The numbers of books and shelves that I recorded in the story were literally what I had at my elbow. Clever critics have worried over those ciphers, and generously endowed them with mystic significance. "The Lottery in Babylon," "Death and the Compass," and "The Circular Ruins" were also written, in whole or part, while I played truant. These tales and others were to become *The Garden of Branching Paths*, a book expanded and retitled *Ficciones* in 1944. *Ficciones* and *El Aleph* (1949 and 1952), my second story collection, are, I suppose, my two major books.

In 1946, a president whose name I do not want to remember came into power. One day soon after, I was honored with the news that I had been "promoted" out of the library to the inspectorship of poultry and rabbits in the public markets. I went to the City Hall to find out what it was all about. "Look here," I said. "It's rather strange that among so many others at the library I should be singled out as worthy of this new position." "Well," the clerk answered, "you were on the side of the Allies—what do you expect?" His statement was unanswerable; the next day, I sent in my resignation. My friends rallied round me at once and offered me a public dinner. I prepared a speech for the occasion but, knowing I was too shy to read it myself, I asked my friend Pedro Henríquez Ureña to read it for me.

I was now out of a job. Several months before, an old English lady had read my tea leaves and had foretold that I was soon to travel, to lecture, and to make vast sums of money thereby. When I told my mother about it, we both laughed, for public speaking was far beyond me. At this juncture, a friend came to the rescue, and I was made a teacher of English literature at the Asociación Argentina de Cultura Inglesa. I was also asked at the same time to lecture on classic American literature at the Colegio Libre de Estudios Superiores. Since this pair of offers was made three months before classes opened, I accepted, feeling quite safe. As the time grew near, however, I grew sicker and sicker. My series of nine lectures was to be on Hawthorne, Poe, Thoreau, Emerson, Melville, Whitman, Twain, Henry James, and Veblen. I wrote the first one down. But I had no time to write out the second one. Besides, thinking of the first lecture as Doomsday, I felt that only eternity could come after. The first one went off well enough—miraculously. Two nights before the second lecture, I took my mother for a long walk around Adrogué and had her time me as I rehearsed my talk. She said she thought it was overlong. "In that case," I said, "I'm safe." My fear had been of running dry. So, at forty-seven, I found a new and exciting life opening up for me. I traveled up and down Argentina and Uruguay, lecturing on Swedenborg, Blake, the Persian and Chinese mystics, Buddhism, gauchesco poetry, Martin Buber, the Kabbalah, the Arabian Nights, T. E. Lawrence, medieval Germanic poetry, the Icelandic sagas, Heine, Dante, Expressionism, and Cervantes. I went from town to town, staying overnight in hotels I'd never see again. Sometimes my mother or a friend accompanied me. Not only did I end up making far more money than at the library but I enjoyed the work and felt that it justified me.

ALEJO CARPENTIER
[1904–1980]

ALEJO CARPENTIER was born in Havana of French-Cuban ancestry. As a child he traveled to France, and he returned there as a young musicologist and writer involved in the Cuban avant-garde. His opposition to the regime of Cuban dictator Gerardo Machado (1925–1933) cost him a period of imprisonment and eventual self-exile to Paris in 1928. There, influenced by the surrealist movement, he published his first book, a collection of poems. Carpentier traveled extensively in Europe, attending antifascist literary conferences in the 1930s, and in 1933 he published his first novel *Ecué-Yamba-O* ["Lord, Praised Be Thou"] in Paris. In this ground-breaking work, Carpentier explored black identity in Afro-Cuban culture.

In 1939 he returned to Cuba and worked for a Havana radio station and later as a professor of music history at the National Conservatory. His second novel, *El reino de este mundo*, 1949 [*The Kingdom of This World*, 1957], was inspired by a 1943 trip to Haiti. Carpentier's best-known novel, *Los pasos perdidos*, 1953 [*The Lost Steps*, 1956], is based on his experiences in Venezuela where he lived in self-exile from 1945 until Fidel Castro's revolutionary movement overthrew the Batista regime in 1959.

Returning again to Cuba, Carpentier was named director of the state publishing house in 1960, and in 1966 he was appointed Cuban cultural attaché in Paris where he made his home until his death.

Carpentier's other major works include stories and novels such as *Guerra del tiempo*, 1958 [*The War of Time*, 1970]; *El siglo de las luces*, 1962 [*Explosion in a Cathedral*, 1963]; *El recurso del método*, 1974 [*Reasons of State*, 1976]; in addition to numerous stories, essays, and even musical compositions. His erudition as a writer may have been responsible for his having never acquired as wide a readership as other Boom contemporaries. Nevertheless, Carpentier's work has been hailed by critics for its portrayal of themes of social struggle and cultural origins in a broad context of Caribbean history.

Among his many essays, the one presented here—published in *Tientos y diferencias*, 1967 ["Preludes and Differences"] and translated here for the first time—was originally a paper delivered at the First Congress of Cuban Writers and Artists in the summer of 1961, a few months after the Bay of Pigs invasion. In consonance with Castro's speeches of the same time declaring (". . . within the Revolution, everything; against the Revolution, nothing . . ."), it reveals a more radicalized Carpentier than in his earlier years. Particularly notable as an effort to trace the history of politically committed literature in Latin America during his lifetime, Carpentier's essay criticizes the earlier, idealistic "Our America" generation and accuses them (and his own earlier self) of well-intentioned escapism and being oblivious to the economic and political realities of the time. Though on other occasions he could appear ambiguous on the issue of committed literature, Carpentier remained to the end a staunch supporter of the Cuban Revolution.

LITERATURE AND POLITICAL AWARENESS IN LATIN AMERICA

Alejo Carpentier
Translated by José Piedra

In the nineteenth century, visual and musical artists from our continent hardly communicated with one another—not even to discuss esthetic principles—simply because there were so few painters and the few musicians (such as Carlos Gómez and Teresa Carreño) who overcame the generalized amateur status as interpreters or composers, entrusted the judgment of their artistry to the European public. Until yesterday our public did not hesitate to treat as geniuses any composers of *joropos* [Venezuelan dance], songs or waltzes for the dancing hall. . . . Writers, however, experienced a very different situation. Since the turn of the nineteenth century, they exhibited their imperious need to search each other out, to find each other, to feel each others' pulse from one end of the continent to the other—naturally I am referring to a continent with its northernmost frontiers in Mexico. Just as humanists from the high Middle Ages knew each other, exchanging their manuscripts and treatises beyond the barriers of feudal states and wilderness, knowing where a Latin scholar or an expert on Horace lived surrounded by illiterate crowds, our writers barely exhibited a national awareness—that is, a sense of creole identity or even a creole will—preferring an exchange of messages, to work in colloquia, their union foretold by their sharing of basic premises. Sarmiento was well aware, on his visit to Havana, where to find Antonio Bachiller y Morales, just as José Martí knew, upon arriving in Caracas, where to meet Cecilio Acosta.

Furthermore, we cannot help but glance with nostalgia at the solidarity of a Latin American humanism, which, through years rich with dictators, encumbered with barbaric caudillos and filled with military coups, generated productive and generous exchanges among men of worth born in neighboring lands of the continent and charged with the highest cultural responsibilities. Let us remember Francisco Javier Yánes, from Camagüey, Cuba, president of the Supreme Court in Caracas, who, in 1811, in full awareness of the situation of the Americas, fought a memorable battle against racial prejudice with words which could have been borrowed a century later by José Carlos Mariátegui. Let us remember the Cuban Heredia, judge of the Supreme Court in Mexico City, and the other Cuban, Pedro de Santacilla, who was Benito Juárez's secretary. Let us remember Andrés Bello, chancellor of the University of Santiago de Chile, and the Argentinian Domingo Sarmiento, director of the Teachers' College in Chile, who, by the way, embarked on a dispute with Bello, which is, in my opinion, the first important debate about issues of transcendental importance to the Latin American writer. Now as we set out to address in this congress similar issues of the writers' craft, we are compelled to evoke the passionate and fascinating 1842 debate in the pages of the Chilean newspapers *Semanario Literario* and the *Mercurio*, where Bello defended the aristocratic concept of art—an overwhelming *respect for form*, and, in addition, the pursuit of purity of language—while Sarmiento spoke to younger writers: "Write about what touches you, what pleases you; it will be good at heart, even though the form might be incorrect. Your work will look like no one else's, and, good or bad, it will be yours and no one can take that away."

All these men knew each other and, even though they sometimes argued in public, they still respected each other. And they respected each other because they were all politically committed. They joined against Spain or, once free from Spain, they overcame their immediate contingencies and shared the same ideas. A great common goal brought together the pioneer Pablo de Olavide, Peruvian friend of Voltaire, and Sarmiento, Juárez and Martí. Among contemporaries everyone knew what company the others kept, and thus could judge who their friends were—validating the saying "one judges a person by the company he keeps." They were all political beings. And if one of them had suffered some political weakness, doubt, hesitation, in the manicheistic distinction between *good* and *evil*—barbarity and civilization, the progressive and the reactionary—his spiritual brothers would have turned their backs on him, after chastizing him. In nineteenth-century Latin America no one could have made today's obsessive and false pronouncement, turned into a cliché by sheer abuse: "We don't know each other." Everyone knew each other then.

The onset of the twentieth century—announced before the turn of the century by changes in trends and techniques—brings forth a phenomenon worth examining. A peculiar lack of morality installs itself in the world of Latin American letters—thankfully preserving for our benefit a good list of authors who rejected contamination. Some of the best poets and prose writers of that time suffered from what we might refer to as the *Oblomov syndrome*, recalling the famous Goncharov novel. Many recognized the lamentable state of the Latin American countries; all recognized that something should be done to remedy this. But this remained nothing more than a vague hope for a messianic occurrence, an apocalyptical event whose absence justified inaction across the board. Like Goncharov's character, such intellectuals are, at heart, full of good intentions; but their repugnance of all systematic activity, of all compromising pronouncements, makes them gaze motionless at the worst injustices or accept, with incredible irresponsibility, any offerings or patronage. Let us reread Rubén Darío's *Memorias*. It is amazing to realize that the great poet accepted gifts from a Central American tyrant, addressing him as his "benefactor," while he reminded those who could blame him for his weakness, that he, Darío, "is not meant to be a judge of history in this world." In San Salvador, he happily accepted the directorship of a newspaper granted by a man who—according to Darío's own testimonial—"was as headstrong and tyrannical as any Central American president." He lived side by side with idiotic and reactionary politicians, whoring generals, whom he found agreeable and even interesting. And, when he praised the city of San José in Costa Rica, he pointed out, as a significant merit, the fact that "its society was among the most Europeanist and prone to the Anglo-Americanist mold. . . ." But Darío's irresponsible behavior is not exceptional. Another great Latin American poet, Porfirio Barba-Jacob (who promenaded considerably around Havana), whose profession it was to offer his "skills of a combative journalist" (and he was brilliant and efficient) to whomever would pay generously for his services, did not worry about ascertaining the legitimacy or honor of the causes being defended. And let us not forget Santos Chocano, who would serve as minister for Pancho Villa as well as counsel to the dictator Estrada Cabrera—Miguel Angel Asturias' model for his *El señor presidente*. Others accepted diplomatic posts, government employment, directorships of magazines and newspapers, without pausing to consider whether or not they were selling their souls to the devil—and we already know from Thomas Mann that it is not necessary to wield a feather pen dipped in one's own blood to sign one's soul away to the devil. It is enough to expose oneself merrily to certain kinds of contamination.

No one should gather that we are attempting to recount the lamentable flaws of the past in order to set ourselves up as posthumous judges of a past generation. The quoted events should only serve as bases for establishing a contrast. Because, even though the *Oblomov syndrome* of the turn-of-the-century generation alienated them from true political commitment, its members were, perhaps, the most seemingly concerned about the future of America as a continent. Let us dismiss the roar of the lyrical puma Santos Chocano, who boasted he "owned the south," while Walt Whitman "owned the north" òf the New Continent. Let us dismiss the indubitable Latin American eloquence and poetics of someone like Porfirio Barba-Jacob. Let us evoke, instead, only the fierce diatribe Rubén Darío hurled at Teddy Roosevelt's face, accompanied by the following rhetorical question: "Are we to be thrown to the fierce barbarians?—So that many millions will speak English?"—as Darío put on our side Moctezuma, Cuauhtémoc's "bed of roses," Netzahuacóyotl's poetry and even Christopher Columbus's God. . . . Never has the word "America" been used so much and so poetically as at the beginning of this century. The concept of "Our America" finally evolved—as once well put by Alfonso Reyes—into a true movement, "Our-Americanism." Nevertheless, that particular "Our-Americanism" emerged as a phenomenon quite distant, to be sure, from Martí's "Our America," in search of whose name, defense and glory, he had sketched an honest ethical profile of the Latin American. Martí made us well aware that "the greatest danger for our America" was "disdain from the formidable neighbor who fails to understand it." He defined the ideology of those with no faith in their nations as "half-baked"; and he pointed an accusing finger at "the delicate types who rejected men's work," and he once more prophesized the wretched path of "deserters who take arms for the United States." Martí's "Our America" encompassed them all: Indians and Blacks, "the natural Creole blood of a country," good and bad times, hopeful of the day in which "the new Americans" could greet one another, people to people, "with the smiling eyes of the working class. . . ." A few years later, Rubén Darío declared that he was not a poet for the masses, and that he abhorred "intellectual miscegenation." And in a revised prologue for his *Cantos de vida y esperanza* [*Songs of Life and Hope*], he explained—or rationalized—the presence in this volume of his already famous poem dedicated to Roosevelt, as well as other poems, with the following words: "Tomorrow we could (and probably will) be Yankees; in any event, my protest should stand etched on the wings of impeccable swans, as illustrious as Jupiter's."

Soon after, intellectuals from our continent would realize that those who had been born and lived there—and as Martí insisted, *lived the life of our nations*—could not protest against the Yankees by writing on wings of impeccable swans, even those as illustrious as Jupiter. Whereas nineteenth-century modernist poets had come together through a joint scorn of political issues, Latin American intellectuals from the twenties established links based on political awareness. Much had happened in the world. Some struggles were becoming urgent. In this, writers were no longer alone with their vehicles of expression. Painting in our continent began to move to a higher plain. It gained a sense of continuity: Mexico

could claim "a movement"—something unknown in Latin American visual arts until that point. The music world experienced a similar phenomenon, as the composer ceased to be an isolated character, without per-
formers or orchestras, as was the case during the nineteenth century.
Besides, Mexico—a pioneering country among many—demonstrated
how understanding and study of their native milieu brought a spiritual
richness to Latin Americans. Our artists naturally continued to visit Europe, but not with the intent of staying on the continent, if they found
work in Paris or Madrid. In spite of the lamentable political climate of
many of our nations, intellectuals only left with the firm commitment to
return. We had to work for ourselves. We knew this well. We envisioned
the forthcoming desire to establish a Latin American *praxis*. Everywhere
there was a renewal of national awareness. The need for communication
among intellectuals from different countries grew greater and greater.
The fact that we continued to read the most important European journals
of the moment did not prevent us from anxiously awaiting the next issue
of García Monge's *Repertorio Americano*, or of certain journals from Buenos Aires and Mexico City. Then two publications became to draw our
interest: *Amauta*, where occasionally we would read an article by José
Carlos Mariátegui, and Diego Rivera's *El Machete*, for which Julio Antonio Mella wrote.

If the generation of the 1900s had been apolitical and prone to the
Oblomov syndrome (Darío, a voice from tiny Nicaragua to be put on the
political map by Sandino, was only interested in "universal politics"), the
generation of the 1920s was extremely concerned about the social and
political destiny of Latin America (Should we remind ourselves that, as
far as Cuba was concerned, the names of Rubén Martínez Villena, Julio
Antonio Mella, Juan Marinello and Nicolás Guillén began to be heard
between 1920 and 1930?). There is a regrouping of efforts. We begin
to know each other in depth. We know who is who and we know people
by the company they kept. But soon some of us find out that politics is
no game, that political commitment breeds trouble. It is then that we
experience "Our-Americanism" once more, this time under the false ve-
neer of novelty, its meaning definitely altered. . . . Some begin to address
the future of "Our America," while avoiding the sensational developments taking place in Eastern Europe by expressing, in the language of
soothsayers and prophets, a much more feasible reality than the remote
projections of turn-of-the-century dreamers. "Something" will soon happen, "something" no one knows yet. But it will happen imminently, for
the sheer mental prowess of our race, its "Latin character" (laughed about
by José Carlos Mariátegui as early as 1923), will change the face of the
continent. A new solution will appear, different from the imagined and
imaginable: an American solution, a super-American solution, part Mir-

anda's neo-Inca state, part Campanella's Heliopolis, with abundant folklore in the background. Amidst this, there will be many an Eldorado and many a Potosi-like city, or else there will be allusions to the shells brought back by pilgrims from Santiago de Compostela and to the myths of an Atlantis, apparently evident in Mayan ruins. All seems to indicate that once awakened, this [Latin] continent will take over the rest of the twentieth century. The means are there. Think of the immense jungles, the endless rivers, the abundance of virgin soil. And then, think of the natural resources, *even* oil. . . . And the people: the Latin American people, the good singers of songs, the creative musicians, true artists when they express themselves. "I have complete trust in the people." We have heard this expression a hundred times in the mouths of people who are well intentioned, sincere, cultured. But these people who demonstrate complete trust in the creative powers, in the intelligence, in the energy of the people, ignore the life conditions of such people, and the evils owed to oil, to metals, to the variants on Eldorado and Potosi, exploited by U.S. firms, or by national interests "associated"—as we now call it—with U.S. firms. . . . And we should also speak of the very important impact of U.S. publications in our languages, written for Latin American readers, which continue to support "Our-Americanism." Naturally, this is not Martí's concept of "Our America," but a vaguely apocalyptical and imprecise "Our-Americanism," projected for a future *sine diae* [without hope] backed by fake references to Bolívar's thought, which some people still put forth while attempting to escape from evermore pressing political commitments, and clinging to the fear of losing their U.S. visa.

The fundamental problems of our continent do not depend on vague bureaucratic theories, deliberations of café society, or erudite colloquia—a continent whose obvious unity cannot be found in the use of a language common to many countries, but in their sharing of similar problems. We must not forget that such problems occur in an immense country where Portuguese is spoken, or in quite a few where the language is English, French, Guaraní or Papiamento. The great nineteenth-century Latin Americans, who learned to empathize through endorsement of the same principles, shared at heart very clear and practical ideas about political emancipation, education of the masses, awareness of their own identity and of human dignity. This was a straightforward, honest form of thought, derived from experiments which were valid then, but looked forward to more "scientific" experiments, that is, more systematic, more firmly based on a deep analysis of the historical and economic development of the societies. . . . Later on—and it is now important to stress it—in Europe and America, certain individuals rejected the insensitivity of many of their colleagues (poet laureates, painters under government contract, musicians who had composed some hymn as a commission) toward social events. They demonstrated some concern for public destiny. They thought about social ills and anguished about the social panorama; they also took upon themselves, in the hope of gaining some understanding of the dangers of free enterprise, a "free-for-all" individualistic process of "socialization" which bypassed the scientific principles of socialism. This brought about a flourishing market of well-intentioned books which, in the final analysis, did not explain or solve any problems. For Rodó's *Ariel* to transcend its being a graceful meditation on democracy and utilitarianism, on "levelling with mediocrity," "the selective processes," "spiritual needs," it would simply have been necessary for the author to study some political science. . . . The idea of "free-for-all socialization" carried not only the risk of cornering us into a "cosmic race," and "the Latin spirit," and other cobwebs in vogue thirty years before but they also push us toward fatal flaws. If the scientific study of socialism is experienced as a "free-for-all socialization," it can take a writer, such as Zola, so well-intentioned and given to noble causes, to trace in *Fruitfulness* a true gospel of the colonization of Africa, in which he sings dithyrambic praises to the French empire (an author like Zola who had written *Germinal* and *Drunkard*, ultimately justifies to a certain extent shooting down natives who would "fanatically" hinder the colonizing effort).

The same process of "free-for-all socialization" took Tolstoy, in spite of the fact that his work was generally useful (as recognized by Lenin) to the October 1917 revolution to invent in his old age a negative and damaging doctrine (again, Lenin's judgment) of "non-resistance to evil," a bucolic and unworkable "return to the land" which even Yasnaia Poliana's teacher could not accomplish by himself. . . . Moreover Romain Rolland, who held an irreproachable stance toward the end of his life, erred in 1914 when, wishing to place himself *au dessus de la mêlée* [above the scuffle], he thought it possible to win over the minds of European writers incapable of linking the burning of the Library at Louvaine with a historical process far more significant than the tragic ruins before their very eyes.

Contemporary history has shown us—probably more eloquently in Latin America than elsewhere—that a simple statistical study, a simple economic report—even an occasional article published by *Fortune* magazine in New York—offers us lessons in contemporary history which are more useful than the speculations of "closet" thinkers who give opinions, according to the "political tone" of their looking glass, on the destiny, present and future, of America. Since Christopher Columbus in his admirable letters of discovery envisioned the newly discovered continent as a universal remedy "to free ourselves from the gold fever," there is a tendency in our America to *mythify*. This tendency, which yields an abun-

dance of fine poetic and artistic fruits, has instead, for our present political needs, served to hide the Molinism [defense of human vis-à-vis
divine will] and Tancredo-esque [resistance to surrender] tendencies of
those who, for fear or for convenience, try to forget that only revolutionary action can liberate us from the evils we have accumulated since
the days of the Spanish conquest.

CLARICE LISPECTOR
[1925–1977]

BORN IN THE UKRAINE, Lispector was only two months old when her family emigrated to Brazil where she grew up in Recife and later Rio de Janeiro. While studying law, she worked as an editor and journalist; the year she graduated, 1944, she published her first novel, *Perto do coracão selvagem* ["Close to the Savage Heart"], which was critically acclaimed as one of Brazil's first introspective novels. Choosing literature over the law, Lispector continued to write and publish while traveling with her diplomat husband and bearing two sons. After a divorce in 1959, she returned to permanent residence in Brazil, writing prolifically, including stories for children, until her early death from cancer.

Often called one of Latin America's most original and important women writers, Lispector's oeuvre includes nine novels and eight collections of short stories. Among her most lauded works are a book of stories entitled *Laços de família*, 1960 [*Family Ties*, 1972]; another collection of stories and reflections, *A legião estrangeira*, 1964 [*The Foreign Legion*, 1986]; and a brief novel, *A hora de estrela*, 1977 [*The Hour of the Star*, 1986], which has recently been made into a prize-winning film by Brazilian director Suzana Amaral. Lispector is credited with revolutionizing the Brazilian short story and bringing a woman's sensibility to the existentialist novel. Rather than focus on narrative events, she emphasizes the repercussion of life's events on the human psyche, particularly on the female, searching for personal meaning in a stifling social environment.

The following excerpts from *A legião estrangeira* reveal Lispector's lyrical approach to writing. She rejects the intellectual in favor of the intuitive, affirming the mystery of life and seeking to illuminate the undefinable. In a metaphor that recalls Virginia Woolf's mystical "moments of being," Lispector has said: "To write, therefore, is the way of someone who uses the word as bait: the word fishes for something that is not a word. And when that non-word takes the bait, something has been written."

As these selections reveal, Lispector's awareness of injustices around her was acute. Writing literature, however, was the only way she could express and protest the toll they took on others and on herself.*

*I would like to acknowledge the special assistance of Dr. Giovanni Pontiero of the University of Manchester, England, in preparing the Brazilian component of this anthology. [*Ed.*]

SINCE ONE FEELS OBLIGED TO WRITE . . .

[Selections from *The Foreign Legion*]

Clarice Lispector
Translated by Giovanni Pontiero

SINCE ONE FEELS OBLIGED TO WRITE . . .

Since one feels obliged to write, let it be without obscuring the space between the lines with words.

REMEMBERING

To write often means remembering what has never existed. How shall I succeed in knowing what I do not even know? Like so: as if I were to remember. By an effort of "memory" as if I had never been born. I have never been born. I have never lived. But I remember, and that memory is in living flesh.

WRITING, HUMILITY, TECHNIQUE

This inability to perceive, to understand, makes me instinctively. . . instinctively what? makes me seek a way of expressing myself which might lead me to a quicker understanding. This way, this "style"(!) has been called a variety of things, but never what it really and exclusively is: a humble search. I have never had to cope with only one problem of expression because my problem is much more serious: that of conception. When I speak of "humility," I am referring to humility in its Christian meaning (as an ideal within or beyond attainment); I am referring to that humility which stems from total awareness of being utterly incapable. And I am referring to humility as technique. Holy Mother of God, even I have been appalled at my lack of modesty; but here there is some misunderstanding. Humility as a technique is as follows: things should be approached with humility, otherwise they will become entirely elusive. I have discovered this type of humility, which ironically is a subtle form of pride. Pride is not a sin, at least not a grave sin: pride is a childish failing which we succumb to like greed. Except that pride has the enormous disadvantage of being a grave error, with all the consequences which error brings into our lives, for it causes us to waste a great deal of time.

ADVENTURE

My intuitions become much clearer as I make the effort to transpose them into words. It is in this sense that writing for me is a necessity. On the one hand, because to write is a way of not falsifying sentiment (the involuntary transfiguration of imagination is only one way of arriving); on the other hand, I write because of my inability to understand except through the process of writing. If I assume a note of hermeticism this is not only because the important thing is not to falsify sentiment but also because I am incapable of transposing sentiment in any clear way without falsifying it—to falsify thought would be to rob writing of its only satisfaction. So I often find myself assuming an air of mystery—a trait which I find extremely irksome in others.

After something has been written, should I not then try to render it more clearly? Here I choose to be obstinate. Besides, I respect a certain clarity peculiar to the mystery of nature which cannot be substituted by any other kind of clarity. I also believe that things can only be clarified with time: just as with a glass of water, whenever something is deposited at the bottom of the glass and the water turns clear.

. . . If ever that water should turn clear, so much the worse for me. I am prepared to take the risk. I have taken greater risks like every other creature who chooses to live. And if I take risks it is not because of some arbitrary freedom or insensibility or arrogance on my part. Each day when I awaken, as if by habit, I take new risks. I have always relished a deep sense of adventure and here I use the word deep to imply inherent. This sense of adventure is what gives me a dimension of security and reality in relation to living, and in some strange way, in relation to writing.

LITERATURE AND JUSTICE

Today, quite unexpectedly, as in any real discovery, I found that some of my tolerance toward others was reserved for me as well (but for how long?). I took advantage of this crest of the wave to bring myself up to date with forgiveness. For example, my tolerance in relation to myself, as someone who writes, is to forgive my inability to deal with the "social problem" in a "literary" vein (that is to say, by transforming it into the vehemence of art). Ever since I have come to know myself, the social problem has been more important to me than any other issue: in Recife the black shanty towns were the first truth I encountered. Long before I ever felt "art," I felt the profound beauty of human conflict. I tend to be straightforward in my approach to any social problem: I wanted "to do" something, as if writing were not doing anything. What I cannot do is to exploit writing to this end, however much my incapacity pains and distresses me. The problem of justice for me is such an obvious and basic feeling that I am unable to surprise myself on its account—and unless I can surprise myself, I am unable to write. Also because for me, to write is a quest. I have never considered any feeling of justice as a quest or as a discovery, and what worries me is that this feeling of justice should not be so obvious to everyone else. I am aware of simplifying the essence of the problem. But nowadays out of tolerance toward myself, I am not entirely ashamed of contributing nothing human or social through my writing. It is not a matter of not wanting to, it is a question of not being able to. What I am ashamed of is of "not doing," of not contributing in an active way. (I know all too well that the struggle for justice inevitably leads to politics, and I should get hopelessly lost in a maze of political intrigue.) Of this, I shall always be ashamed. But I have no intention of doing penance. I have no desire, through oblique and dubious means, to achieve my own absolution. Of this, I wish to go on feeling ashamed. But, of writing what I write, I am not ashamed. I feel that if I were to be ashamed, I should be committing the sin of pride.

Two Ways

In trying to ignore immediate life in favor of a deeper existence, I have two ways of being. In life, I observe a great deal and I am "active" in my observations. I have an eye for the absurd, I am good-humored and ironic and fully capable of participating. But when writing I have insights which are "passive" and so intimate that they "write themselves" the very instant I perceive them almost without the intervention of any so-called thought processes. For this reason, I make no choice when writing. I am incapable of multiplying myself a thousand-fold. And despite myself, I can sense my own destiny.

WRITING

I no longer remember how it started. It was, in a manner of speaking, all written at a single stroke. Everything was there or ought to have been there as in the temporal space of an open piano . . . on its simultaneous keys. I wrote, cautiously pursuing the words which formed themselves within me, and which only after the fifth copy had been patiently drafted, I was able to absorb. My great fear was, that out of impatience with the slowness with which I understand myself, I might somehow be forcing things unduly.

I had the distinct impression that the more time I allowed myself, the more readily the story would narrate what it had to narrate without any crisis. More and more, I discovered that everything is largely a question of exercising patience, of love begetting patience and patience begetting love. The entire text came to life at once, with greater clarity emerging here and there. I would interrupt a sentence in chapter ten, let us say, in order to resume the writing of chapter two, interrupted in its turn while I devoted myself to the writing of chapter eighteen. I found that I had the necessary patience and it taught me a great deal: for example, how to bear the frustrating discomfort of disorder, without any guarantees.

Yet it is also true that order constrains me. As always, the greatest difficulty was that of waiting. (I am feeling unwell—the woman would explain to the doctor. You are about to have a child—he would say. And to think that I imagined I was dying—the woman would reply.

The deformed soul, growing, swelling, without even realizing that this is waiting. Sometimes, faced with stillbirth, one knows that it was expected.)

In addition to the trial of waiting, there is the laborious task of reconstructing the vision that was instantaneous. And, as if this were not enough, alas I am incapable of "drafting" a manuscript. I am incapable of "relating" an idea or of "dressing up an idea" with words. What comes to the surface is already expressed in words or simply fails to exist. Upon writing the text, there is always the certainty (seemingly paradoxical) that what confuses the writer is the necessity of using words. This is the real trouble. If only I could write by carving on wood or stroking a child's hair or strolling though the countryside, I should never have embarked upon the path of words. I should do what so many people who are not writers do, and precisely with the same happiness and the same torment as those who write, and with the same deep, inconsolable disappointments: I should avoid using words. This might prove to be my solution. And as such, it would be most welcome.

PABLO NERUDA
[1904–1973]

KNOWN BY HIS PSEUDONYM—his real name was Ricardo Neftalí Reyes—Pablo Neruda was a native of Chile, a career diplomat, and a member of the central committee of the Chilean Communist Party. Above all, he was an exceptional poet. Neruda was awarded the Nobel Prize for Literature in 1971.

His first collection of poems won him his earliest literary prize, in 1921. Thereafter, Pablo Neruda's poetry was as abundant and expressive as his energy for life. Yet the prolific Neruda also found time to serve as diplomatic consul—in Burma, Ceylon, Java, Buenos Aires, Cambodia, Madrid, and Mexico—and he was active in aiding refugees from the Spanish Civil War. Outspokenly opposed to United States economic exploitation in Chile in the 1940s, Neruda's work became increasingly politicized in the 1950s during which time he was awarded the Lenin Peace Prize. He died shortly after the overthrow of the Socialist government of his friend and democratically elected president of Chile, Salvador Allende, a coup backed by the United States.

Neruda's most celebrated works of poetry include *Veinte poemas de amor y una canción desesperada*, 1924 [*Twenty Love Poems and a Song of Despair*, 1969]; *Residencia en la tierra*, 1925–1935 [*Residence on Earth*, 1946]; *Alturas de Machu Picchu*, 1966 [*The Heights of Machu Picchu*, 1966]; *Canto general*, 1950 ["General Song," selections available in translation]; and *Odas elementales*, 1954 [*Elementary Odes*, 1961]. Many bilingual editions of his poetry have been published in the past twenty-five years.

His roots were deeply planted in his native country, yet his poetry held appeal for all Spanish-speaking peoples. The most admired poet of his generation, he was the ubiquitous voice of Latin America's intrepid past and protean present.

He was referred to as a surrealist, and his poetry was often obscure. But Neruda was instinctively sensitive to the heartbeat of his continent and always willing to put the personal ahead of the intellectual. He was, he claimed, a poet of the people. According to his compatriot José Donoso, "He created himself in his own lifetime. Neruda's work constitutes one of the great poetic autobiographies of literature, a kind of vast Whitmanesque 'Song of Myself' in which his imagination acts as a reverberator for the whole world."

The pages which follow—including his prose poem "The Word"—are extracted from Neruda's autobiography, *Confieso que he vivido*, 1974 ["I Confess I have Lived," published as *Memoirs*, 1976].

MY FIRST BOOKS

(From *Memoirs*)

Pablo Neruda
Translated by Hardie St. Martin

I sought refuge in poetry with the intensity of someone timid. The new literary movements hovered over Santiago. I finished writing my first book at 513 Maruri Street. I used to write two, three, four, five poems each day. In the late afternoon, outside my balcony, there unfolded a spectacle I never missed for anything in the world. It was the sunset with its glorious sheaves of colors, scattered arrays of light, enormous orange and scarlet fans. The middle section of my book is called "Maruri Twilights." No one ever asked me what Maruri is supposed to mean. Maybe a very small number of people know it's only a modest street frequented by the most extraordinary twilights.

In 1923 my first book, *Crepusculario*, appeared. I had setbacks and successes every day, trying to pay for the first printing. I sold the few pieces of furniture I owned. The watch my father had solemnly given me, on which he had had two little crossed flags enameled, soon went off to the pawnbroker's. My black poet's suit followed the watch. The printer was adamant, and in the end, when the edition was all ready and the covers had been pasted on, he said to me, with an evil look, "No. You are not taking a single copy until you pay me for the entire thing." The critic Alone generously contributed the last pesos, which were gobbled up by my printer, and off I went into the street carrying my books on my shoulder, with holes in my shoes, but beside myself with joy.

My first book! I have always maintained that the writer's task has nothing to do with mystery or magic, and that the poet's, at least, must be a personal effort for the benefit of all. The closest thing to poetry is a loaf of bread or a ceramic dish or a piece of wood lovingly carved, even if by clumsy hands. And yet I don't believe any craftsman except the poet, still shaken by the confusion of his dreams, ever experiences the ecstasy produced only once in his life, by the first object his hands have created. It's a moment that will never come back. There will be many editions, more elaborate, more beautiful. His words will be poured into the glasses of other languages like a wine, to sing and spread its aroma to other places on this earth. But that moment when the first book appears with its ink fresh and its paper still crisp, that enchanted and ecstatic moment, with the sound of wings beating or the first flower opening on the conquered height, that moment comes only once in the poet's lifetime.

One of my poems seemed to break away from that immature book and go off on its own: "Farewell," which many people, wherever I go, still know by heart. They would recite it to me in the most unlikely places, or ask me to do it. I might find it annoying, but the minute I was introduced at a gathering, some girl would raise her voice with those obsessive lines, and sometimes ministers of state would receive me with a military salute while reciting the first stanza.

Years later in Spain, Federico García Lorca told me how the same thing kept happening to him with his poem "La casada infiel" ("The Faithless Wife"). The greatest proof of friendship Federico could offer anyone was to repeat for him his enormously popular and lovely poem. We become allergic to the unshakable success of just one of our poems. This is a healthy and natural feeling. Such an imposition by readers tends to transfix the poet in a single moment of time, whereas creation is really a steady wheel spinning along with more and more facility and self-confidence, though perhaps with less freshness and spontaneity.

I was now leaving *Crepusculario* behind me. Deep anxieties stirred my poetry. Short trips to the south renewed my powers. In 1923 I had a strange experience. I had returned home to Temuco. It was past midnight. Before going to bed, I opened the windows in my room. The sky dazzled me. The entire sky was alive, swarming with a lively multitude of stars. The night looked freshly washed and the Antarctic stars were spreading out in formation over my head.

I became star-drunk, celestially, cosmically drunk. I rushed to my table and wrote, with heart beating high, as if I were taking dictation, the first poem of a book that would have many titles and would end up as *El hondero entusiasta*. It was smooth going, as if I were swimming in my very own waters.

The following day, filled with happiness, I read my poem. Later, when I got to Santiago, the wizard Aliro Oyarzún listened with admiration to those lines of mine. Then he asked in his deep voice: "Are you sure those lines haven't been influenced by Sabat Ercasty?"

"I'm pretty sure. I wrote them in a fit of inspiration."

Then I decided to send my poem to Sabat Ercasty himself, a great

Uruguayan poet unjustly neglected today. In him I had seen realized my ambition to write poetry that would embrace not only man but nature, its hidden forces: an epic poetry that would deal with the great mystery of the universe and with man's potential as well. I started an exchange of letters with him. While I continued my work and mellowed it, I read with great care the letters Sabat Ercasty addressed to me, an unknown young poet.

I sent Sabat Ercasty, in Montevideo, the poem I had written that night and I asked him if it showed any influence from his poetry. A kind letter from him promptly answered my question: "I have seldom seen such a successful, such a magnificent poem, but I have to tell you: Yes, there are echoes of Sabat Ercasty in your lines."

It was a flash of light in the darkness, of clarity, and I am still grateful for it. The letter spent a good many days in my pocket, wrinkling until it fell apart. Many things were at stake. I was particularly obsessed with the fruitless rush of feelings that night. I had fallen into that well of stars in vain, that storm of stars had struck my senses in vain. I had made an error. I must be wary of inspiration. Reason must guide me step-by-step down the narrow paths. I had to learn humility. I ripped up many manuscripts. I misplaced others. It would be ten years before these last poems would reappear and be published.

Sabat Ercasty's letter ended my recurrent ambition for an expansive poetry. I locked the door on a rhetoric that I could never go on with, and deliberately toned down my style and my expression. Looking for more unpretentious qualities, for the harmony of my own world, I began to write another book. *Veinte poemas* was the result.

Those *Veinte poemas de amor y una canción desesperada* make a painful book of pastoral poems filled with my most tormented adolescent passions, mingled with the devastating nature of the southern part of my country. It is a book I love because, in spite of its acute melancholy, the joyfulness of being alive is present in it. A river and its mouth helped me to write it: the Imperial River. *Veinte poemas* is my love affair with Santiago, with its student-crowded streets, the university, and the honeysuckle fragrance of requited love.

The Santiago sections were written between Echaurren Street and España Avenue, and inside the old building of the Teachers Institute, but the landscape is always the waters and the trees of the south. The docks in the "Canción desesperada" ("Song of Despair") are the old docks of Carahue and Bajo Imperial: the broken planks and the beams like stumps battered by the wide river; the wingbeat of the gulls was heard and can still be heard at that river's mouth.

In the long, slender-bodied, abandoned lifeboat left over from some shipwreck, I read the whole of *Jean Christophe*, and I wrote the "Canción desesperada." The sky overhead was the most violent blue I have ever seen. I used to write inside the boat, hidden in the earth. I don't think I have ever again been so exalted or so profound as during those days. Overhead, the impenetrable blue sky. In my hands, *Jean Christophe* or the nascent lines of my poem. Beside me, everything that existed and continued always to exist in my poetry: the distant sound of the sea, the cries of the wild birds, and love burning, without consuming itself, like an immortal bush.

I am always being asked who the woman in *Veinte poemas* is, a difficult question to answer. The two women who weave in and out of these melancholy and passionate poems correspond, let's say, to Marisol and Marisombra: Sea and Sun, Sea and Shadow. Marisol is love in the enchanted countryside, with stars in bold relief at night, and dark eyes like the wet sky of Temuco. She appears with all her joyfulness and her lively beauty on almost every page, surrounded by the waters of the port and by a half-moon over the mountains. Marisombra is the student in the city. Gray beret, very gentle eyes, the ever-present honeysuckle fragrance of my foot-loose and fancy-free days, the physical peace of the passionate meetings in the city's hideaways.

Meanwhile, life was changing in Chile.

The Chilean people's movement was starting up, clamoring, looking for stronger support among students and writers. On the one hand, the great leader of the petite bourgeoisie, Arturo Alessandri Palma, a dynamic and demagogic man, became President of the Republic, but not before he had rocked the country with his fiery and threatening speeches. In spite of his extraordinary personality, once in power he quickly turned into the classic ruler of our Americas; the dominant sector of the oligarchy, whom he had fought, opened its maw and swallowed him and his revolutionary speeches. The country continued to be torn apart by bitter strife.

At the same time, a working-class leader, Luis Emilio Recabarren, was extraordinarily active organizing the proletariat, setting up union centers, establishing nine or ten workers' newspapers throughout the country. An avalanche of unemployment sent the country's institutions staggering. I contributed weekly articles to *Claridad*. We students supported the rights of the people and were beaten up by the police in the streets of Santiago. Thousands of jobless nitrate and copper workers flocked to the capital. The demonstrations and the subsequent repression left a tragic stain on the life of the country.

From that time on, with interruptions now and then, politics became part of my poetry and my life. In my poems I could not shut the door to the street, just as I could not shut the door to love, life, joy, or sadness in my young poet's heart.

"The Word"

. . . You can say anything you want, yessir, but it's the words that sing, they soar and descend . . . I bow to them . . . I love them, I cling to them, I run them down, I bite into them, I melt them down . . . I love words so much . . . The unexpected ones . . . The ones I wait for greedily or stalk until, suddenly, they drop . . . Vowels I love . . . They glitter like colored stones, they leap like silver fish, they are foam, thread, metal, dew . . . I run after certain words . . . They are so beautiful that I want to fit them all into my poem . . . I catch them in mid-flight, as they buzz past, I trap them, clean them, peel them, I set myself in front of the dish, they have a crystalline texture to me, vibrant, ivory, vegetable, oily, like fruit, like algae, like agates, like olives . . . And then I stir them, I shake them, I drink them, I gulp them down, I mash them, I garnish them, I let them go . . . I leave them in my poem like stalactites, like slivers of polished wood, like coals, pickings from a shipwreck, gifts from the waves . . . Everything exists in the word . . . An idea goes through a complete change because one word shifted its place, or because another settled down like a spoiled little thing inside a phrase that was not expecting her but obeys her . . . They have shadow, transparence, weight, feathers, hair, and everything they gathered from so much rolling down the river, from so much wandering from country to country, from being roots so long . . . They are very ancient and very new . . . They live in the bier, hidden away, and in the budding flower . . . What a great language I have, it's a fine language we inherited from the fierce conquistadors . . . They strode over the giant cordilleras, over the rugged Americas, hunting for potatoes, sausages, beans, black tobacco, gold, corn, fried eggs, with a voracious appetite not found in the world since then . . . They swallowed up everything, religions, pyramids, tribes, idolatries just like the ones they brought along in their huge sacks . . . Wherever they went, they razed the land . . . But words fell like pebbles out of the boots of the barbarians, out of their beards, their helmets, their horseshoes, luminous words that were left glittering here . . . our language. We came up losers . . . We came up winners . . . They carried off the gold and left us the gold . . . They carried everything off and left us everything . . . They left us the words.

MIGUEL ANGEL ASTURIAS
[1899–1974]

GUATEMALAN WRITER MIGUEL Angel Asturias came to the world's attention in 1967 when he became the second Latin American author to win the Nobel Prize for Literature. Asturias' literary output prior to that time had been remarkably abundant considering his active career as a diplomat for much of his life, culminating in his appointment as ambassador to France from 1966 to 1970.

Educated as a lawyer in Guatemala but forced to flee the country for political reasons for the first time in 1923, Asturias studied South American cultural anthropology at the Sorbonne and earned a living as a journalist until his return to Guatemala in 1932. As a diplomat he traveled throughout Latin America and Europe. But after the CIA-backed overthrow of the Arbenz government in 1954, Asturias was stripped of his citizenship by the Castillo Armas military regime and forced into exile. After a long stay in Argentina, he returned to Guatemala in 1966, once again entering the diplomatic corps and spending his last years in Paris.

Among his most famous works are *Leyendas de Guatemala*, 1930 ["Legends of Guatemala"]; and the novels *El señor presidente*, 1946 [*The President*, 1963]; *Hombres de maíz*, 1949 [*Men of Maize*, 1975]; *Viento fuerte*, 1950 [*Strong Wind*, 1968]; and *Mulata de tal*, 1963 [*Mulata*, 1967].

"Questions and Realities," the brief piece translated here for the first time, was published in a book of essays entitled *Latinoamérica y otros ensayos*, 1968 ["Latin America and Other Essays"]. As Asturias said to the Swedish Academy in 1967, "My work will continue to reflect the voice of the peoples, gathering their myths and popular beliefs and at the same time seeking to give birth to a universal consciousness of Latin American problems."

QUESTIONS AND REALITIES

Miguel Angel Asturias
Translated by Doris Meyer

In my condition as a Latin American writer who lives in Europe I often get interview questions that, if our reality weren't so tragic, would make the harshest schoolmaster laugh out loud. And if not, let the reader judge the kind of questions that journalists generally ask. Here are some examples: What is the greatest happiness? What is the greatest misfortune? Is conjugal love constant or perishable? Do you think that oppression will someday be completely eradicated? How would you symbolize evil? How would you symbolize good? Can censorship be justified? When? Why? What about the death penalty? When? Why? Does there exist an exclusively or preferentially masculine virtue? A defect? What are they? With what legend do you sympathize most: that of Christ or of Prometheus? If, as in the case of Xenophon's Hercules, you found yourself between the goddesses Pleasure and Virtue, which would you choose? What is your primary passion? If you could only ask one question, what would it be? Other interviewers ask: What are your favorite colors? Your favorite countries? The TV programs you like most, the number of times you go to the movies, how you write: sitting down? standing up? in the morning? afternoon? evening? Do you have friends? Do you believe in friendship? And so on, endlessly, with this type of question which—as we said earlier—doesn't make us laugh because the answers our reality gives are too tragic.

How can we, having our feet on the ground, answer these journalistic questions when we know that in the United States the average life span of a man is sixty-five years whereas in the twenty countries of Latin America it's only thirty-five? And what are the causes? Well, let them ask us. They're there. Misery, exploitation, abandonment, bad food, tropical diseases, alcoholism, malaria, militarism, changes of climate forced on the Indians, etc.

Do you know, Mr. Journalist—we feel like saying—that while you are asking me if "conjugal love is constant or perishable," in Latin America, in Guatemala, a child drinks a glass of milk every ten days; that what a North American woman spends on beauty products in one year equals or exceeds the annual income of a South American family, without factoring in that one-half of the population of Latin America is illiterate?

You can't publish this, you say? Ah, then, how can you talk to me about censorship, if I am for or against censorship? And where does this censorship come from? The editorial board? No. It comes from the advertising pages. If these things were said, many advertisers would withdraw and would even go so far as to boycott the paper, as happened in the case of *El Nacional* in Caracas, and others. If instead of answering this gentleman as to whether Christ or Prometheus stirs my sympathy more I were to tell him that in the Northeast of Brazil half the population never reaches thirty years of age, that 200,000 children die before they are one year old, and that two-thirds of this human mass doesn't know what a pair of shoes is, while a Brazilian congressman and landowner spends ·20 million—I repeat, 20 million—cruzeiros on his daughter's wedding, and 4 million cruzeiros on a meal . . .

And as for Good and Evil, and the way they could be symbolized, why not talk instead of the slanderous, cruel dictatorships looking to perpetuate themselves in Nicaragua, Paraguay, and Haiti? Aren't these dictatorships the very image of Caliban? Why search for other images? And as for "good," it has fled from Latin America, which in 1980 will have 100 million more inhabitants, of which only 18 million will have the possibility of work, thus increasing the number of unemployed and undernourished.

Solutions? Very well, better to talk of the solutions that are offered for these problems than what you were asking me, "if human nature is immutable or changeable." Three solutions to these problems are put forth: ignore them, the military, and elections. When a problem is so vast, better not to think about it. Ostrichlike. Of course. The military solution is, nevertheless, possible. The slap of·a hand. Barracks in power. Colonels. They come, they go, they rise up, proffer proclamations, decide, threaten, attack, conclude, and since the problems aren't solved, representative democracy is dragged in as a last resort and elections are convened, taking care, naturally, that the ruling thugs retain key positions. Political agitation, closely scrutinized by internal and external police, grows in proportion to the capitulation to interests of the wealthy, who always want to continue enjoying their money; to those of the privileged office-holders or concessionaires who consider themselves unmovable; and to those on the right who maintain vigil against any dangerous idea that might seep through. And then come the elections. Ballot-boxes. Result: a shot in the pants for those who govern by the shots with which they threaten, or the shots they fire against students, protesters, and now against guerrillas.

Neither the military nor elections are any longer the solution to the problems that Latin America has to resolve. If the results of elections were respected by unleashed gorilla-ism, they would of course open the way at least to examining problems in their exact terms. But as long as that's not possible, perhaps you are right, Mr. Journalist. It would be better to dwell on what you were asking about Xenophon's Hercules: which goddess to prefer, that of Pleasure or of Virtue?

❖ VICTORIA OCAMPO
[1890–1979]

VICTORIA OCAMPO, the eldest of six daughters of a wealthy and powerful Argentine family, was educated at home by governesses and taken on yearlong excursions to Europe. She learned French and English as a small child and wrote naturally in French as a young woman, but her mature works, written in Spanish, have been called the most *criollo*—or authentically Argentine—of any writer of her generation.

Her passion for reading and love of the theater made her aspire as a young woman to a career as an actress. Her family, however, would not hear of it, and Ocampo turned instead to literature. In 1908 she confided in a letter to a female friend:

> Literary ambitions? . . . My dear friend, if you only knew where I'm aiming, how far I'd like to go, whom I'd like to equal . . . and all without knowing how to go about it! I *feel* I can demand a great deal of myself. I *adore literature* frantically. I *feel* I have something unusual inside me. I'll have to work, persevere, arm myself with patience and resignation if I want to achieve the goal I've set for myself.

Such determination and devotion were characteristic of Ocampo throughout her life.

After an unsuccessful marriage, she scandalized proper Argentine society by living alone, writing for *La Nación*, and working for women's rights in the 1920s and 1930s. In 1931, she founded the literary review *Sur*, which became the most influential journal of its kind in Latin America. Ocampo's aim was to build cultural bridges between Europe and North and South America, encouraging the best native talent and bringing the finest foreign minds to the attention of readers at home. In order to commission and publish translations, she founded a publishing house under the same name. With friends like Eduardo Mallea, Waldo Frank, Jorge Luis Borges, José Ortega y Gasset, Alfonso Reyes, and María Rosa Oliver on the editorial board, *Sur* achieved a reputation for internationalism at a time when Argentina was becoming more nationalistic and xenophobic under the Perón government. In 1953, Victoria Ocampo was arrested without explanation and imprisoned for a month until pressure from friends and admirers around the world forced her release.

Ocampo was the author of ten volumes of essays—which she called *Testimonios*, 1935–1977, ["Testimonies"]—numerous short books on a variety of topics from Dante and Bach to Tagore and Virginia Woolf, and the translator of many works from French and English. She also wrote a multivolume autobiography (*Autobiografía*) published after her death; the details of her own life, her involvement with the arts and her close friendships with artists the world over, make her memoirs fascinating reading and a valuable cultural document.

The following essay, translated here for the first time, was originally delivered as a speech in 1966 when Ocampo was awarded the prestigious Vaccaro Prize in Argentina. Eleven years later, she became the first woman to be elected to the Argentine Academy of Letters.

Woman's Past and Present

Victoria Ocampo
Translated by Doris Meyer

The Vaccaro Prize, granted to me by the commission headed by Dr. Bernardo Houssay (and his presidency says it all), rewards such notable merits that—although for different motives—it might justify on my part an attitude like that of Sartre toward the Nobel Prize. This is not just empty talk. There have been occasions when I've turned down flattering recognitions because they seemed inappropriate to my person.

I feel compelled to explain to you why I thought it legitimate to accept this Vaccaro Prize, which means so much not only because of the unique personality of its founder but also because of those charged with choosing the candidates. I believe that no one would understand better than Vaccaro himself what I am going to say to you. That man knew the cost—in whatever activity—of persevering effort undertaken in adverse circumstances. And he also knew that it isn't easy to begin at zero. His life is an admirable and comforting example of energy and generosity. I feel that, in addressing myself to you, I lean on him.

Before continuing, I'd like to take this opportunity to say again publicly how much the review *Sur* owes to Eduardo Mallea. Without him, it probably wouldn't exist. He helped more than anyone to get things underway, and once in motion, he helped maintain the rhythm of the step. Words are inadequate to thank him for the total selflessness he always showed in this consuming work.

When the Vaccaro Prize was announced, *La Nación* mentioned that this was the first time it was given to a woman. This struck me as important. The most important thing of all. Not because I was the one chosen, but because I feel all women share it with me.

What *little* I have done in my life (and I don't call it little out of false modesty, but because my plans were more ambitious) I have done in spite of being denied the advantages of being a man. But I wouldn't have achieved this little bit without having the unshakable conviction that it is necessary to fight to win the place that belongs to half of humanity. In my case, the struggle consisted of following a vocation: that of letters. To be victorious in this sector—even if the victory were insignificant—would mean helping the great movement for emancipation that was underway.

I don't consider it meaningless to look back, on this occasion, toward what the life and education of a *niña*, or "young lady," was like at the end of the nineteenth or beginning of the twentieth century. Even if she belonged to the privileged class. Those privileges of fortune did not change one iota the injustices to which a woman was subjected. You may say that I'm wasting my time commenting on a bygone age, but I do so out of the belief that this isn't the case yet. The horrors of the last World War appear to have been overcome. Nevertheless, it isn't prudent to be so sure they won't recur in some new form.

Let's return to the destiny of the young lady sheltered from all economic hardship, spoiled in her infancy and adolescence, born into an environment in which traditions were respected. Such advantages concealed serious disadvantages, rarely taken into consideration. Especially in our era.

I should also point out that it was easier to declare open war on a household without love—in any social class—than on a home in which the love and care lavished upon a child or adolescent reached the limit. This tends to create a subterranean tragedy. Like the one I happened to experience.

I was born in the last years of the Victorian era. This is essential to establish since my namesake represented in the world a whole index of taboos, prejudices, conventions, and falsehoods with respect to the nature of women (and, consequently, that of men), which was not limited to the British Empire. It extended to almost the entire civilized world. Here in Argentina we suffered from it, and it lasted longer than in England.

In her way, Victoria was a great queen. I underline: in her way. Her reign was unusually long: sixty-four years. She happened to cross paths on the streets of Brussels with a young teacher from Yorkshire, unknown at the time. A girl who didn't dare sign a novel, *Jane Eyre*, with her woman's name. It wasn't seemly that Charlotte Brontë should write. This encounter doubly impresses me, due to the fact that I, too, saw the same queen pass by. As I looked at her from a London balcony, her appearance disconcerted me. I associated the word *queen* with the splendors of youth and beauty, not imagining anything other than the queens of fairy tales I had been told. I was too young to read at the time. It was natural, therefore, that I not suspect how great my disillusionment would become with the passage of years. It wouldn't stem from an appearance, but from concrete facts of another order. This woman, on whom the hazard of birth had conferred the maximum power in the most powerful empire on earth, who had accepted for herself the exercise of a supreme authority, was violently opposed to her sisters'—women—conquering rights that any male (with the exception of criminals and the insane) enjoyed as a matter of course. When she ascended the throne, by what merits did such responsibility fall on her inexpert eighteen-year-old shoulders? None.

During her reign, the much-ridiculed suffragist movement grew, and in 1870 the sovereign wrote to Theodore Martin: "The Queen is anxious to recruit all those who can speak, write or help to restrain this crazy and perverse madness of *women's rights*, with all its retinue of horrors to which a poor and weak sex is included, making them forget all sense of feminine modesty."

In writing this, Victoria was reflecting the feelings and thoughts of the majority of her subjects, and if such is the function of those who rule and those who govern (as we are assured today), she was right and complied with her duty. She also complied with her duty when in the same letter she declared that Lady Amberley deserved a whipping for having spoken publicly of the need to grant women equal political and educational rights.

Who were those wicked women, leaders of the emancipation movement, who so provoked Victoria's wrath? Extraordinary women like the well-known Mrs. Pankhurst, and the little-known and admirable Josephine Butler. The daily chores of the latter (her struggle to put an end to white slavery and the laws that legalized such commerce) prevented her from working in the ranks of the suffragists. But her work formed part of that campaign. These two women were living proof that the sex to which they belonged wasn't exactly weak. They, like Elizabeth Barrett, George Eliot and, in current times, Virginia Woolf, had the good fortune to be adored and respected by their husbands. George Eliot's never became her husband, sadly, for though he devoted his entire life to her, he could never marry her as they both desired. In the Victorian era, that would have meant ostracism.

Elizabeth Barrett, who found it necessary to flee from her family home with Browning; Charlotte Brontë, who lived under the dictatorship of her father and later her husband; and Virginia Woolf have all suffered—to a greater or lesser degree—from patriarchal tyranny. What they endured would have defeated women less strong than they. Spiritually strong. The health of all three writers was fragile.

I have insisted on remembering a great queen, and her influence on the era in which she reigned, because the example is a perfect one. No one could have changed the course of things the way she could have. Her daily work habits, her concern for government policy, the amount of time her tiring labor endured—all clearly proved how resistant our sex can be: Nevertheless, she would not, or could not, accept that woman's time had arrived and that opposition was useless. She impeded the suffragist movement in every way possible. How much pain could have been avoided with more understanding on her part!

When I asked a woman from India if women in her country had had to struggle a great deal for the emancipation of women, she answered: "Not at all. Gandhi and Nehru were in favor of it. They were more convinced than anyone." For Gandhi and for Nehru, emancipation was not synonymous with perversion and madness, as it was for men of Victorian mentality, whatever their nationality might be. They placed things on another level.

The ruler or monarch is a kind of father. In the nineteenth century when the suffragist campaign began to intensify, and at the beginning of the twentieth when it continued and won its case, those fathers of nations were opposed to equal rights. The same thing was happening at home, even in the homes of refined and highly cultured people. Educated fathers (I don't know from personal experience how others reacted), however much they loved their daughters, behaved like tyrants—or petty tyrants. Without even being aware of it, they exercised their dictatorship like a divine right. This created serious problems when the daughters refused to acquiesce. Naturally only famous cases have passed into history. In our era, Virginia Woolf said that, if her father hadn't died when she was young, she probably wouldn't have written anything. And Virginia's father, whom she loved dearly and portrayed in *To the Lighthouse*, was not a monster. Nonetheless, Leslie Stephen—talented essayist, friend of great writers of his era—had an inhibiting effect on his daughter (the loveliest and most literarily talented woman I have ever known).

That's enough about fathers. They weren't the only ones who were against equal rights: mothers, daughters, sisters weren't far behind. The majority out of ignorance. John Stuart Mill said that all forms of tyranny have seemed natural, not just to those who imposed them, but to those who endured them. Whatever becomes part of usage and custom always seems natural to the majority.

But there was a minority among women who, in showing indifference to our struggle or opposition to our Cause, were unpardonable. Their intelligence, their culture—acquired through familiarity with the most illustrious personalities of the century—their privileged situation in the economic sense, made their animadversion, their blindness, or their apathy more reprehensible. I refer to cases like that of the Countess de Noailles. This charming, spiritual, talented woman was a vehement enemy of the emancipation of her own sex. She used to expound on the subject in terms more disdainful and intransigent than the severest Victorian father. It was her opinion that talented women were an exception (as if it weren't likewise with men). Of course, she was the exception. Her case was, in a certain sense, like that of Queen Victoria, except that the Queen was more humble (at least with the Prince Consort) due, I suspect, to a lack of physical beauty, which Anne de Noailles had in abundance. Beauty tends to give most women an aplomb born of the effect it produces even on the most egregious (in the words of the *Revista de Occidente*) representatives of the stronger sex. Let it be stated that I believe no woman can use this as a weapon without prostituting herself.

Anne de Noailles' favorite hero was Napoleon. Our preferences are revealing, as I always say. Only an antifeminist could feel a predilection for the Bonaparte responsible for a Civil Code in which a woman's incapacity is established in so many areas. According to this code, a woman cannot inherit, sell, travel, learn a profession, etc., without her husband's authorization. And even worse: this code prohibits the investigation of paternity. In all of this, Napoleon functioned like Queen Victoria. I mean to say that he conformed to the opinion and interests of the majority (especially the masculine majority). Strange legislation for a country that had just proclaimed—with drums, cymbals, and considerable blood— liberty, equality, and fraternity as the only ideal. Articles twelve and nineteen of this code impose on wife-serfs the husbands' nationality, as if by marriage they were bought or colonized. A good example bears fruit. This law has been the rule in many countries, and still applies in some.

Je suis romaine. Hélas! Puisqu' Horace est romain . . .

I point out this *hélas* that Corneille puts in the mouth of Sabine. As early as the seventeenth century, a Frenchman, the father of dramatists, called a woman who could not keep her nationhood, or remember it as such, an "enchained slave." ·

When I witness the mental tumult occasioned by the (so-called) burning question of the self-determination of peoples, I can only look with irony at the men who are agitated and inflamed by the problem. For centuries half of humanity has lived deprived of the most elemental rights of self-determination without causing the blink of an eye. Where was the male sense of justice? The female sense of dignity?

The Catholic writer Emmanuel Mounier stated that the largest proletariat in the world, without class distinctions, was that of women. Errors have been corrected in this chapter. Important reforms have been enacted. But let's not forget that we in Argentina waited while thirty-nine nations gave the vote to women before the one who decreed it here* tried to pass it off as an *innovation*. I emphasize that the case was won long before that. Even on our underdeveloped continent, Bolivia,

*Juan Perón, ratified by the Argentine Congress in 1947. [*Trans.*]

Costa Rica, Cuba, the Dominican Republic, Ecuador, Panama, and Uruguay had taken that step before Argentina.

When the event occurred in our country, the women who for years had struggled to obtain equal rights were not even mentioned. Their names were unjustly silenced, eclipsed by the only name that was allowed to be pronounced. (It should be made clear that I do not say this out of personal bitterness. I fought the battle in a sector removed from politics.)

In a recently published biography of Josephine Butler, the author tells how a young Cambridge professor went to give a lecture on astronomy to a group of women. The topic was aseptic. (In the nineteenth century no astronaut had walked in space contaminating its purity.) The lecturer invited his female audience to ask questions. A scandalous invitation. It was considered improper for a woman—married or single—to ask a professor in public about astronomical phenomena.

This took place in Liverpool in the year 1869. Closer to 1920, shortly before the six-hundredth anniversary of Dante's death, for a woman to speak of heavenly (and infernal) things was still considered taboo. The following anecdote will prove it. A young Argentine woman took an essay of hers about La Divina Commedia to a male friend who was a writer. She had tried to write her own spiritual guide to the poem, without greater pretensions. The young woman thought the anniversary might be a good occasion for publishing it. The friend read her jottings and advised against publication for fear of the criticism it would provoke. Her commentaries on La Divina Commedia would be interpreted, he assured her, as an autobiographical confession. The essay was entitled De Francesca a Beatrice, and I was the consternated author. But once I had digested the rejection, I refused to be placated. La Nación published those pages, and several years later Ortega y Gasset generously brought out a separate edition in his press, Revista de Occidente. I have kept the friend's letter as a document of the era. The character Jim, from Look Back in Anger, would have called this friend of mine stingy. I think he was simply Victorian. He was right about one thing: Hell, Purgatory, and Paradise are, of necessity, autobiographical subjects for any human being.

This kind of mishap wasn't the most serious thing. It was even more deplorable that a woman didn't devote herself seriously to any field of study. She was destined to be an aficionada at everything (except cleaning floors, cooking, washing, ironing, etc.), even though she might show talent for other occupations. If she was artistically gifted, if she accomplished something in the arts, that something remained confined to the circle of family and friends, or, if not, it caused a scandal. We know that one field was open to her: matrimony. With unusual good luck, she might end up with an admirable husband, like Elizabeth Barrett's or Virginia Woolf's. With bad luck, a caveman. Between these two extremes was a whole gamut of possible mates, which I won't describe.

But for a single as well as a married woman, to publish an article— not to mention a book—was frowned upon (at least in Argentina), just as in the era of the Brontë sisters. There was no better way of getting pilloried. Consequently, no parent dared to wish that fate on a daughter. And if any did, they were rare.

To go out alone on the street with a girlfriend of the same age, to talk for a long time with a boy of the same age, to write him, telephone him, to read freely what we wanted to were all absolutely prohibited actions. Virginia Woolf has told how the celebrated archaeologist and traveler Gertrude Bell reached the age of twenty-seven without having walked alone through Piccadilly.

Why talk about things of the past? Because I don't consider them overcome yet. The defeat of Nazism didn't eradicate totalitarianism or racism; they still afflict a planet that is on familiar terms with the Moon. In spite of Madame Curie and Golda Meir, I don't believe that women have yet come to occupy the place that belongs to them.

I have chosen to recall a past that is both distant and near because it has been my own as well as other women's. What little I have done, I repeat, I have done in spite of being a woman. I understand that having been born in a difficult era isn't excuse enough for my deficiencies. There are those who, with an identical handicap, have reached the summit.

In summary, and conclusion, I have lived in an age when medicine, law, architecture, philosophy, letters, and acting were not careers for a truly "decent" woman. When truly "decent" women didn't walk alone on Piccadilly Square or Florida Street. Today, a Russian woman has gone on her own around and around the block we call our planet. Soon, her North American sisters will jump into space, and they won't lose face by doing so. The Moon won't be shocked to see them leave the capsule wearing pants.

Yes. Things have changed. Gabriela Mistral began life in a worse situation than the Brontë sisters—in the Valley of Elqui, surrounded by obstacles that seemed insurmountable. She was a teacher in pitiful schools in Chilean hamlets. Nobody dreamed that the Nobel Prize awaited her. Referring to difficult times, she wrote to me: "I have chewed stones with woman's gums." All women of the nineteenth and early twentieth centuries—those who desired a radical change and struggled to achieve it— have chewed stones.

I see no worthwhile reason for receiving from you, my male friends, the Vaccaro Prize if not for having—myself also—chewed stones.

I have always dreamt that woman might be for you, my male friends, an equal and a partner. I have never made peace with those who didn't wish this, friend or enemy. The Victorian situation seemed to me as humiliating for men as for women. To see man diminished by persisting in this injustice hurts me, since I like to admire him and love him. Only in admiring and loving have I found happiness. To admire and to love leads us to accomplish work (whatever its nature), which is the palpable proof of our admiration and our love. I know that my work has been none other than that; it has no other meaning or reason for being. It is the result of a very intense and always renewed need to admire and to love. Had there not been in the world of men (and I mean men) those worthy of this admiration and love of mine, my life would have been very different. They have helped me in my struggle, and I didn't always need their physical presence. With those living as well as dead I was not only in communication but in communion. Never have so few gained pardon for so many things done by others.

When in 1953 a group of women was locked up in Buen Pastor prison, Mother Gertrude asked all of us to sew a sign on our smocks, for identification. It occurred to us then that it would be better to write our whole name and wear it on our chest, where it could be clearly seen. One cellmate, María Rosa González, embroidered mine with green thread on a piece of white ribbon. When I left the prison, I tried to buy my smock as witness to an unforgettable experience. They wouldn't give it to me. So I unstitched my name-tape and took it with me. It's one of the most prescious souvenirs I have.

Gentlemen, friends: I shall keep the Vaccaro Prize medal with that piece of ribbon.

GUILLERMO CABRERA INFANTE
[1929–]

CABRERA INFANTE was born in the town of Gibara in Oriente province, Cuba. Although he has been a journalist, film critic, and translator, he is most celebrated as a writer of fiction. Cabrera Infante's best-known novel is the humorous and verbally inventive *Tres tristes tigres*, 1965 [*Three Trapped Tigers*, 1971], set in prerevolutionary Havana and banned both in Franco's Spain and Castro's Cuba. Cabrera Infante is also the author of a collection of stories, *Así en la paz como en la guerra*, 1960 ["In Peace as in War"]; *Vista del amanecer en el trópico*, 1974 [*View of Dawn in the Tropics*, 1978]; and *La Habana para un infante difunto*, 1979 [*Infante's Inferno*, 1984], the latter two based on personal experience.

Cabrera Infante has said that he meant to be a doctor but found success in literature through a natural inclination toward parody:

> I wrote many short stories, parodies all, in the coming years. Then I tried writing on films, movies being central to my life, which was not the case with books. Later the crooked arm of the law intruded in my plans and I was accused of publishing a short story with four-letter words in English (which was true) and of corrupting Cuban morals (which was false: they were already corrupt) and I was put in jail, tried, and fined for what the judge called "writing English profanities." Harder than the sentence was the penalty: I couldn't write with my own name in the best

Cuban publications—but there was a kind of loophole: I could use a pseudonym.

This he did until 1960 when, after the overthrow of Fulgencio Batista, he published his first book under his own name.

In the first few years after the Castro revolution, Cabrera Infante was one of Cuba's best-known young writers. An editor of the avant-garde literary supplement, *Lunes*, part of the official newspaper, *Revolución*, his heterodoxy eventually brought him into conflict with the government, and in 1961 the magazine was banned. Cabrera Infante was given a diplomatic post in Brussels, but in 1965, after attending his mother's funeral in Havana, he left Cuba once and for all, eventually settling in England where he has become a naturalized British citizen. His most recent book, *Holy Smoke*, 1985, was written in English.

Since his exile, Cabrera Infante has often spoken out against censorship in Castro's Cuba. But he was also familiar with intellectual repression under Batista. The essay/story "English Profanities," translated into English for this collection, was originally titled "Obsceno" and was published in 1975 in a collection of autobiographical stories called *O*. Slightly reworked by the author in collaboration with the translator, it bears witness, with Cabrera Infante's typically mordant wit and humor, to a writer's travails in pre-Castro Cuba.

English Profanities

Guillermo Cabrera Infante
Translated by Peggy Boyers

One day in October 1952 the Secret Police paid me a professional call. They arrived in the afternoon, having found me by devious detours. They had already been to *Bohemia* (then a very popular magazine in Cuba and the most important in Spanish America) in which I had published a short story the previous week containing foul language. One of the characters, an American, cursed in English: realism was all the rage then.

At *Bohemia* they had questioned the fiction editor, Antonio Ortega, whose private secretary I was. Ortega had given them my unlisted phone number but had feigned ignorance of my address. Nice touch of his this. With my phone number in hand the detectives next directed their search to the Cuban Telephone Company, which in turn refused to divulge any further information—police or no police—even though the country was ruled then by Batista and his military band.

Shortly before the imminent arrival of the police I received a phone call from the telegraph office. They had a cable for me from New York but only had my phone number. Would I be so kind as to give them my address so that they could deliver the message? Not suspecting that anything was up, I gave my address not to the cable company but to the Secret Police. Crafty bastards! Within ten minutes of the phone call they were knocking at my door. Inside the apartment there promptly reigned the kind of panic that rules a sinking ship. My melodramatic mother tore at her hair and threatened to throw herself out the fourth-story window. My father rambled on about something vaguely pertinent, but no one listened. My brother accused me of being innocent. In the meantime the plainclothes policemen stayed in the doorway, apparent shyness rendering them incapable of entering or leaving. But they were not ashamed of sending us into a state of despair. One policeman wore a long dirty-white *guayabera*, which almost covered his beige and brown pin-striped trousers. The other had on gray trousers and a gray shirt

61

underneath a dark-blue nylon jacket. Both wore hats: felt and fake Panama respectively. But they did not search the house's "every nook and cranny," as reported by a journalist some time later.

All they wanted was for me to come with them, *now*. I asked permission to put on a coat and tie—which at the time was the costume worn by those who respect the law, but which years later would be the opposite: the garb of the guilty. The police said it wasn't really necessary; I was fine as I was. Come as you are, pal. Finally at the center of this storm—a relatively calm moment—my father was able to gather his rambling into a question. He asked the visitors if he could come with me. The visitors again answered that this wouldn't be necessary. Apparently, nothing was necessary to them, only my singular company. But the police promised that my stay among them would be short. Only time enough to sign some paper or other. That was all. "You'll be out in a jiffy." But it was with a feeling more akin to fear than resignation that I went with them to the headquarters of the Secret Police—an agency not to be confused with the Bureau of Investigations, the SIM (Service of Military Intelligence), with the yet to be created BRAC (the Bureau for the Repression of Communist Activities), or with the national police. They were *La Secreta* and virtually omnipotent.

The Secret Police Building was an old dark house on Simón Bolívar Avenue, named after the liberator of South America. But for some reason the street was still known by its old name, Calle Reina. (Perhaps the association between the great liberator and *La Secreta* was too much for the people to swallow.) When we went in, the faces of the policemen at the front desk turned toward us. What did they expect? A hardened criminal? (Here I have to interpolate that at the time I was so small, skinny, and beardless that I looked closer to sixteen than to my actual age, twenty-two.) The policeman in the *guayabera* or perhaps the other uttered a memorable phrase, *"Aquí etá éte"*—meaning "Here he is"—in broken Spanish. Another interpolation: language is my business.

With that sentence he set in motion the machinery of police bureaucracy. They took fingerprints. They also took my belt, my shoelaces, and a few cents from my pocket. Later they made me go into a room where they took my picture, profile and front: mug shots all. Finally they made me return to the front desk where they read me the accusation made by one "Armando Senis" or "Denis," whom I later spent years searching for to find out who he was and why he had done this to me. In the original letter of denunciation by "Denis" or "Senis" to the Minister of the Interior, there were more references to *Bohemia* as a scandal sheet than to me. But the magazine had refused to comply with the warrant and so the accusation came to fall literally on my lap. Yet another interpolation: I was considered guilty until proven innocent.

Later they transferred me to a cell that overlooked a treeless patio. Its complete furnishings consisted of a narrow wooden bench and a bucket in the far corner. The entire cell reeked of urine. Even the polished iron grating, which was about level with my face when I stood, stank. It was a stenchtrap. They locked me up in there but not for long—and not out of compassion. Another policeman opened the door and ordered me to follow him. We climbed to the second floor where they made me sit before yet a third policeman, who was older and had a kinder face. He began to question me instantly. Soon he sounded wounded, the way certain policemen do. You see, they take the commission of any crime as a personal offense and they feel hurt. As for me, fear of the police combined with a general fear of publishing made me respond nega-tively—negatively, that is, for me.

"What made you write that trash?"

That was the policeman asking. Swiftly dismissing his literary ap-praisal, I told him I believed the crime was in the publishing, not in the writing of the piece.

"Well then, why did you publish this crap?"

He had the magazine on top of the desk open to the page that read "Ballad of Bullets and Bull." Now he pounded on the admittedly poor illustration with his swollen index finger. He was looking more and more like a literary critic than a policeman.

"Aren't you ashamed?"

He meant of the language, of course, not the story. I told him that I was not. I used a cunning variation of the *ad authorem* argument. You see, that was the sort of down-to-earth language used by the characters in the story, not by me. He didn't buy it.

"And what if your sister should read this?"

I told him I was sorry, but I did not have a sister.

"And how about your dear old mother?"

I answered—and this was my final contribution to the inquest—that my mother was not old, but rather young, in fact. Besides, she did not speak English. After this the policeman began to turn red from his gray head of hair down to his trembling mustachioed upper lip and at last burst out furiously, "You'll pay for that, smart ass! Hey you," he called out to the policeman standing nearby who had brought me up to him, "take him down and lock him up!" Then he hissed at me: "You can't mess around with the police, mister!"

Back to the cooler. By then it was high noon. The stench had also peaked. At about a quarter after, there appeared a familiar face who looked at me a moment and then went on without stopping. It was Noe Noah, a friend whom they must have allowed to go to the men's room behind the far wall of the courtyard. (*La Secreta*'s secret was that it had more urinals than cells.) At six—it was already getting dark (October is a dubious month)—Antonio Ortega came to see me. He stayed only two minutes. (Days later, after I was freed, he told me that in my cell I had looked like a guinea pig in a cage. I was about to remark on the rabbit face he would have had in my place—he was, like Juan Blanco, somewhat hare-lipped—but I kept quiet out of respect and because I was then out of prison. He was an older man—and my boss to boot.)

After a short while, Juan Blanco, a lawyer and future in-law, appeared. He assured me he'd get me out quick as a flash—and then vanished like a flash in the pan. But someone came from a nearby cafe with a hero sandwich and a sad *café con leche*. Courtesy of Juan Blanco, not the law.

It was soon after that that hammering began. As if the situation weren't dramatic enough, Havana was being threatened by what seemed to be, according to the Weather Bureau, either a hurricane or a tidal wave or flood-level tides—or perhaps a combination of all these sea scourges at once. In order to protect the decaying headquarters of *La Secreta*, also known as *La Decrépita*, from the record-breaking storm, invisible carpenters were busy nailing shut the doors and windows all over the place. But no carpenter came to my cell to secure it against the rain, which began to stream in sideways from the open patio. The din of the hammering continued practically through the night. Resigned, I decided to curl myself up in the corner farthest from the steel bars—but closer to the shit stink. Between the foul smell and the awful noise I hardly slept. Now the wind, full of foreboding, came rushing in and added itself to another, more distant hammering: thunder. Policemen prepared.

Like all Cubans I used to welcome hurricanes as occasions for celebration but feared their calamitous aftermath: fiestas turned funerals. But increasingly it was only calamity which I saw now in the form of a water spout and surf which would flood my cell and surely drown me between the steel bars and excreta. *La Secreta!*

But by morning the weather cleared and the sun was shining bright. The hurricane had not even hit Havana, having changed course at dawn and gone westward. But I was still a prisoner, in fair weather as in foul.

Outside in the street my friends were gathering, as I learned later: Carlos Franqui (the revolutionary and future editor of the most influential daily paper in Cuban history), whom they had not allowed in to see me (Franqui held that this was just as well for jail would do me good both as a person and as a writer) Noe Noah (whom I saw henceforth with paranoid persistance; anyone capable of going into the inner sanctum of the police urinals, even to urinate, I suspected had to be either police or a desperate victim of polyuria), Rine Leal (an old friend and future relative), and others whom I'd rather not remember. Not now anyway.

Round about late afternoon the cell opened and yet another police-man ordered me to follow him. He walked toward the entrance, or to the front desk rather—though this wasn't exactly a hotel. There was my father, smiling, small and meek as ever, but too weak to be genuinely supportive. A sergeant handed me a form and said, "Sign here." Sure that it was the work of Blanco's *habeas*, I took pen and prepared to sign.

"Not so fast, boy." It was a lieutenant or captain, someone of a higher authority, in freshly donned civilian clothes, who watched the scene, be-mused, from behind the sergeant:

"Never sign anything without first reading it, young man."

I don't know if I smiled. I only know that I looked at the form, trying to read the small print. But my reading was interrupted by the sergeant:

"First sign; then read." They all laughed. I managed to sign, and they gave me back my shoelaces, my belt, and my pennies. I dropped the change in my pocket, put on my belt, and tied my shoes standing up: I was raring to go.

"Hey, where are you going?"

It was the sergeant. He had raised a hand like a traffic cop.

"Wait, wait, *muchacho*. We're not done with you yet, no sirree."

Then he added over his shoulder, "Take him away, boys."

He was addressing the police pair from yesterday—or was it from the day before yesterday? In any case, the fat one still was in his dirty shirt but the thin one was in a raincoat. Each grabbed me by an arm and together they lifted me off the ground and bore me away. My father stayed behind, still smiling meekly. In front, by the entrance, were my friends. I didn't see Juan's *corpus*. The two agents made me get into a car which took me posthaste toward Old Havana. We were headed com-pletely in the opposite direction from where I lived. They weren't taking me to my house, but rather to the emergency tribunal, as I learned later. Post*hate*.

In the street there were still signs of the hurricane that never came: boarded-up doors, masking-taped windows, and here and there a *ciclo-nera*. In Cuba, *cicloneras* were women who used to take to the streets in borrowed trousers right after hurricanes or whenever there was the slight-est sign of a cyclone, an occasion universally regarded as an orgy: a time for high partying and slight panic. In hurricanes we lived Decameron days. Now, as we entered Havana proper, an improper twelve- or thir-teen-year-old girl alone and dressed in particularly tight trousers, crossed the narrow street. The driver in his raincoat stopped the car to let her pass. Even he could be courteous. But when she had crossed the street he shouted at her:

"Save those tight little pants for me, sweetie. But don't take 'em off till they're good and dirty." He laughed; they both laughed. It occurred to me that for a lesser obscenity in a foreign language I was being driven to court by this lawman—outlawman, rather—when the car skidded and tilted dangerously. Due to the excitement of the driver, flushed with sudden sexual arousal, we had fallen into one of the trenches dug for the waterworks. Or for the hurricane. Whatever, we were stuck. This meant uncivil war.

"Everybody out!"

We all got out to see the car's two front wheels well into the ditch.

"Shit!"

The driver continued to curse his luck and his mother alternately. The second policeman, the one in the dirtier shirt now suggested that we lean against the body to lift the vehicle. The first policeman ordered a passerby to help and we began our attempt to haul the car out of the ditch, with the first policeman inventing new groupings for old word combinations, tedious though predictable. Suddenly it occurred to me that now that the policemen were so busy getting the car back onto the road, I could walk away without anybody's noticing my absence. Luckily for me, I rejected the idea. Policemen in Cuba used to be handier with guns than with cars. Happier too. I helped the boys get the car out.

When we got to the courthouse, which was adjacent to the port, the enormous wooden doors of the old palace were closed shut. There we stood, before the gates of the law.

"Fuck!"

"Now what?"

"Back to *Reina*, right?"

"Better we should leave him in El Príncipe once and for all."

"Good."

While the policemen discussed my destiny I reflected that it was no coincidence that we had arrived at the courthouse late, that my transferral to El Príncipe prison, where I should wait until Monday to be formally arraigned before the court, was a way of thwarting my *habeas corpus*. From the start I had been destined to El Príncipe. Everything, undoubtedly, had been preordained at the Ministry of the Interior: from the Secret Police right down to these ditchdiggers, they had only been fate's factotum.

When we arrived at the fortress on a Havana hill that was El Príncipe castle, it was late afternoon. The sentry guard stood at attention behind a lattice door.

"Who goes there?"

"Friends."

"Who?"

"The Secret Police."

"We're going to leave you a customer here until Monday."

"Come forward and be recognized."

The door opened, we came in and then began to climb an old narrow stairway to the castle. Behind me the iron door banged shut with an echo of the sort one used to hear on radio melodramas: the clanging was a message, a sound effect from fate. I have never felt worse than I did climbing those steep old stone stairs. I was sure I was being committed not to a temporary cell but to a real prison fortress: El Príncipe could be my Colditz, my Castle of If. If If, then Dante's or Faria's— which?

In the antechamber my constant companions provided my credentials and their identical IDs. The head guard yelled in my direction, addressing someone I couldn't see:

"One for one!"

I entered cell number one more diminished and meek than my father had entered life. They assigned me to a bed—a cot rather—by the door. I sat down. This time they had taken neither my shoelaces nor my belt, but they'd appropriated my freedom and something else besides, something even less tangible but important. I stayed on my cot for quite a while. Then mealtime arrived unexpectedly. Two prisoners came around dishing "dinner" out of a huge pail that resembled a gargantuan grub bucket. They informed me that I should take the plate and spoon from behind my bed, which I did. Suddenly from above there fell upon my plate a huge ball of grayish-yellow droppings. It was the food. I stared at it long after the waiters had gone. I tried to eat, but it tasted worse than it looked: I was unable to get down even a bite. For a moment I felt like crying. But only for a moment, since someone put a hand on my shoulder and said:

"A gourmet, eh?"

I turned to find a tall, strong, dark inmate with a striking resemblance to Steve Cochran, the movie villain. He held out his very real hand to me. He was not wearing the prison's uniform but a sport shirt, trousers, and loafers. He was as casual as his clothes.

"My name's Jorge Nayol Nasser."

I told him mine.

"Why are you here?"

I explained. He smiled with his full set of perfect white teeth: "You'll be out in a jiffy."

Where had I heard that before?

"You sure?"

"Before a week's over. You'll see. But first we'll fix dinner for you."
He turned around.

"Hey you! Two fried eggs with rice for my friend here."

He was speaking to someone who started to walk toward a very definite place at the back of the large cell. In the cell there were at least ten prisoners and some fifteen beds: prisons were not crowded in Cuba then. The direction in which Jorge Nayol Nasser called was a sort of cell within the cell. In it there was a kitchen complete with a refrigerator, jars of preserves and canned goods, and of course a stove and cook. Everything (including the cook) belonged to Jorge Nayol Nasser—and now let me explain who Jorge Nayol Nasser was, for though he didn't know me, I had certainly heard of him.

Toward the end of the 1940s, or perhaps the early 1950s, a big bank on the Paseo del Prado in Old Havana was held up. The thieves succeeded in taking one million clean pesos, which in those days meant a cool million in American dollars: a hefty haul. The robbers were a two-time loser named Guarina, a first-offender taxi driver named Chino Prendes—whom I had known briefly around 1948 as the boyfriend of a girl from my hometown who lived in the tenement of Zulueta 408—and Jorge Nayol Nasser, born in Lebanon. The robbers, who had escaped without difficulty, were discovered because Guarina had hidden part of the loot in his father's house. There the soldier-boyfriend of one of his sisters found out about the sacks stuffed with bills and notified the police. They were all apprehended. Chino Prendes and Guarina had drowned in a swamp trying to escape from the Isle of Pines prison, while Jorge Nayol Nasser, all cunning and savvy, still waited for his trial in preventive custody in El Príncipe—where he lived like a prince. His handsome outlaw photo had appeared many times in the newspapers, always linked to violence and law-breaking. He was a tough guy and looked the part. So did Steve Cochran.

Now Jorge Nayol Nasser was the boss in cell number one. After dinner and cigars he invited me to gather with the others around the bed in his small private cell within the big cell. The other inmates accepted me with instant warmth that contrasted sharply with the steady scorn of the police. We talked about what Jorge Nayol Nasser, a born leader, talked about, and he talked about what all common prisoners in the underworld talk about: their criminal obsessions. In jail you are what you dream. Jorge Nayol Nasser's recurring dream had to do with the perfect holdup. He had been in prison in the United States, in Sing-Sing of all places. He used to tell us how when he arrived in prison as one of a threesome and saw its six or seven stories from the courtyard—cells all—he said to himself, "Jorge, brace yourself. Here you'll have to be real tough." He survived the jail. Not so those who arrived with him:

one had committed suicide by throwing himself head first to the courtyard from the top floor and the other had gone mad.

But Sing-Sing, more than a jail for Jorge Nayol Nasser, had been an
education. There he had met several prisoners who came to form a part
of his personal mythology. They were the elders: the safecracker who was
freed by the governor in exchange for opening a federal strong-box containing valuable government documents (you see, the combination had
been lost); the bank robber with a thousand consecutive years in Sing-
Sing and still playing it cool; finally, the veteran criminal who became
an advisor to young inmates. It was thanks to the latter that Jorge master-
minded the Havana bank robbery. It was in Sing-Sing that the plan had
taken shape after the veteran's having learned how badly guarded Cuban
banks were. It was the master criminal who taught him how to do it.
"But I never should have trusted a queer," Nayol Nasser would finish.
He was referring, of course, to the thief who had the name of a local
queen, Guarina.

Another member of the criminal circle was the unsuccessful robber
of the hideous Miramar bank heist. The botched job had ended in a
messy shootout with the police and had been featured in the newspapers
not long before. The gangster had been wounded in the leg and only
recently had left the prison hospital. He came over to speak to me.

"You the guy who wrote that article in *Bohemia*?"

He said, very clearly, "article" rather than story. He was one of those
people, of whom there are many, who are unable to accept fiction. Just
like Defoe's readers. For them the printed word is always a mirror to
reality. But the following observation nevertheless surprised me:

"You don't know what you're talking about man. That's not how
you go about knocking off the opposition."

My story, the one that had landed me in jail, was about political
gangsters who "knock off" the wrong man but never regret it. Their only
concern is for the waste of time involved. In the end they simply resolve
to aim better next time.

"I'm gonna tell ya how it's done."

He never did. But he added an afterthought:

"What we have more than enough of here is people to kill."

He probably had meant to say people capable of killing—killers—
but that's how it came out. Then he continued telling me about the
robbery: the perfect heist that went wrong. Finally he finished with a
brief reference to his crippled leg.

"But I *will* walk like you again. You'll see."

Thus in their conversation each expressed his most immediate wish.
For Jorge Nayol Nasser it was to have another shot at the perfect bank
robbery. This time it won't fail: no queers, no stoolies, see? For another

inmate it was to go instantly free. For the lame bank robber it was to be able to walk again without limping. When the man who wanted to be set free at his impending trial left the group, Jorge Nayol Nasser said to me:

"That one, believe me, will get at least thirty years."

That's how it really was. But the most painful part of the conversation came when the crippled crook left the group to walk back to his bed. I could see that his left leg was much shorter than his right.

"You can see for yourself," Jorge Nayol Nasser added. "Not even the Surgeon General could make him walk like a man again."

Jorge Nayol Nasser was firmly convinced that he was a man the judges couldn't touch: he had a perfect alibi and he would go free at his trial. We all love symmetries, and indeed that's what happened. A few months later he was free and roaming the streets of Havana: the man who robbed a bank and lived to tell it. Then he decided to go to Venezuela, where they told him that robbing banks was like taking candy from a baby. He was killed while trying to rob a bank in Caracas. Obviously, he had been misinformed.

Night came and then again the day. In prison one has to lead a regular life: early to bed and early to rise, though nobody is any healthier, wealthier, or wiser for it. But the new day brought me a surprise. Shortly after ten a guard called me and ordered me to go to the front gate. There, in the dilapidated visitor's room, was Juan Blanco with a white paper in his hand:

"Your *habeas corpus*, pal. Don't ask me how I got it. Here it is. Let's go!"

I didn't understand. Did he mean go away? For good? Until the guard at the gate barked at me that I could leave, I didn't really understand that I was free. I could shout like the genie in the bottle: Free! Free at last! But knowing what happened next to the genie, I didn't. I went back to the cell to pick up my things and left in silence. I didn't say good-bye to a single one of my new but already fleeting friends. Not even to Jorge Nayol Nasser, *número uno* in number one.

Outside, poised anachronistically atop the castle ramparts, was a taxi. Leaning against it, waiting for me was Rine Leal, smiling. He had the best teeth of all. All three of us went to my house which, ironically, was very near the prison.

At home my girlfriend was waiting for me, crying for joy—as Juan Blanco said to my mother, "What I promise, I deliver." But it wasn't a happy ending. It was this girl that I married hardly eight months later, perhaps having been moved by such a tearful display. Shortly before the wedding the trial took place. Since my crime was a minor one the case had passed from the emergency tribunal to a justice court. The justice of the peace, so-called, had a reputation for being a hanging judge and a man about town who visited the Havana brothels every night. In the courtyard, in open cells corroded by time and weather, several caged prostitutes waited, motley-feathered, for their trial. No doubt two or three additional child molesters biting the bars and more than one pimp to boot were in other cells I didn't see. But so foul did my case seem to this judge, so severe, that he made us pass to another, dustier room while the usher announced loudly to the crowded courtroom:

"Now hear this! The next case the judge will try *en camara, in the bedroom.*"

He had meant *in camera*, behind closed doors—and that's how the proceedings took place. I hardly had anything to say, but I had to listen a great deal. The good old judge delivered me a lecture on the virtues of writing without including what he called "the amenities of everyday life." He finished up with a sentence worthy of his reputation.

"So that you won't do it again (take note of this secretary): one hundred and fifty pesos in fines. Case dismissed. Have a good day, gentlemen."

He disappeared to a higher calling and into the next room.

And that was that. No appeal and no reprieve from the governor at the eleventh hour. I could pay the equivalent in time, of course: for the judiciary, time is money. In those days a hundred and fifty pesos was one hundred and fifty dollars; no less, no more. But for me it was a fortune. I had saved up only seventy pesos for the trial. Between them Juan Blanco and Antonio Ortega came up with the difference, payable to the bailiff with a hungry hand.

But the punishment didn't end there before the judge convening *in camera*, ready with a sentence and damning remark, but rather in the open ostracism to which the publication of the short story would condemn me. For two years I was prevented from pursuing my degree at the School of Journalism; nor could I publish another story, feature, or article under my real name for a long time. Perhaps this was the origin of my passion for pseudonyms (I've written under at least six pen names) and the successive transformations my proper name has undergone over the years. All because of what the jovial judge called "English profanities."

JULIO CORTÁZAR
[1914–1984]

BORN IN BELGIUM—where his father was assigned as a diplomat—Julio Cortázar held dual citizenship in Argentina and, many years later, after 1981, in France. Educated in Buenos Aires, he first earned a living as a high school teacher of French and as a translator. In the meantime he wrote poems, a play, and his first short stories, the latter published under the titles *Bestario*, 1951, *Final del juego*, 1956, and *Las armas secretas*, 1959 (later translated into English in editions entitled *End of the Game, and Other Stories*, 1967, and *Blow-up, and Other Stories*, 1968). Among his other works, most of which are available in English, are novels such as *Los premios*, 1960 [*The Winners*, 1973]; *Rayuela*, 1963 [*Hopscotch*, 1966]; *62: Modelo para armar*, 1968 [*62: A Model Kit*, 1972]; *Libro de Manuel*, 1973 [*A Manual for Manuel*, 1978]; and further collections of short stories, essays, and poetry.

Cortázar, master of the style known as "magical realism" (also called "the marvelous real" by Alejo Carpentier when he first drew critical attention to the natural juxtaposition of the fantastic and the everyday in Latin America), achieved international fame with the publication of *Rayuela*. A novel that has been referred to as "a turning point for Latin American literature," this seminal work explores the craft of writing itself, inviting the reader to take part in the creative process. His later works continued to play with new literary forms and increasingly expressed Cortázar's concern with social, economic, and political crises in Latin America. Rejecting "overly naive forms of realism," as he put it, out of the belief in a "more secret and less communicable" order, Cortázar attempted to jolt a complacent reader through humor, satire, unexpected inversions of the commonplace, and overt social protest.

The essay/letter included here, written in 1967 for the Cuban literary journal, *Casa de las Américas*, and translated for this anthology, testifies to the importance of Cortázar's visits to postrevolutionary Cuba in awakening his commitment to socialism and the cause of the people's revolution. Cortázar was a member of the editorial board of the journal, whose editor was Roberto Fernández Retamar. This piece was written at the height of a period of ideological controversy in Cuba over the role of the intellectual in a revolutionary society. That period would culminate in 1971 with the government crackdown on "pseudo-revolutionary leftist intellectuals."

During the last years of his life, spent in Paris where he had made his home for three decades, Cortázar also voiced his commitment to Sandinista Nicaragua. Visiting Nicaragua, he read to a stadium full of enthusiastic admirers; in return, he expressed his own admiration for the Marxist revolution and its efforts to improve the living standards of the average citizen. As a tribute to him after his death, his friends have mounted an international effort to raise funds for a medical center there in his name.

Letter to Roberto Fernández Retamar

Julio Cortázar
Translated by Jo Anne Engelbert

Saignon (Vaucluse)
May 10, 1967

My dear Roberto,

I owe you a letter and also some pages I promised you for the magazine on the situation of the intellectual in Latin America today. As you will see almost immediately, it was easier for me to combine both things; if I can just talk to you—even from a piece of paper sent across the sea—I think I can say a few things that would come out too starchy if I put them in the form of an essay, and you know that starch doesn't agree with me very well. Let's just imagine that we're back in the car together headed for Trinidad and that we've managed to grab the best seats for ourselves, to Mario's annoyance, with Ernesto and Fernando jammed in the back, and that we're just continuing that conversation we kept up for three marvelous days last January and which you and I will always find a way to keep going.

I prefer this tone because words like "intellectual" and "Latin American" automatically make me put up my guard, and if they happen to appear together they immediately sound to me like somebody's dissertation bound (I almost said "bound and gagged") in Spanish leather. Add to this the fact that I've been away from Latin America for almost sixteen years and that I consider myself above all a *cronopio* who writes stories and novels with no other objective than the one pursued by all *cronopios*—their own personal enjoyment. I have to make a great effort to understand that despite those peculiarities I am a Latin American intellectual. And I hasten to tell you that until just a few years ago that classification aroused in me the muscular reaction of making me shrug my shoulders until they touched my ears; I think the everyday facts of this reality that oppresses us (*reality* this unreal nightmare, this dance of idiots at the edge of the abyss?) make it necessary to quit playing games, especially word games. I agree then to accept my status as a Latin American intellectual, but I must make one qualification: it is not on account of my being one that I will say what I intend to say here. Circumstances place me in this context and I must speak within it, but I would like to have it understood that I do so as a moral being—let us say as plainly as possible, as a man of good faith, without my nationality and my vocation being the factors determining my words. That my books have been present for years in Latin America does not invalidate the deliberate and irreversible fact that I left Argentina in 1951, and that I continue to reside in a European country for no other motive than my sovereign desire to live and write in the way that seems the most complete and satisfying to me. Certain events of the past five years have moved me to renew my personal contact with Latin America, and that contact has been made because of Cuba and from Cuba. But the importance that that contact has for me does not stem from the fact that I'm a Latin American intellectual; on the contrary, I assure you that it stems from a concern that is more European than Latin American, more ethical than intellectual. If what follows is to be of any worth, I have to be totally frank, so I had to start out by saying these things to the die-hard nationalists who have often reproached me directly or indirectly for my "distance" from my country, for my refusal to physically return to it.

In the last analysis, you and I know very well that the problem facing the intellectuals of our times is the single, universal one of achieving a peace based on social justice, and that preoccupation with the national origins of individuals only subdivides the problem without changing its character. An author far away from his country necessarily has a different perspective on things. When a writer lives at the periphery of local circumstances, outside the inevitable dialectic of daily challenge and response provoked by the political, economic and social problems of a particular country, which demand an immediate commitment on the part of the conscientious intellectual, his sense of the human process becomes more planetary; it operates by synthesis, attempting to see things whole. If this global perspective means loss of concentrated force in an immediate context, it affords a lucidity that is sometimes unbearable but always instructive. It is obvious that as far as mere world information is concerned, it doesn't matter whether you live in Buenos Aires, Washington, or Rome, whether you're living in your own country or outside it. But I'm not talking about information but about vision. As a Cuban revolutionary you know very well that local imperatives, your country's daily problems, form a vital first circle in which you must operate as a writer, and that this first circle, in which your life and your destiny are at stake as well as the life and destiny of your people, is at the same time a point of contact and a barrier with respect to the rest of the world—contact because our battle is that of humanity, and barrier because in a battle it is not easy to attend to anything but the line of fire.

I know there are writers with full awareness of their national mission who also struggle for something that transcends and universalizes that mission; but there are many more intellectuals who, yielding to the conditioning of circumstances, act from the outside inward, latching onto a set of universal ideals and principles and making a country, a language, a national character conform to them. I am not advocating a watered-down, abstract universalism—people becoming "citizens of the world" in order to avoid concrete responsibilities in places like Viet Nam, Cuba, all of Latin America—the sort of universalism that is more comfortable because it is less dangerous. On the contrary, my own personal situation tends to make me participate in what is happening to us *all*, to make me attentive to all voices that approach the compass rose, whatever their angle of origin. At times I wonder what my work would have been like if I had remained in Argentina; I know that I would have continued writing because I'm no good at anything else, but judging by what I had done by the time I left my country, I am inclined to believe that I would have continued along the crowded thoroughfare of intellectual escapism I had traveled until then and which is still the path of a great many Argentine intellectuals of my generation and my tastes. If I had to enumerate the causes for which I am glad I left my country (and let it be very clear that I am only speaking for myself as an individual and not as any sort of model), I believe the main one would be the Cuban revolution. For me to become convinced of this it's enough to just talk from time to time with Argentine friends who pass through Paris evincing the saddest ignorance of what is really happening in Cuba; all I have to do is glance at the newspapers read by twenty million of my compatriots: that's enough to make me feel protected here from the influence that is wielded by U.S. information in my country and which an infinite number of Argentine writers and artists of my generation do not escape, even though they sincerely think they do; every day they are stirred by the subliminal mill wheels of United Press and "democratic" magazines that march to the tune of *Time* or *Life*.

I'd like now to speak in the first person since what has been asked for is a personal testimony. The first thing I will mention is a paradox that may be of value if it is considered in the light of the previous paragraphs, in which I have tried to clarify my situation and your situation. Doesn't it seem really paradoxical to you that an Argentine oriented from birth almost entirely toward Europe, to the point of burning his ships and going to France, without a clear idea of his destiny, should have discovered here, after a decade, his true condition as a Latin American? But this paradox raises a deeper question: Whether or not it was necessary to be situated in the most universal perspective of the Old World, from which everything seems to be perceived with a kind of mental ubiquity, in order to gradually discover a little the real roots of what is Latin American without thereby losing a global vision of history and man. Age and maturity are factors, of course, but they are not sufficient to explain that process of reconciliation and recovery of original values; I insist on believing (and I'm speaking for myself and only for myself) that if I had remained in Argentina, my maturity as a writer would have been translated another way, probably more perfect and satisfactory for literary historians, but certainly less provocative, challenging, and in the last analysis, fraternal for those who read my books for vital reasons and not with an eye on a file card or an aesthetic classification. Here I would like to add that in no way do I believe myself to be an example of that "return to the roots," national, telluric, or whatever, so characteristic of a main current of Latin American literature—for example, *Los pasos perdidos* or, more specifically, *Doña Bárbara*. This atavism as it is understood by someone like Samuel Feijoó, for example, seems profoundly alien to me because it is so narrow, parochial, and I would even say provincial; I can understand it and admire it in people who don't achieve, for a multitude of reasons, a global vision of culture and history, and who concentrate all their talent on a "regional" focus, but it seems to me to be a preamble to the worst advances of a negative nationalism when it becomes an article of faith for writers who because of a cultural deficit insist on exalting the values of the "land" against values in general, raising up their country against the rest of the world, their people (because this is what it comes down to) against other peoples. Can you imagine a man of the stature of Alejo Carpentier converting the thesis of his above-mentioned novel into a belligerent battle standard? Of course not, but there are those who do just this, just as there are circumstances in the life of a people in which that sentiment of return, that almost Jungian archetype of the prodigal son, of Odysseus at the end of his voyage, can lead to an exaltation of what is theirs in which, through a kind of breakdown of logic, they feel the profoundest scorn for everything and everyone else. And then we know what happens, what happened in 1945, and what can happen again.

Let's say, then, getting back to me, since I am, reluctantly, the theme of these pages, that the paradox of rediscovering from a distance the essence of what is Latin American implies a process that is very different, not at all like a hasty, sentimental return to one's old stamping grounds. Not only have I not returned to my old stamping grounds but France, which is my home, continues to seem to me the ideal place for a temperament like mine, for tastes like mine, and I hope, for what I still intend to write before I devote myself exclusively to old age, a complicated and absorbing activity, as we know. When I say that I was privileged to discover my condition as a Latin American, this was only one of the aspects of a more open and complex evolution. This is not an autobiography, so I'll summarize that evolution by simply enumerating its stages. A writer left Argentina who believed, as Mallarmé did, that reality ought to culminate in a book; in Paris a writer was born who believed that books ought to culminate in reality. That process embraced many battles, defeats, betrayals and partial successes. I began by becoming more aware of my fellow man on a sentimental and, in a manner of speaking, anthropological plane; one day I woke up in France to the abominable evidence of a war in Algiers—I who as a boy had understood Spain's war and later the World War as events in which what was essentially at stake were ideas and principles. In 1957 I began to be aware of what was happening in Cuba (previously through news articles from time to time, I had gained a vague notion of a bloody dictatorship like so many others, but I had no strong commitment of feeling, despite my sympathy for the principles involved). The triumph of the Cuban revolution, the first years of the government, were no longer a mere historical or political satisfaction; suddenly I felt something else, an incarnation of the cause of man as I had finally come to understand it and yearn for it. I understood that socialism, which until then had seemed to be an acceptable and even necessary historical current, was the only current in modern times that was based on the essential facts of human existence, on the fundamental ethos that was systematically ignored in the societies in which it had been my destiny to live—the simple yet inconceivably difficult principle that humanity will begin to be worthy of its name on the day in which the exploitation of man by man comes to an end. I was incapable of going further than that, because, as I have told you and demonstrated to you on many occasions, I am completely ignorant of political philosophy; I have not come to feel myself a writer of the left as a result of an intellectual process but as a result of the same mechanism that makes me write the way I write or live the way I live— a state in which intuition, some magical sharing of the rhythm of men and things, charts my course without giving or asking explanations. With Manichaean oversimplification I can say that almost every day I run into people who are thoroughly familiar with Marxist philosophy and who nevertheless behave on a personal plane in a completely reactionary manner, while I, who have been steeped in bourgeois philosophy my whole life long, nevertheless venture farther and farther along the avenues of socialism. And what is being asked about in this present survey is by no means easy to define—the *situation* in which I find myself at the moment. A text of mine "Casilla del camaleón," recently published in your magazine, could demonstrate a part of that permanent conflict of the poet with the world, of a writer with his work.

But returning to my situation as a writer who has decided to assume a task he considers indispensable in the world around him, I want to complete the description of the road that ended in my new awareness of the Cuban revolution. When I was invited to visit your country for the first time, I had just read *Cuba, Prophetic Island* by Waldo Frank, which struck a responsive chord in me, awakening a kind of nostalgia. I felt a sense of lack, as if I were out of touch with the world of my times, although in those years my Parisian world was as full and exultant as I had always wanted it to be, something I had achieved after more than a decade of living in France. Personal contact with the achievements of the revolution, friendship and dialogue with writers and artists, everything I saw, positive and negative, on that first trip had a double impact on me: on one hand I was again touching Latin America, from which I felt so far away at the personal level, and on the other hand I was witnessing the hard and at times desperate task of building socialism in a country so ill prepared for it in many ways, so open to the most imminent danger. But then I realized that that double experience actually wasn't double at all, and that sudden discovery amazed me. Without previous analysis, without thinking about it, I suddenly came to the marvelous realization that my ideological path coincided with my return to Latin America; the revolution, the first socialist revolution I was privileged to follow firsthand, happened to be a Latin American revolution. I hope that on my second visit I showed you that my amazement and joy did not remain on the level of mere personal satisfaction. I felt that somehow my belief in a socialist future for humanity and my individual and emotional return to Latin America, which I had left without a backward look many years earlier, were finally reconciled.

When I returned to France after those two trips, I understood two things much more clearly. On one hand, my personal and intellectual commitment to the fight for socialism, which up to that time had been rather vague, would enter, as indeed it did enter, a phase of concrete definition, of personal collaboration wherever I could be of use. On the other hand, my work as a writer would continue on the course that my character and temperament set for it, and although at some moment it might reflect that commitment (like an occasional story that takes place in your part of the world), this would be a consequence of the same principles of aesthetic freedom that are leading me at the present moment to write a novel that is set almost outside of historical time and space. At the risk of disappointing the catechists and the defenders of art at the service of the masses, I continue to be that *cronopio* who, as I said at the beginning, writes for his own pleasure or his own personal suffering, without the slightest concession, without "Latin American" or "socialist" obligations understood as a pragmatic a priori. And it is here that what I tried to explain at the beginning finds its greatest justification. I know very well that living in Europe and writing as an "Argentine" scandalizes those who demand a kind of obligatory classroom attendance for the writer. Once to my utter stupefaction a foolish jury awarded me a prize in Buenos Aires; I found out that a certain celebrated woman novelist from those parts had said with patriotic indignation that Argentine prizes ought to be given only to residents of the country. This anecdote epitomizes in all its stupidity an attitude that appears in many forms but which always has the same objective: even in Cuba, when it could make little difference whether I live in France or in Iceland, there are those who are mildly disturbed about my supposed exile. False modesty is not my forte. It astonishes me at times that people don't see that the reason my books have had some resonance in Latin America is that they postulate a literature whose national and regional roots are nourished by a more open and complex experience of reality; each evocation or recreation of what was originally my experience reaches its maximum tension precisely when it opens outward onto and inward from a world that transcends it—a world which, in the last analysis, chooses it and perfects it. What Lezama Lima has done in Cuba, that is, assimilate and Cubanize in a poetic synthesis the heterogeneous elements of a culture that embraces everything from Parmenides to Serge Diaghilev, I would like to do through tangible experiences, direct contacts with a reality that has nothing to do with information or erudition, but which is its *living* equivalent, the lifeblood of Europe. And if one could say about Lezama Lima, as Vargas Llosa has just done in a beautiful essay appearing in the magazine *Amaru*, that his Cubanness is profoundly affirmed by his assimilation of foreign elements into the vital juices, the very voice of his country, I also feel that the Argentinity of my work has gained rather than lost because of this spiritual osmosis. A writer in this state neither renounces nor betrays anything. Rather he establishes a vantage point from which his original values become part of a perspective infinitely wider and richer. From it, these values—as I know very well, although others may deny it—gain in richness, in amplitude, recovering the deepest and most valuable elements they have to offer.

Because of all this you will understand that my "situation" doesn't concern me simply on the personal plane; I am quite willing to go on being a Latin American living in France. Exempt for the moment from any kind of coercion, from the censorship or self-censorship that restricts the expression of those who live in highly polarized environments, my problem continues to be, as you must have sensed when you read *Ra-yuela*, a metaphysical problem, a continual struggle between the monstrous error of being what we are as individuals and as people of this century, and the possibility of an ideal: a future in which society will finally culminate in that archetype of which socialism provides a practical vision and poetry provides a spiritual one. From the moment I gained awareness of the essential human condition, the quest for that ideal has been my commitment and my duty. But I no longer believe, as I once could, so comfortably, that literature of mere imaginative creation is sufficient to make me feel that I have fulfilled myself as a writer; my notion of that literature has changed. I now believe that that literature embraces the possibility of representing the conflict between individual realization as humanism understood it, and collective realization as socialism understands it—a conflict that achieves what is perhaps its most devastating expression in Peter Weiss's *Marat-Sade*. I will never write expressly for any one faction, minority or majority, and the repercussion that my books may have will always be a secondary phenomenon unrelated to my task. Nevertheless, I now know that I write *for the sake of, in order to*, that there is an intentionality directed toward a hoped-for reader in whom the seed of the future man resides. I cannot be indifferent to the fact that my books have encountered a vital response in the young people of Latin America. This strikes me as the confirmation of a potential, the possibility of insights, intimations—apertures upon mystery, wonder, the astonishing beauty of life. I know of writers who surpass me in many ways and whose books, nevertheless, do not engage the people of our lands in the fraternal combat that mine do. The reason is simple. If, once upon a time, a man could be a great writer without feeling like a participant in the immediate history of mankind, this is no longer true. No one can write today without this participation: it is a responsibility and an obligation. Works that assume this obligation, even though they are imaginative works displaying the entire gamut of games writers can invent, are the only ones that can approach greatness. Even though they never allude directly to that participation, in some ineffable way they will contain that tremor, that presence, that atmosphere that makes them recognizable and enduring and awakens in the reader a sense of contact and closeness.

If this is still not sufficiently clear, let me add an example. Twenty years ago I saw in Paul Valéry the highest exponent of Western literature. Today I still admire him as a poet and essayist, but he no longer represents that ideal for me. No one could represent it who, throughout a lifetime dedicated to meditation and creation, arrogantly ignored the dramas of the human condition which were given expression in the eponymous work of an André Malraux, and which in a devastating, contradictory way, but in a way that was far more admirable precisely because of the devastation and the contradictions, were being portrayed by an André Gide. I insist that I demand of no writer that he make himself a tribune of the struggle being waged against imperialism in its many forms; but I do demand that he be a *witness* of his own time as Martínez Estrada and Camus tried to be, that in his work or in his life (how can they be separated?) he bear witness in his own way. It's no longer possible to respect, as we once could, the writer who takes refuge in an ill-conceived freedom in order to turn his back on his own human sign, his pitiable and marvelous condition as a man among men, of a privileged spirit among the martyred and the dispossessed.

For me, Roberto, and with this I will close, none of this is easy. The slow, absorbing, infinite and egoistic traffic with beauty and culture—life on a continent where a few hours put me in front of a fresco by Giotto or a Velázquez at the Prado, the curve of the Rialto of the Grand Canal or those London salons in which it seems that the paintings of Turner reinvent light, the daily temptation to return as in other days to a total, feverish absorption in intellectual and aesthetic problems, to lofty games of thought and imagination, to creation with no other finality than the pleasure of the intellect or the senses—all this sets off in me an interminable battle with the feeling that none of it is ethically justified if at the same time it is not open to the vital problems of peoples, if it does not resolutely assume the condition of the intellectual of the third world to the extent that every intellectual nowadays potentially or effectively *belongs to the third world, since his mere vocation is a danger, a threat, a scandal for those who are slowly but surely resting a finger on the trigger of the bomb.* Yesterday in *Le Monde*, a cable from UPI transcribed the declarations of Robert McNamara. These are the exact words of the U.S. Secretary of Defense: "We consider that the explosion of a relatively small number of nuclear devices in fifty urban centers of China would destroy half the urban population (more than fifty million persons) and more than half of the industrial population. Moreover, the attack would eliminate a large number of persons occupying key positions in government, in technical areas and in industrial management, along with a high proportion of skilled workers." I quote this paragraph because I think that after reading it, no writer worthy of the name would be able to return to his books as if nothing had happened. I cannot keep writing with the comfortable feeling that a writer's mission is accomplished in the mere exercise of a vocation as novelist, poet or dramatist. When I read such a paragraph, I know which of the two elements of my nature has won the battle. Incapable of political action, I do not renounce my solitary cultural vocation, my obstinate ontological search, the games of the imagination in their most dizzying planes. But all this does not merely revolve about itself; it no longer even resembles the comfortable humanism of the Mandarins of the West. In the most gratuitous thing I might write there will always appear a will to make contact with the historical present of man, to share in his long march toward excellence as a collectivity and as humanity. I am convinced that only the work of those intellectuals who respond to that impulse and that rebellion will become part of the consciousness of peoples and so justify this profession of writing for which we were born.

A very strong *abrazo* from your

JULIO

❦ ROSARIO CASTELLANOS
[1925–1974]

ROSARIO CASTELLANOS was born in Mexico City, but she spent her youth in Comitán, Chiapas, a region of southern Mexico which figured prominently in her work as did her abiding interest in its Indian population. She studied at the National University in Mexico City where she was one of a group of writers known as the "Generation of the 1950s."

In addition to her work as a journalist and a teacher, Castellanos held positions at the Institute of Arts and Sciences in Tuxtla and at the National Indigenist Institute in Mexico City. After teaching in the United States at several universities, she was appointed to the chair in comparative literature at the National University.

Certainly one of Mexico's most outstanding authors—appreciated even more following her untimely death by electrocution while serving as Mexico's ambassador to Israel—Castellanos's first book of poetry was published in 1948 and was followed by eleven more poetry collections; there were in addition three books of short stories, two novels, four volumes of essays and literary criticism, and a long satirical play entitled *El eterno femenino* [The Eternal Feminine], published posthumously. There is no way to prove her death was not accidental, but the obsessive presence of death in her writing seems tó indicate a premonition of suicide. Her life was marked by sadness and loneliness, from the death of her brother when she was a child to the loss of two of her three children as well as an unhappy marriage. Her writing was an outlet, and it contains much testimony to the suffering she experienced as a woman; but Castellanos was also vitally concerned with the plight of the uneducated and poor Indians of her country, and she was equally committed to the advancement of women's rights in a society notoriously obsessed with *machismo*.

Her most celebrated works include the novels *Balún Canán*, 1957 [translated as *The Nine Guardians*, 1960] and *Oficio de tinieblas*, 1958 ["Occupation of Darkness"]; the short-story collections *Convidados de agosto*, 1964 ["The Guests of August"] and *Album de familia*, 1971 ["Family Album"]; and the collection of essays *Mujer que sabe latín*, 1973 ["Woman Who Knows Latin"] from which the following piece is taken and translated here for the first time. Her poetry has been published in a volume entitled *Poesía no eres tú*, 1971 ["Poetry Is Not You"].

In a 1985 essay-portrait of Castellanos, Elena Poniatowska wrote this tribute to her friend and colleague:

> I believe that Rosario Castellanos was a great Mexican writer, if not great in all she wrote, great in her aspirations. And great above all for the love she inspired and continues to inspire in us. Before her, no one except Sor Juana truly devoted herself to her vocation. No woman lived to write like her. Rosario is faithfully that: a creator, a maker of books. Her books—poetry and prose— are the diary of her life.

EARLY WRITINGS

Rosario Castellanos
Translated by Maureen Ahern

I can't conceive of the discovery of a literary vocation as an act of the intelligence that reveals a fact which, up to that point, had remained hidden, and which, thereafter, is exposed to scrutiny, subject to the rules of development, ever striving to achieve fulfillment.

No, I understand the discovery of a literary vocation as a phenomenon that takes place on much deeper and more elementary strata of the human being: at the levels where instinct, blind but effective, finds an answer to situations of sudden emergency or extreme danger. When it's a matter of life or death and a person bets everything on a single card . . . and wins.

I'm not talking about myself, yet. I'm remembering the narrator of *Á la Recherche du Temps Perdu*, who, during his infancy, observes with curiosity and wonder, family preparations for a formal dinner, which, of course, he is forbidden to attend because these are ceremonies not yet appropriate for a child of his age.

Naturally the prohibition disappoints him. But what causes him intolerable anguish is the certainty that his mother will not leave her place at the banquet table to come upstairs, as she always does, to give him his goodnight kiss.

And still, contrary to all the foresight of logic and custom, the narrator waits impatiently for what could only be a miracle. To make it happen, he sends a little handwritten message, an imperious "Come!," which a servant carries to its addressee who never replies, much less satisfies his request.

Nevertheless, the narrator—by the mere fact of having written that note—feels the tension he struggled with diminish, as though writing had acted upon him (not on external circumstances) like a balm. Something mysterious has happened: a liberating change.

How could one not repeat the attempt and try to relive this unexplainable event? The narrator will do it every time the world closes in, every time the abyss opens, every time the sky falls; there, within reach of his lips, is the word, the spell. Once pronounced, it restores peace to the spirit, and order to chaos—two realities that interrelate and complement one another.

But as for myself—as in Cernuda's poem, at the same age as the narrator of *Á la Recherche du Temps Perdu*—"I didn't say words." I dwelt in a realm prior to them, one of pure sounds, which afterward I found out harmonized in sequences and correspondences. It was then that I began to recite the alphabet.

What counterbalances vertigo? Vowels. Yes, as long as they are uttered, movement slows down—like a merry-go-round that begins to run down—until whatever was making me dizzy or confused comes to rest, as if inviting me to get on. Because the machine is going to start up again and it's better that we spin with it rather than standing aside looking at it.

I get up onto the merry-go-round—with the magic incantation melting in my mouth—and each time that a thrust derails it, I set it back into orbit with the pure successive utterance of *a, e, i, o, u.*

And its rhythm is so regular and gentle that it resembles the breathing of a sleeping child. Yes, I've fallen asleep and I'm dreaming that my brother is not dead, that my parents are with me, that my house is a small one without a single empty space to be used by ghosts, bats, and witches.

A house for my size . . . not this excess that must be filled up with consonants. Twenty-two of them. Nor are they enough nor do I manage to invent more. Some of them will therefore have to be repeated: the best-sounding, most emphatic and clearest ones. Dogmas don't exist. Every night I freely decide according to whatever needs must be satisfied. As long as I perform this task (so similar to that of the child whom Augustine surprised on the beach trying to empty the sea with the aid of a small bowl), I'm not the girl death passed over so it could select a better person, my brother. I'm not the child whose parents deliberately abandoned her in order to carry on their mourning. I'm not that pitiful figure who wanders through empty halls and who doesn't go to school, to outings or anywhere at all. No, I'm almost a person. I have the right to exist, to appear before others, to enter a classroom, to go up to the blackboard and subtract fractions, to climb onto the stage decorated with crepe paper and recite the nursery rhyme that goes,

Hey ho,
Where can poor little Perlín be hiding?

Granny has searched for him
all through the house.

Perlín is a cat, the rest is an anecdote . . . set to music. Couldn't it be imitated? Well, imitation is still a task far beyond the resources at my disposal. But on the other hand, a copy. . . . Not an exact copy, of course. I'm not capable of that either. But an acceptable likeness. Let's begin by saying Perrin, instead of Perlín. But by saying Perrin, we've evoked the very pet that is antagonistic to the cat: its natural enemy, the dog. So from here on the story takes another turn, will have another plot, and will produce a different climax.

But, on second thought, the dog doesn't convince me in the least. The one I met once was too lively and high-strung, too difficult to handle. As a matter of fact, I would choose a toy dog. Or better yet, an imaginary dog. One that's never had any density, volume, bark, or weight. A dog that I've invented. His name is Rin-tin-tin.

The sound of these syllables evokes something familiar to me. Until I finally determine the coincidence: Yes, Rin-tin-tin is the hero of a thousand adventures grandly acclaimed by the only magazine that was published for children then: *Paquín*. The couplet comes into being with the fatality of the inevitable:

I like to read *Paquín*
because it has Rin-tin-tin.

I write it down on the pages of a school notebook, and when I read it I realize that this pair of lines, composed in my innermost heart, have just severed their umbilical cord, have freed themselves from me, and now they face me like autonomous units, absolutely independent, and what's more: like strangers.

I don't recognize them as objects that once upon a time belonged to me but simply as objects that are there and that challenge me to achieve a wider and more perfect existence: a public existence.

They refuse to go on existing in the pages of that notebook where only my eyes can read them: they aspire to continue somewhere else, where they are exposed to the sight of everyone. So I obey and copy the two lines on letter paper, put it in an envelope, and send it to the address of the children's magazine. There they have a page dedicated to spontaneous submissions from readers. There, once the required time has passed, I will stare astounded at the two lines—now set into printed letters and repeated infinitely in the infinitive number of copies—and at the bottom, my name. I am the author of what others read and comment on. Of what they appropriate and consider their own and recite in their own way and interpret however they like. I can't do anything to stop it or change it. I'm set apart, separated forever from what I once sheltered within myself as one shelters . . . no, I refuse to use the conventional simile: a child, which one's oeuvre is always compared to. At that time I lacked the slightest experience of what maternity is. But on the other hand, I did know what sickness was. So let's agree that I sheltered the couplet within me as one harbors an illness.

And now I'm cured of it. But exposed to the onslaught of so many afflictions. It's no longer a dog that barks around my feet, begging me to utter his name. It's I myself who wants to see me represented in order to know myself, recognize myself. But, what is my name? Who do I look like? Who am I different from? With pen in hand I start a search that has found its respite in proportion to its discoveries, which are still not over.

HEBERTO PADILLA
[1932–]

HEBERTO PADILLA is the author of many collections of poetry, published between 1948 and 1971; numerous essays written for Cuban and foreign journals; and an autobiographical novel—*En mi jardín pastan los héroes*, 1981 [*Heroes Are Grazing in My Garden*, 1984]—begun in Cuba and completed in the United States. Selections of his poetry have been translated into English under the title *Legacies*, 1982. He was born in Pinar del Río, Cuba.

An early supporter of the Cuban Revolution and an editor with Cabrera Infante of *Lunes de Revolución*, which was shut down in 1961, Padilla was sent to Prague and Moscow as correspondent for Castro's *Prensa latina*. Later he became disenchanted with the restrictions placed on writers and artists, and he expressed his reservations in a book of poems, *Fuera del juego*, 1978 ["Out of Play"], which resulted in his being charged with "conspiracy against the state" and detained in 1971. After a short imprisonment, he was obliged to retract his words in public, and for the next nine years he lived under virtual house arrest, forced to work as a translator and ghostwriter and unable to publish any works in Cuba. The "Padilla affair" touched off widespread protest from intellectuals on both continents, and it disillusioned many former Castro supporters in Latin America. In 1980, Padilla was allowed to join his wife—the poet Belkis Cuza Malé—and son in the United States, where they had emigrated several years before.

Padilla had begun writing *En mi jardín pastan los héroes* in Havana in 1970, before the government accusation against him. He kept his manuscript hidden and, despite a copy having reached police hands, Padilla managed to smuggle it out with him when he left Cuba. The "Afterword" to this novel, reproduced here, describes his initial imprisonment and later departure from Cuba. It underscores the ironies and indignities of the circumstances, the atmosphere of artistic repression under Castro to which the novel testifies.

Today, Padilla lives with his family in Princeton, New Jersey. He and his wife founded and edit a literary journal, *Linden Lane Magazine*, primarily devoted to Cuban-American artistic expression. Padilla is also executive director of the Center for Hemispheric Affairs of the Institute for Contemporary Studies in San Francisco. His most recent publications include *Autoretrato del otro*, 1987 ["Self-portrait of the Other"], a volume of memoirs and essays; *Un cielo perdido*, 1987 ["A Lost Sky"], a book of poems; and a novel, *Prohibido el gato*, 1987 ["No Cats Allowed"].

AFTERWORD

Heberto Padilla
Translated by Andrew Hurley

I was lying on one of those wooden boards hung from the wall by two thick chains, like those in medieval dungeons, in a narrow cell of the Department of Security of the State of Cuba, when I heard the big steel door creak open. A guard ordered me to stand. It must have been very early in the morning; there was no sound from the neighboring streets. I was surprised once again that the man was heavily armed, since at every door in that stronghold with its labyrinth of hallways there was a guard who challenged you and gave you permission to pass. I walked again the long stretch that separated me from the small, cold, overly bright office of Lieutenant Alvarez. I was his "case."

Each prisoner is always interrogated by the same officer. The socialist world's outstanding contribution to jurisprudence is that policeman, investigator, and examining judge are one and the same person. Perhaps they do it that way to speed up the work of the tribunals, whose only function is to hear the charges of the prosecution and deliver the sentence, without ever considering how the investigation might have been conducted or its conclusions arrived at. The defense lawyer merely pleads for clemency in the name of the generosity of the Revolution.

Before entering the office, I went once again through the ceremony of abasement, simple and brief, to which all political prisoners are submitted. The guard grabs you by the bare shoulders (since the prison uniform is a kind of sleeveless overall, the color of baby shit, given you at random, so that one week it may swallow you up and the next squeeze you like a straitjacket), shoves your nose against the wall, and stands at attention before the closed door. Then, pitching his voice in a guttural tone he thinks of as martial, except that some speech defect makes what he says imcomprehensible, he exclaims: "Tinint, priznr jacintf'r sere byndmi!"

The phrase, which he has memorized, is too pompous for the national temper; the guard pauses for a split second and, almost choking, finishes: "Mission tletiminter."

Of course, if one is Cuban and has heard it often, he may manage to decode the phrase as follows: "Lieutenant, the prisoner you sent for is here behind me. Permission to let him enter."

From within is heard an imitation of Fidel Castro's voice, since every Cuban policeman's aesthetic and emotional goal is at least to *sound* like Fidel. "Permission granted, comrade. Have him come in."

The first time I was taken to his office, Alvarez was wearing a dress uniform and he behaved with the ceremonial air he might have adopted to receive a captive general after a long battle, but today he wore U.S. Army fatigues. His fatigue jacket was held at the waist by an imposing green belt, from which a no less imposing pistol hung. I was afraid that something had happened, since he seemed ready to go into combat. His silence and angry look added to my uneasiness. Moreover, this time he didn't order me to sit down. He was standing before the desk flanked by the two chairs we always occupied. Behind him I saw the door, ajar for the first time, which had intrigued me from the beginning, through which could be heard the incessant pecking of several typewriters, doubtlessly making copies of recorded interrogations that would be submitted later to expert analysis.

"We've had Mesié Pier Golendorf, notorious enemy agent, here for a month. We know what you said about his detention: 'To convince me Pier is guilty, you have to show me proof of his guilt.' And who are you that we have to show you any proof?"

I remained silent, but Alvarez didn't stop. "We have in our possession all the notebooks you keep your 'literary notes' in—which are nothing but reports to the enemy. You don't believe me?"

I said that Golendorf was a member of the French Communist Party and a friend of Cuba.

"Like you, right?"

He shouted then and abruptly took the manuscript of my novel *Heroes Are Grazing in My Garden* out of a desk drawer. I recognized it immediately by the two thick, hard, plastic covers that Soviet export companies use for their catalogues and I used for bindings. It was unmistakable.

"We've found all your copies. You made more than they do for *Granma* magazine, except *Granma* spreads the ideas of the Revolution and you spread CIA poison."

He stroked the shining covers and smiled as he looked toward the door. "Your wife should be here with you. You two are cut from the same cloth. She says she has claustrophobia, so the doctor has diagnosed her as a hysteric."

I said she had nothing to do with what I said, did, or wrote, that she didn't have to suffer my fate, much less be held for no reason at all.

"Is that a challenge?"

I said no, but I knew what I was saying was wasted breath, they had certainly picked her up moments after me. And they had. A cold chill ran through my body when I heard her tense, anguished voice emerging from a tape recorder, refuting the accusations this very officer was throwing at her. What did she have to do with my poems, my novel, my opinions? Why had she been unjustly locked up in one of those cells? Truly, I could never have imagined that they would resort to such tactics, dictated by blind hatred. If my imprisonment for "conspiring against the state" was an outrageous hoax, her imprisonment—when they knew she suffered from a nervous condition—could only have been the result of "policy," the term they use for high-level decisions which, though unjust, are considered necessary. In fact, they were taking their revenge, two years afterwards, for not having been able to stop the Cuban National Union of Artists and Writers from unanimously awarding me the national poetry prize. The jury, made up of both Cubans and foreigners, insisted so strongly on its decision, in spite of political pressures, that my book *Out of Play (Fuera del juego)* was published by the Writers Union itself, though reluctantly. My novel was said to be only an attempt to create a new international scandal. The title *Heroes Are Grazing in My Garden* infuriated them: only *animals* graze—horses, for example, which was Fidel Castro's nickname in those days.

To get an idea of the paranoia with which State Security reads the work of Cuban writers, consider the case of Virgilio Piñera. He published his collected poems under the title *A Whole Life*, and included "The Horse's Path," originally published in the magazine *Silver Spur* in 1941. The police suppressed the poem at the last moment, even though Virgilio had shown them the collection. Ironically "The Horse's Path" *did* appear in the index, since the efficiency of the police censors didn't reach that far.

I took the title of my novel from a brief poem by Roque Dalton, which begins and ends with the line "heroes are grazing in my garden." Roque was a friend of many years, member of the Central Committee of the Communist Party of El Salvador, dead under circumstances that have never been completely clarified. He had a great sense of humor, of irreverence, and he was greatly amused that one of his lines might be used as a book title. But whenever the novel was mentioned in high-level gatherings of the police, the clever line was taken as an insult.

Well, there was no doubt now that vengeance and hatred could be converted into "policy," though I couldn't see the need to extend it to my family. There was a knot in my throat and tears came to my eyes. Alvarez looked at me condescendingly. "Cry if you want to; it's all right for a man to cry. But before you declare war on us you'd better ask yourself if you're ready for the bullets. You're intelligent, of course we recognize that. But we have to do something about this state of affairs with regard to the intellectuals of Cuba—if we don't want to wind up like Czechoslovakia. In Czechoslovakia, intellectuals are all standard-bearers of Fascism, like that little Russian friend of yours Yevtushenko, who's anticommunist and anti-Soviet."

Yevtushenko had cabled me from Moscow, congratulating me on the prize awarded to *Fuera del juego*. "It is a bitter book," he said, "but bitter truths are still truths."

I replied, though I was convinced it wouldn't do me any good, that history would be the judge. Alvarez shouted, "Counterrevolutionaries have no history!" I poured out my objections. I insisted that no one could ever prove that my wife and I were anybody's agents; I had sent the novel that was so irritating to everyone to the rector of the University of Havana, under whom I was working, so he could read it and give me his opinion; I had no intention in writing it other than to mirror some types and conflicts which emerge only in a revolutionary process: the very fact that we were being held in detention for a novel that had not yet even been published illustrated my point better than anything else. "You know that I've been to almost all the socialist countries," I said, "and worked in two of them. And in every one of them I saw very clearly that the political apparatus in the end becomes a force of unquestioning authority, political leadership unfailingly becomes alienated from its popular base. Instead of being here in a cell like criminals, my wife and I, I should be discussing my book at the Writers Union with my colleagues and the political leaders of my sector, not with the police."

"Yes, of course, over a cup of coffee and a good cigar, so you could then become president of the Union."

"You have a very bad opinion of writers, Lieutenant."

"Because they're all the same."

"All of them?"

"All," he said, "without exception. Did Che make exceptions when he said all writers are in a state of original sin?"

It was Raúl Castro's reasoning, too. Years before, in Prague, speaking to the Cuban diplomatic and commerical mission I was with, Raúl had referred to the controversy raging around Solzhenitsyn in the USSR. He had said, even then, "In Cuba, fortunately, there are very few intellectuals, and those there are do nothing but get bogged down belaboring the obvious."

The real motive behind an article entitled "The Provocations of Herberto Padilla" in *Olive Green* magazine was that the magazine, the official organ of the Cuban Armed Forces, was at that time publishing editorials which clearly implied that Raúl Castro was at last purging the cultural sector of the country. This was an old ambition of his; he had done it for the morals of the country when he created the infamous Military Units for Aid to Production (MUAP), forced-labor camps into which hundreds of homosexuals were crowded in Camagüey province. Both purges showed his style—coercion, repression, jail. I will never forget the impression of Raúl that Waldo Frank left me with in Havana in 1960: "There is some deep abnormality in Raúl. He's cold and cruel and might even be capable of crime." A Cuban writer who was with us gave me a terrified look. We were both frightened by the vision of Raúl, but we believed it was subjective. After all, Frank was an old man and in the habit of judging men and stories by his own brand of religious ethics.

"The moment will come," Alvarez went on, composed once again, "when every citizen will be a member of the Interior Ministry, as Fidel wants. Then no one will have to be detained. But today the Party has assigned us this job and we are doing it."

He took the novel and thumped it on his desk. "Do you know what the title of your novel ought to be? Can you guess?" He came to within a few steps of me. "The inconclusive novel, buddy, in which nothing happens, nothing *can* happen. A few pages read by a tight little group. But it'll wind up where it deserves, in the trash—because what good is something fragmentary, unfinished, incomplete? Fidel doesn't like this poisonous shit, the leaders don't like it, the Party, nobody likes it."

And he seized the manuscript with a fury I'd not witnessed until then. I didn't see or hear anything more. When I came to, I don't know how much later, I was no longer in his office. A huge weight seemed to press down on my head. Next to the board I was lying on, a doctor was taking my pulse, listening to my lungs and heart; then he left without a word. For a few moments I tried painfully to reconstruct the scene, but my head felt three times its size and all the blood rushed to it; my ears rang; it was a struggle to breathe. I managed to get up and went to the water tap, tucked into a corner of the minuscule lavatory, no more than a hole in the floor. I splashed cold water on my face, all over my head, and I pissed blood while my nose also bled.

A cold unusual for March filtered through the three chinks high on one of the walls, openings to the outside for air; the cell was filled with a kind of mist through which I could make out walls scribbled with the end of a spoon—poignant inscriptions, farewells to the world, scraps of prayer, which I forced myself to stop reading. There was a light bulb above the doorway, protected by a steel mesh. I heard voices coming down the hall they herded all of us political prisoners through when they led us to an interrogation. We never saw one another; to avoid that possibility, the guards used whistles to signal that some prisoner was being moved. Once, when I was about to run into another detainee, two whistle blasts sounded simultaneously and they pushed my nose into a wall until they could hide the other man and I could go on down the hall.

I felt terribly weak, terribly tired, and went back to the wooden board, but when I tried to get up on it, my strength failed me and I fell full-length on the floor of the cell. My feet must have knocked against the door, the noise must have been heard, I don't know; the light of a flashlight shone through the peephole. Then the door was opened.

I found myself in the Military Hospital at Marianao. The place was roomy, airy, and you could see trees through a high window. The nurse had finished taking my electrocardiogram. A man's booming voice filled the whole place. "I'm a friend of Ramirito Valdés and Sergio del Valle." And he went on adding names of political leaders to an inventory nobody was paying any attention to—the guards, doctors, and nurses carried on with their duties. In a while the iron grating of my room opened and a fairly young nurse came in—unattractive but cheerful-looking—and put a thermometer under my arm, in the Cuban manner. I took advantage of the occasion to ask about the man; she would tell me only that he was under psychiatric observation.

"But if he's crazy, what's he doing here?"

"He's being treated—but of course his case is different from yours. I've read your books, we talked about them when we were young—your influence can be harmful to young people. But we have instructions to give you the best treatment we can in this hospital. I have orders to let you choose your own lunch and dinner."

She took the thermometer and looked at it with concern. I snatched it from her.

"That wasn't necessary," she said. "You have a fever of 104. I'll give you two aspirins to bring it down."

Now the man was jumbling together all sorts of political figures—those in the government and those in exile. He was a friend of Raúl Castro and Raúl Chibás, of Ramiro Valdés and Hubert Matos. It was maddening.

"He's crazy," I said to the nurse, and she turned before she left: "But he had his own explosives factory."

She came back with two aspirins, and in half an hour the fever began to subside. As it did, I felt a growing lassitude that brought me images of my wife locked up in a cell at State Security; of my children, who wouldn't have gone to school, to avoid questions and taunts from the teachers and the other children; of the friends who would be in danger because of my arrest—I had no doubt that this was the beginning of the iron-fist policy Raúl Castro had so strongly advocated, had so keenly desired to direct personally. Vitali Voroski, the first correspondent *Pravda* sent to Cuba, who used to visit Raúl often, said to me one day as we were walking along the Avenida del Puerto: "Be very careful of what you say—be very careful." He said it warily. Vitali had an intense nature, a sharp intelligence; he was a cultured man who had fought in World War II and was a member of the Soviet Communist Party. Knowing what I now know of such things, I have no doubt that he was an agent of Soviet intelligence. That day he was accompanied by a young writer, whose name I don't want to disclose now, but with whom I have more than once discussed those words. Why did he warn us that way, leading me to imagine the most terrifying possibilities?

He said to us: "*Pravda* has sent me word that in a few days a young Russian poet, more or less your age—Yevgeny Yevtushenko—will arrive in Cuba. I have not met him, but his poems are published in *Pravda*, and that means a lot in the USSR."

We didn't know the name either. Was Voroski trying to warn us against Yevtushenko?

"The Cuban Communist Party is still Stalinist," Voroski added. "The newspaper *Today* has not even published Krushchev's speech to the 20th Congress, and looks with some disfavor on Yevtushenko's trip. They say the anti-Stalinists of today are the anticommunists of tomorrow. It horrifies them that Yevtushenko might become friends with any of the young comrades from *Revolution Monday*." *Lunes de Revolución* was Cuba's most influential literary magazine, and apparently Fidel Castro didn't want Cuba's young literary talent "corrupted" by Yevtushenko.

Vitali paused, adding in a low voice: "Listen to this and listen carefully. Enemy number one to all of you is Raúl, and one of his biggest phobias is culture in general. They say the only thing cultural whose existence he recognizes is the waltz."

This iron-fist policy knew no scruples. The first signals came from *Olive Green* magazine—defamation, insults. Why did Fidel Castro tolerate, or perhaps back it? We Cuban writers were not unconscious of the hostility with which foreign intellectuals, who almost unanimously defended the Cuban Revolution, reacted to the revolutionary government's support of the Soviet invasion of Czechoslovakia, even though, after that first statement, the Cuban press published the broadest, most objective version of the facts—which led one to assume fairly certainly that Cuba condemned the invasion. Fidel Castro himself, in the speech in which he admitted the "bitter necessity" of approving the invasion, noted that his words would let a lot of people down. If he accepted this, why his fury at the international condemnation of his behavior, why take it out on us? We weren't even permitted Yevtushenko's luxury; he condemned the invasion from abroad during one of his many literary tours, and he hadn't suffered the least repercussion when he returned to Moscow. Was this a symbolic act—was knocking me around and throwing my wife and me in prison a way, in morbid reflection, of subjecting Jean-Paul Sartre and Simone de Beauvoir to the same harsh treatment? It wouldn't surprise me: Fidel Castro has been obsessed all his life with the thought of doing away with all distinctions of worth and superiority. He equates himself with Lenin, casts me as a tropical Sartre, and turns Cuba into the whole African continent. The political weight of a country makes the international stature of its leaders, its artists, even its critics and deserters. Che Guevara himself told me that, in so many words—at meetings of the Steering Committee of the Ministry of Foreign Trade, which on Thursday midnights would be down to its chief, the minister Alberto Mora, and me. Our conversations were always about philosophy and literature: "This boom of Latin American writers is a result of the Cuban Revolution. Without the Revolution, those guys would be just a bunch of assholes running around Paris."

Standing up to a perfectly orchestrated, unscrupulous maneuver is utterly futile. There is no courage more impotent and unrecognized than a Cuban's as he tries to shout his truths at a police squad armed to the teeth. Your friends will tell you not to get stirred up; they know how much a petty official can count on to provoke you, and how much a victim has to lose. The only weapon against a bully is intelligence, cunning. Before bullies it's not a question of balls. The Chief of State's balls are beautifully protected by a repressive apparatus, whereas a jailed writer's are highly vulnerable to blows and torture. "The Spanish shout, 'I swear it, by my balls!' Well, a bull's are bigger yet, and they cut'em off," Galán, an old Asturian who loved the British crown, would declare. "England!" was to him a symbol of all the world's wisdom. "Viva England!" he would cry in a stifling Cuban beer hall where piss couldn't have been a more horrible color than the stream of beer they poured for a peso into whatever was handy (there were no beer mugs), nor could beer have smelled more like piss. The old man got on the nerves of my friends Hubert Martínez Llerena and Alberto Martínez Herrera, but all three of us felt the menacing knife.

So Security was right from the beginning—the title of these pages should be *An Inconclusive Novel*. And everything that happened to me in Cuba was so grotesque and paradoxical that when I tried to redo the lost chapters of my novel I inevitably went back to my own experiences. The fates of these characters, as well as the situations they are involved in, are inconclusive, because everything written in a suffocating political atmosphere is inconclusive and fragmentary. In such a world, the pages of a book must be hidden, and "the absolute time of literature" that critics speak of, out of which they claim quality of genius comes, becomes secondary. What counts is the furious weight of the *message*. Books written under socialism are generally imperfect; the country's reigning, or for that matter clandestine, aesthetics stamps books with a feeling of desperation or neurosis. They are accepted abroad out of solidarity, rather than literary recognition; they are adopted books—adopted for the scandal they cause.

I was living in New York when the furor over Boris Pasternak's novel broke out. I can never forget the face like an angry hawk's that was displayed in all the bookshops of New York. I read the novel then, like many of my friends, with no heed to its other values. Years later, traveling and living in various socialist countries, I saw how people in those countries were reading the book, which circulated clandestinely among them. They read it with bated breath, heart throbbing, tears in their eyes. In Spain, the avant-garde publisher Carlos Barral, praising Pasternak's poetry, called the novel "mediocre and disproportionately famous." And the novelist Juan Goytisolo wrote: "To make a judgment about the novelty and importance of these writers, we consider only their thematic audacity, without taking into account, as in the case of *Dr. Zhivago*, for example, or Solzhenitsyn's novels, that in structure, order, syntax, almost unvaryingly they repeat the narrative ploys of the nineteenth century— a world predating Marx, Freud, Ferdinand de Saussure," because, according to Goytisolo, "in countries with freedom of expression, there are no longer, as we all know, any provocative themes."

The Joke, by Milan Kundera, was published in London in 1965, I believe, due to the scandal that its publication caused in Czechoslovakia, but its editor restructured it to make it "accessible" to the English public. I remember the letter Kundera wrote to *The Times* asking people not to read that version, which was barely his at all. The defects in Solzhenitsyn's novels are often excused because of the urgency with which he wrote. Few people point out that those books require an impossible reading by an impossible reader, since no reader will have the kind of knowledge required for their understanding. It's a kind of writing for the blind.

This novel [*Heroes Are Grazing in My Garden*] was saved by a miracle. Five copies of the manuscript had been discovered, but the original remained untouched in a wicker basket, among toys and bric-a-brac. The policeman's hand was suspended in midair—just as in a detective novel— when his superior, satisfied with the plunder so far uncovered, ordered an end to the inspection.

When Fidel Castro let me know that I had been authorized to leave Cuba, I took the manuscript and put it in a nylon bag among hundreds of letters my wife had sent me from the United States during the year we were separated. I showed the bag to Gustavo Castañeda, who had charge of me, and who had done all the paperwork for my exit. I told him I wanted to keep these letters with me. Of all the people who saw me off at the airport, only my friend Alberto Martínez Herrera knew the manuscript was hidden among the letters. He was tense and pale, and every second we had to wait made him more and more anxious. The plane for Montreal was unusually late, so that I paced the waiting room endlessly under the watchful eye of the Security officer dressed in his blue safari jacket that only clumsily concealed a pistol. I had the impression that he was looking at the bag with marked interest; but Fidel Castro had given orders to let me go. What would he gain by searching it? The news of the authorization for my departure had been broadcast internationally. Jan Kalicki, Senator Kennedy's foreign affairs adviser, was waiting for me that night in Montreal; the novelist Gabriel García Márquez had traveled to Havana expressly to interview me before I left.

Wanting to ease the tension of the wait, I remarked on the items the tourists—mostly French-speaking Canadian girls—were buying. I saw the rum bottles lined up for sale, and I told Gustavo I was going to buy one, but the cashier said they could be bought only with dollars. The Security man turned pale. He said he was going to the washroom, and when he came back, he offered to buy me a beer. Minutes afterwards, from a corner of the waiting room, someone signaled him. I pretended I hadn't seen; I went to the washroom myself. The plane was to leave in a few minutes, and I would be the first person on board, I had been told. The Security man led me through a side door and we walked across the strip toward the boarding steps. I saw a man approaching with a package; it was a bottle of rum.

"Our gift to you. Send us a picture when you drink a toast in the United States," the officer said to me. "No hard feelings, I hope." The fat, pink-cheeked, clean-shaven young man was smiling, as though he were seeing off a high official on a daring mission.

I have no hard feelings. Castañeda was my natural enemy, he had orders to be just that—to dog my steps, to inform himself of my opinions, to make veiled threats over the telephone whenever a foreign visitor expressed an interest in seeing me. Now his impassivity whenever I shouted angrily at him seems to me admirable. He never lost his composure, not even when he tried to prevent Gabriel García Márquez from interviewing me, a year earlier, in the Havana Riviera Hotel. I saw him approaching with two policemen posing as tourists, and I turned to García Márquez and said, "Gabriel, this is a State Security officer and two of his agents. He's come to keep me from asking you to help me leave Cuba. His name is Gustavo Castañeda." And Gustavo offered his hand to García Márquez—he didnt't try to hide his profession, and he ordered his agents away.

He was a short man with a pale complexion, lank blond hair, and light eyes. Sometimes he was quite heavy and sometimes quite thin, depending on the ups and downs of his kidney disease; the last time I saw him he was in deep suffering. He had been divorced and was trying to make a more pleasant life for two little girls, his child and his new wife's. His brother had committed suicide in his office in the Philosophy Department of the university, where he worked. But Gustavo loved his job, felt enormous pride in it, and the truly great misery of his life was not being able to show off, at the Ministry of Culture or the Writers Union, where he was always hanging out, the major's uniform which was his glory.

I got on the plane and sat next to a window. I could see the airport I had freely passed through to go in and out of Cuba for many years, which one day was suddenly closed to me again. The observation decks were full of people waving goodbye to those like me who had been set free—I saw it all with a sensation of unreality. Still standing a few yards from the plane, a few steps from the Canadian tourists walking up the steps, the Security officer contemplated the scene. I saw him for the first time not from a moral but from a physical height. He was physically, below, like the dead time of my anxieties.

My first encounter with Fidel Castro in my cell at the Ministry Hospital came back to me—the clamor of opening iron bars and the spectacular movement of the escort opening way in a place where even inanimate objects would have knelt to let them pass. I remember him shouting at the guards—"Get out, all of you, and wait in the hall!"—at which his body guards faded away, and he waved a dossier, a shiny folder, and paced back and forth with great strides, but did not look me in the eye. "We two are the only ones who have to be here," he commanded. "Because today I have some time to talk to you, and I think you do, too; and we have a lot to talk about."

Yes, we had time to talk: time for him to talk his head off, to heap abuse on all the world's literature, because "getting revolutionaries to fight isn't the same as getting literary men to fight. In this country they have never done anything for the people, not last century, not this century. They're always jumping on history's bandwagon. . . ." He must have seen himself as an impressive leader standing magnificently before a no less impressive adversary dressed in a faded uniform, a scar still bleeding on my forehead, my whole body aching from the kicks of this moment of history. Unforgettable encounter! I describe it in detail in my *Memoirs*, and I trust someday he will write his version of this and all our other meetings, so we can both rest easy in our consciences.

I remember the morning when I saw the most impressive face history can show any man. That man was me. It was about six in the morning, and Lieutenant Alvarez appeared with another officer, named Gutiérrez. They ordered the nurse to give me back the clothes I'd been wearing when I was arrested, and ordered me to get dressed. "We're going to the beach; you need a little air."

At that moment, the crazy inmate stirred in his bed and gave a long wail. His anguish-filled inventory would begin again now, name after name. . . . The officers turned toward the voice, and the chief (Gutiérrez) made a comment, but I didn't get what he said.

We left and got into a car that was ordinary in every way except for a remote-control device that relayed its location to headquarters. At the end of Guanabo, in a heavy thicket opening onto a lovely solitary beach lit by the sunrise, we stopped. "Don't you feel better already?" Gutiérrez asked me. Alvarez sat on a boulder and he invited me to sit down too, but I refused, saying I preferred to stand.

"Well, if you want to *keep* standing, you'd better think seriously about what you're doing. We can destroy you. We can destroy you even though you know that, legally, we have absolutely no reason to. You haven't done anything, haven't planted any bombs or committed sabotage or smuggled foreign currency. The Revolution will recognize all this in its own good time and we'll have no choice but to rehabilitate you—but today you represent a dangerous tendency in the country, and we have to eliminate that tendency. So there's only one thing for you to do— come around to our way of seeing things . . ."

We returned to the hospital cell in silence, and they left without another word. They had already said it all. The nurse came in, smiling as always, with a clean uniform for me. As she went out, she stopped for a second. "You'll feel calmer from now on, so you can think. . . . That madman isn't here anymore. They've transferred him to Security. So you'll have peace and quiet."

And in the plane I thought again, too, of the poor, wretched man whose shouts I then began to miss, as the silence of solitude heightened my desolation. I was about to leave all that behind, down there, where the policeman was. I held on to my nylon bag, where my manuscript was; the plane's engines began to turn. At last we were rolling over the runway, and the officer disappeared from view. The plane took off, and I heard the stewardess' voice ask us not to smoke during takeoff. The plane gained altitude and leveled off; I looked out the window at the great brilliant expanse, that amalgam of greenness and luminosity that was my native land.

NICOLÁS GUILLÉN
[1902–]

BORN IN CAMAGÜEY, Cuba, Nicolás Guillén is Cuba's most nationally and internationally acclaimed poet. As a young man he began to study law, but economic hardship forced him to turn to journalism, like many aspiring Latin American writers of his own and subsequent generations. A founder of the Society of Afro-Cuban Studies and a pioneer in this field in his native country, Guillén started writing poetry in the spirit of the "son," a popular Cuban rhythm derived from African music and folklore. His earliest collections—*Sóngoro cosongo*, 1930, and *Motivos de son*, 1931 ["Son Motifs"]—capture the rhythms and expressions of rural Afro-Cuban culture, reflecting Guillén's long-standing concern for the poor and oppressed of his race.

A committed antifascist, Guillén was imprisoned in 1936 in the early years of Fulgencio Batista's power in Cuba but was later acquitted and released. He traveled in the same year to Spain, where he joined other leftist writers at the First International Congress of Writers for the Defense of Culture, later traveling on to other parts of Europe and Latin America. Guillén became a Communist in 1937, and in 1953 he was awarded the Stalin Prize.

After the Castro revolution, he achieved prominence in Cuba as "poeta nacional" as well as being named president of UNEAC (Union of Cuban Writers and Artists). Guillén has represented Cuba at many foreign conferences. It was in 1971 at a conference in the USSR that he delivered the speech published here for the first time in English. His words reflect the attitude of Marxist Cuba toward the role of literature in the context of a society in revolution. It should be noted that this address was given in the same year that Heberto Padilla was detained.

Among his many other published works are *España, poema en cuatro angustias y una esperanza*, 1937 ["Spain, Poem in Four Anguishes and One Hope"]; *El son entero, suma poética*, 1929–1945 ["The Entire Son, Poetic Summary"]; and *El gran zoo*, 1968 [*The Great Zoo and Other Poems*, 1973].

Words of Greeting

Nicolás Guillén
Translated by Cynthia Ventura

On behalf of the Union of Cuban Writers and Artists, over which I preside, and on my own behalf, it is a great pleasure to offer a warm and supportive greeting to the Fifth Conference of Soviet Writers. I should also express my gratitude—and hereby do so—to the board of directors of the Writers Union of the USSR for the singular distinction conferred upon me at being expressly invited to this event.

I remember with emotion meetings like this one in which I have participated. They were great experiences and a great help to me, for they contributed in no small measure to educating me and giving me a vision of what creative work is like in a great socialist country like the Soviet Union, the noble goals it always pursues and its great accomplishments. Furthermore, this conference meets at an especially tense moment in world history. On the one hand, an aggressive imperialism headed by North America entirely ignores the small countries—although it must be said that their smallness is only geographic, as is evident in the cases of Vietnam and Cuba. On the other hand, one can see the growth and development of the countries of the so-called third world, already in open rebellion and unrestrained struggle to affirm and extend their nascent personalities, to such a point that it wouldn't be an exaggeration to say that before the end of the twentieth century all of them will have shaken off the yoke imposed by a multitude of enslaving exploiters who consider themselves superior and who will have to relinquish the hard way (which in this case is the "good way") the treasure of human work, blood, sweat, and tears that they have been withholding.

In Latin America, the great land I have just come from—the creole and mestizo America (and so I call it "our America," as José Martí named it forever)—a popular rebellion is seething in such a way that it could be said we are living today as in those days which preceded the uprising of the Spanish colonies at the beginning of the nineteenth century, following the example and principles of the great, willful Simón Bolívar. Only one who is blind or deaf would not pay attention to such a subterranean clamor, such hurricanelike winds, such quivering and trembling as shake the American countries. No one doubts that Cuba, Chile, and Peru will not be the only ones to give—each in its own way, each according to its history—proof that they are ready to be free and independent once and for all. Because the truth is that the independence of Latin America was not consummated at Ayacucho when the great Marshal Sucre defeated the Viceroy's troops, nor much less almost a hundred years later in the waters of Santiago de Cuba and Cavite where the Yankee battleships destroyed the weak Spanish fleet guarding those ports and the declining power of the old Hispanic lion gave way to the dirty wing-flapping of the North American eagle, which occupied the position left by Spain in America. That is, imperialism replaced colonialism. We won the first battle for our independence against Spain, but the last, second, and definitive one will have to be fought not against Madrid but against Washington. This had already been observed by the watchful eye of José Martí. A battle with weapons in hand, for our enemy brandishes them and we can't respond to bursts of machine-gun fire with speeches and theories. That's what happened in the Bay of Pigs and that is what should happen in all bays where imperialism attempts to invade our dominion.

Now then, no writer can forget or not know what his role is in such a confrontation. His role is to struggle with all the resources in his power to defeat world imperialism, for the recognition of the right of countries to determine their own destinies, for a world peace that can only draw strength from justice.

I can't imagine, and I say so with all sincerity, comrades, how a writer of our times—above all, one who comes from a country in undeveloped rebelliousness—could turn his back on that struggle, that country, surrendering himself to sheer games of the imagination, to inconsequential verbalisms, to hateful polychromes, to amusing crossword puzzles, to deliberate obscurities, to the romantic treatment of realities or themes that correspond precisely and are pleasing to the very imperialists who asphyxiate and exploit us. It's a kind of cultural contamination that attempts to make us into individuals dependent on norms and methods alien to our anguish and our dreams—and worse yet into our own executioners. Nor can I understand how a genuine contemporary writer could, without blushing, present to a miner, a sugarcane cutter, an oil worker, texts that truly are hieroglyphs, when that writer has not struggled enough to have that worker understand them. This is not only mockery, but worse than a mockery, it is a betrayal.

I don't believe, and I hasten to say it again, that the fact that a writer puts his little typewriter (it needn't always be a pen) at the service of a popular struggle diminishes the artistic quality of his work. That's a reactionary judgment, because if the artist is genuine, he can and should find and show beauty wherever it may manifest or even hide itself. Engels was very right about this, as about everything, when he said that the political intent of a poem, a painting, in short, a work of art should be disguised, not appear in the foreground, because that was the worst propaganda that could be made. Propaganda should derive from the effectiveness of the work of art as such, not sacrificing beauty for politics but making them come together and harmonize. It should be the political— that is, propaganda—which is facilitated by the beautiful.

Dear friends, we have just celebrated in Cuba an important conference convened to define and specify the cultural politics of our revolution. I won't begin to explain here and now all the details of that great meeting, but I can tell you that the role of an intellectual revolutionary, and above all a Cuban intellectual revolutionary, was established there. We Cubans don't forget that Cuba is not only a country in revolution but a country at war, and at war with the strongest power of the imperialist world. This forces us to be implacable in the maintenance of a correct point of view with regard to a revolutionary culture. We reject whatever contributes to undermining or destroying our historical personality, and therefore we confront whatever comes from abroad and clashes with the national spirit. This doesn't mean we suffer from cultural chauvinism and that we bristle like a porcupine, rolled into a ball of spines, when faced with foreign cultural manifestations. We know what literary and artistic influences are; we understand very well the theory of cultural inheritance proposed by Lenin. We will not renounce the treasure that for us constitutes the Cuban bourgeois nineteenth century which produced Heredia, Martí, Avellaneda, Plácido, Zena; nor are we against the knowledge and assimilation of figures unequaled in universal culture. But we are ready to defend tooth and nail the preservation of our personality, which comes from the union or commixture of two human and fundamental nuclei: the black slaves and the white Spaniards, and their descendents. That blend of cultures is our seal; it constitutes our identification and our most intimate way of being, and we raise it like a defensive wall when faced with the penetration of decadent influences from countries destroyed by their vices, whose bright colors, as has been said, are precisely those of decomposing organic matter.

It is a secret to no one that, along with armed aggression, imperialism employs a type of intellectual aggression by sending out politically trained cultural attachés who undermine, or attempt to undermine, the spiritual bases of undeveloped or unsuspecting countries. They relegate authentic values to a secondary plane and take advantage by creating a subtle inferiority complex that makes everything emanating from the creative sources of our national spirit look bad, deficient, and incomplete. In this manner, countries subject to this type of power become true cultural colonies with representatives who are really subjects of the colonizing country and, therefore, tributaries of that colonization.

During the period that comprised republican life in Cuba, that is, the fifty or so years of feigned independence, Yankee imperialist policies not only made an attempt against our economy, exploiting us to the marrow of our bones, but also imposed upon us a type of language, a type of *slang* plagued with barbarisms, as a substitute for pure words and native expressions. Well then, we have decided to complete our political independence with cultural independence. Just as we have an ideological profile in our country that differentiates what was before the revolution from what is now, we are also willing to create our own art and literature that express our authentic way of being, our most genuine concerns, our struggles, our conflicts and hopes. We are not unaware of all the slander, all the insults that such an attitude, that such a decision provokes among imperialists, and of course among their most submissive servants. But that convinces us that we are standing on firm ground and that this ground will lead us to a final victory.

Dear friends, I would also like to say how much we Cuban artists feel sustained and encouraged by popular support. I can tell you that not even a day goes by without receiving at our worktable contributions by anonymous poets, short-story writers and even musicians and painters, who have recently become literate—common people who express in that way their interest in artistic creation. Of course, they're not always good works; to the contrary most of them aren't, due to defective style, an evident absence of technique or craftsmanship. However, they are highly promising and they testify to a sentiment of beauty that lives in the Cuban people and to the resources they possess which allow them to express themselves. Scarcely twenty years ago, more than one popular artist died with inspiration still inside him, lacking an outlet for his creative impetus because the conditions imposed first by colonialism and later by imperialism made him an intellectual invalid.

Last month I visited my hometown of Camagüey, and I was in the Mella library looking through old newspapers. Among them I found one more than a hundred years old which carried an announcement placed by the guardians of a slave poet, asking for public support to publish his verses and buy his freedom with the earnings. I couldn't find out how this effort had concluded because the newspaper collection was incomplete. But it made me think of the many talents, and even geniuses, who were frustrated under the Colony, not just by being black slaves but simply by being illiterate, even if they were free and white—peasants and workers deprived of any schooling—without counting those who suffered this lack under the Republic, a Republic divided by classes and even by the color of the selfish, colonial skin. How much genius, how many works will never be known, buried in oblivion!

Now then, how can a writer, a poet, a painter, far from such a moving spectacle, speak in a sibylline language to men who are beginning artists about Proust, Joyce, and Kafka, before Martí, Heredia, Luz Caballero, or Varela? How can one not develop in them, before anything, a national consciousness of art, a national consciousness of literature that allows them to know first who they are, where they came from, and where they are going? Cubans should not learn to read starting where others end, submerged in deprived decadence.

Dear friends, I don't want to delay this session any longer by abusing the kindness and courtesy you have granted me. But I couldn't resist telling you all this because I know it is good news for you. There are many viewpoints shared by the Cuban and Soviet peoples, and consequently by Soviet and Cuban artists. There are many tasks we have in common. I know, by personal experience and from everything I've seen, that Soviets and Cubans contemplate the same reality with eyes full of sympathy and understanding. Of course there are also traits that make us different without separating us, much less making us oppose one another, and which are highly positive because they affirm and define our respective personalities within a common sphere, a sphere of revolutionary struggle, of artistic creation at the service of the people, of the construction of the new man who lacks selfishness, who is all generosity and love. I reiterate then my most fervent hopes for the success of this conference, which I am convinced will produce conclusions of great interest for the writers of the socialist world in general. Thank you very much.

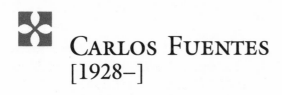

CARLOS FUENTES
[1928–]

CARLOS FUENTES is the Mexican-born son of a career diplomat. As a child, however, he lived in Washington, D.C., Santiago, Chile, and Buenos Aires, thus learning English as well as Spanish at an early age. After receiving his higher education in Mexico and Switzerland, he began a diplomatic career in the 1950s which he later put aside for writing and lecturing, although he served as Mexico's ambassador to France from 1975 to 1977. Fuentes, recipient of major international literary prizes, has been singled out by José Donoso, in his book on the Boom, as "the first active and conscious agent of the internationalization of the Spanish American novel" in the early 1960s.

Today Fuentes is Mexico's foremost novelist, known primarily for his richly textured portraits of Mexican social history from the late nineteenth century to the present. Focusing on Mexico City in the years after the Mexican Revolution of 1910, Fuentes' early novels probe the psyche of his mestizo nation, most notably in his portrait of the fictional Artemio Cruz, an amalgam of Mexico's best and worst character traits. Fuentes has written short stories, essays, plays, and screenplays. It is his widely translated novels, however, that are his major accomplishment. An innovative stylist, Fuentes was influenced by cinematic technique, and his narratives often experiment with multiple voices and montage effects to reflect the density of human memory and experience.

His most famous works include *La región más transparente*, 1958 [*Where the Air Is Clear*, 1960]; *La muerte de Artemio Cruz*, 1962 [*The Death of Artemio Cruz*, 1964]; *Cambio de piel*, 1967

[*Change of Skin*, 1968]; the ambitious epic novel *Terra nostra*, 1975 [same title, 1976]; *La cabeza de hidra*, 1978 [*Hydra Head*, 1978]; and *El gringo viejo*, 1985 [*The Old Gringo*, 1985]. His latest novel, *Cristóbal Nonato*, 1987 ["Christopher Unborn"], is inspired by the approaching fifth centennial of the discovery of America.

The essay which follows was originally delivered in English in 1974 as a speech at the annual dinner of the American Center of the PEN Club (an international organization of poets, essayists, and novelists). Fuentes' opening remarks were made in response to an introduction by the Polish-American novelist Jerzy Kosinski, then president of PEN's American branch.

CENTRAL AND ECCENTRIC WRITING

Carlos Fuentes

The wily old dictator, Porfirio Díaz, who ruled my country over three decades and who did not delete his expletives, once remarked: "Poor Mexico, so far from God and so near to the United States." I believe, my dear Jerzy Kosinski, that with one toponymical change, this singular remark could equally well be applied to Poland. But if applied to you, I would word it thus: "Poor God, so far from Poland and so near to Jerzy Kosinski."

A case could be made for the view that Mexico is the Poland of Latin America, and Poland the Mexico of Europe—when things go badly for us. When they go well—well, then we are both Finlands of the mind and can start counting our blessings.

My purpose tonight is to offer some random reflections on what I call central and eccentric writing, on writers who are either near to God and far from the Devil, or the other way around. A writer born in Poland or Mexico, so far from the gods and so near to the devils, realizes before he is out of knee pants that it is one thing to write from within a culture that deems itself central and another thing to write from the boundaries of eccentricity—an eccentricity defined by the central culture's claim to universality. The central culture tends to believe that it speaks with the words of God or, at least, that it has a direct and open line to the ear of the Divinity. With the voice of Jupiter, Whitman spoke of Democracy with a capital D; Jean-Paul Sartre argues as though he were the proprietor of dialectics; John Galsworthy wrote his novels as though he were the final arbiter of good manners; not to mention that imperialist Atlas, Rudyard Kipling, who regarded three-fourths of the world as "the white man's burden." In this way, the central culture is seen by the marginal cultures as offensive, self-serving, devouring, one that imposes its own values and is scornful of any values that are alien to it.

This arrogance of culture is compounded by other factors. If you are a Pole or a Mexican, you are also very conscious that your country has suffered grievous humiliations, territorial mutilations, aggressions and menaces of all sorts. We have had to develop a resilience to the constant pressures of the mighty, and we know the very concrete meaning of the principles of nonintervention and self-determination. We know, furthermore, the efforts and sacrifices it takes to maintain a national identity. It must be understood that our nationalism is not an aggressive force, but a way of preserving our values: we wish to enrich, not to impoverish, ourselves and others. If we have developed a defensive stance, it is because of the offensive one of the central culture which has put us in the situation of the scalded cat: we are wary of boiling water.

But rather than deal in these generalizations, I wish to explain my own views. Let me say at once that I have no Manichaean visions to offer, only an account of my own complicated experience as a writer from a marginal culture traveling the paths of the central culture. Permit me, then, to be frankly autobiographical.

It is hard for a Mexican *macho* to admit that he was led into the knowledge of literature and society by two women. But the fact is that the kidnapping of the logos by Western culture first became apparent to me when, in my early teens, I read Jane Austen. Here were these locally determined early-nineteenth-century products of white, European, middle- and upper-class civilization speaking with the assurance that they represented a fixed, universal, and eternal human nature. "It is a truth universally acknowledged," Miss Austen tells us at the beginning of *Pride and Prejudice*, "that a single man in possession of a good fortune must be in want of a wife." Though the statement is meant to be droll, it rests upon an assumption that it is not love that brings men and women together, nor even sexual desire. Property is the universal category, and love is defined by possession: of a good fortune, then a good wife.

Perhaps Jane Austen is the perfect example of a writer in harmony with the predominant values of her society. She is the novelist of means in a society of means, in both senses of the word. Everything, in her novels, is a means toward a means: courtship a means toward marriage, marriage a means toward economic security and social respectability, and these a means toward raising children who will once more repeat the round of middleness. *In medio stat virtus*: Miss Austen, the median novelist of the middle class, never concerns herself with ends; no one ever dies in her novels, no one ever questions God or is distressed by the lives of the less than fortunate and privileged. Nothing, in fact, is more distressing than the elopement of a nice girl with a dashing captain of the guard or the snub suffered by a spinster at the county ball.

What would Darcy and Elizabeth have had to say about the repres-

sion of the workers in Manchester in 1819? If forced to contemplate the
brutality with which the riots were handled, they would have found a
justification favorable to their social order. Darcy would not have had to
sacrifice his pride to colonize India or Elizabeth Bennet her prejudice to
accompany him and recreate Miss Austen's amiable world within their
closed walls in Delhi. There is no way for the oppressions conducted for
the benefit of her class to enter the world of her novels. And there was
no way for my particular quest for identity as the son of a Mexican
diplomat, living abroad yet trying to keep alive my allegiance to the
realities of Latin America, to accept this exclusion of the world I knew
in the jungles and mesas and rivers and faces of my land.

Behind Jane Austen's unself-conscious attitudes, I came to realize,
stood the weighty conviction, elaborated by the philosophy of the Enlightenment, that human nature is always one and the same for all men,
although imperfectly developed, as Locke put it, in children, madmen,
and savages; and that this true human nature is to be found, permanently
fixed, in Europe and the European elites. Only Europe, declared Herder,
is capable of living historically. After the French Revolution, to be universal meant to be a part of the dominant classes, conditioned by the
limited geography, the linear time, the future-oriented and progress-im-
bued culture of the commercial and industrial West. And the elites of
the West certainly needed this justification and certainly made full use of
it. Externally, they imposed their universal human nature on the imperfectly developed savages of their colonial empires. Internally, they put
their imperfect children to work in sweatshops and their imperfect madmen—William Blake and Emily Brontë, Nerval and Nietzsche, Poe and
Baudelaire—remained outside the glowing hearth of the law of human
nature, under which all men were equal insofar as all were men of means.

In effect, demanded Montesquieu, how is it possible to be a Persian?
Or, indeed, a Nigerian tribesman, a Peruvian peasant, a Chinese coolie,
or a Mesopotamian soothsayer and also aspire to the true, universal human condition as embodied by the well-bred croquet players on a well-
cut Sussex lawn?

I continued to read. I discovered that the first protagonist of the
modern European novel was a mad Spanish gentleman who believed
everything he read and who dreamed of himself as an epic hero in the
age of chivalry. I also realized that the penultimate hero of the modern
European novel is an all-too-lucid Czech Jew who cannot even believe
he is a man and wakes up to find himself transformed into a bug. Between
Don Quixote and Gregor Samsa, the hero of modern literature first
doubts himself as Hamlet and asserts himself as Don Juan, within the
Renaissance culture in which all was possible yet all could be questioned.

But once he has doubted away the old medieval order and affirmed the brave new world of modernity, he came in the bourgeois era to adapt to it in the fashions of David Copperfield and Becky Sharp, Julien Sorel and Frederic Morel, Rastignac and the diabolical thaumaturge of the bourgeoisie, Vautrin, a criminal who becomes cop and confidante.

These heroes and heroines had lost not only the dramatic greatness of Hamlet, Don Quixote, and Don Juan, but also the perfect sense of belonging of Jane Austen's characters. King Lear could not be compensated for his daughters' ingratitude. But Père Goriot could be compensated by monthly allowances from his ungrateful daughters. The tragic dimension had been lost. I saw that the bourgeois hero's claim to universal significance dwindled more and more into the mediocrity of particular customs, particular incapacities, particular pretensions. The norms of bourgeois society were completely at variance with Emma Bovary's passionate dreams, and condemned her to mediocrity and a sordid end. Elizabeth Bennet's provincial paradise had become Mme Bovary's hell. The greatness of Proust's narrator was that he finally realized that the promises of the modern world had come to naught. (And what greater optimism than Condorcet's, who could write on the eve of his death, condemned by the Jacobins, that the Golden Age of Man now lay in the future?) A culture driven, since the French Revolution, by its hunger for the future, was suddenly halted in its tracks, and when, as with Proust's hero, it dared look back on its past, it sadly recognized that even the past had ceased to project the glow that the modern hero once called his future. My compatriot, Octavio Paz, has pertinently remarked that the story of the modern novel can be told between two titles: *Great Expectations* and *Lost Illusions*.

I was raised in the Catholic faith, educated in classics at the severe English schools of Santiago de Chile and Buenos Aires, and swam the tides of Marxian revolt at the University of Mexico. In my twenties these conflicting influences seemed to jell in the following perspective. As Nietzsche had written, when you believe that all is rational, an exception suffices for everything to become irrational. Between the *Divine Comedy* that closed the theological order and the *Human Comedy* that opened the sociological order, tragedy was banished from modern culture, which was dominated by a double rationality.

Man is reconciled with God by the Christianity of deism. Man is reconciled with reason by history itself. But men maintain only abstract relationships with God or history when these refuse to admit within their purview the concrete human lives that persist in their conflicts and anxieties despite the canons of reason. In pagan tragedy, the gods provoked conflict, the unreasonable the unexplainable. The tragic hero fought against this intervention, actually his destiny, in a concrete manner: he dealt with ambivalent, mockable subornable gods: the gods were the Other, often enemies, part of the project of evil. But the Christian God was not responsible for the Fall: evil was a purely human project; a guilty God would be a monstrosity. Turning their backs on God, the children of the Goddess of Reason could now debate what was authentic human nature within the dialectical framework of history. Once having found it, they could then proceed rationally toward the full accomplishment of being in an ever-ascending progress that led to the synonymous Hegelian paradises of history, the future, and freedom.

Caught among the perspectives of classical antiquity and the Christian faith and the ideologies of reason, I struggled to find my own convictions as the terrible decade of the 1940s came to an end. It seemed to me that, banished from history by history itself, tragedy had found refuge in the actor of history: in each man, author of his own history, as Marx said, but finally, and tragically, capable of being both free and wrong, of mastering the machine of progress only to see it spout death, of setting foot on the shore of the future only to find that this paradise bore the infernal names and the satanic shapes of Buchenwald or Hiroshima and the Siberian camps. Yes, we have seen the future . . . and not only did it not work, it was a charnel house.

The modern tragedy appeared to me then as the tragedy of a freedom that can err: disastrously and evilly. I was caught in the bewildering realization that believing myself liberated from fate as an implacable, blind, and alien force, I could not separate myself from myself: a self subjected to the evil of the world I lived in and also to the sources of that evil within myself. I was, in this total sense, my own fate. And the burden was no less heavy than that imposed by the concerted gods of my heritage: Zeus, Jehovah, and Huitzilopochtli. I read Hegel: fate is the awareness of self, but of an enemy self. I felt this, and started to write.

An enemy within. An enemy without. Great expectations. Lost illusions. Jane Austen had led me into the impasses that I have just outlined; Emily Brontë showed me a way out of it. For it was on rereading *Wuthering Heights* in the mid-1950s that I came to understand the *other* possibility of that Western culture I had come to see as both mine and alien, nurturing and poisonous, magnificent and decadent. But, above all, this other possibility enabled me to make use of my Western inheritance without giving up my own Latin-American, mestizo, Indian-colored realities. For what was Emily Brontë but the outcast within the center, the visionary writer who dissolved the hypnosis of the future by the consecration of the instant of passion, preferred love to property, clung to the reality of myth as a constant present, and shunned the illusion of progress. In the enduring myth of the couple, the body, its transfigurations, its splendors and miseries, she confirmed for me the tragic knowledge of the enemy self, the self battling with itself and so capable of accepting the embrace of the enemy outside the self, and recognizing it as one's own demonic lover: Cathy, Heathcliff, the fallen angels, the exiled lovers on the lonely moors, the woman and the man in whom I could recognize all the women and all the men uninvited to Jane Austen's tea parties or having to disguise themselves at the soirée at the Duchesse de Guermantes'.

The revolt against the central culture's monopoly of universality became for me the story of our common literature, no longer "modern," hardly "contemporary," as yet unlabeled, it was as ancient as the epic of Gilgamesh or the sacred books of the Maya, as recent as the writing of Susan Sontag or LeRoi Jones: a literature not of linear progression but of circles and simultaneities, capable of receiving the eccentric contributions of our total humanity. A revolt, yes, of the angels who dared to be the ambassadors of God before the court of the Devil and the emissaries of the Devil before the court of God: the bearers of the tragic oppositions, the secret dreams, the dark follies, the lost innocence, the outlawed loves, the murdered children, the comical defeats, and the savage languages that the religion of Reason, the bedrock of the bourgeoisie, with its discreet charms and righteous crimes, had exiled from the life of man.

Discrete charms and righteous crimes: when I was thirty, my friendship began with a man who was to influence me profoundly from then on: Luis Buñuel, the great artist of Surrealism, who in films such as *L'âge d'or* and *Los olvidados* made marginality his central concern, and revealed the humanity of the eccentric.

And so, on the margins of the central development I had first come to know, thrusting upward and outward from within the central culture itself—Emily Brontë and William Faulkner, Jean Genet and Allen Ginsberg—or infiltrating from the dim outskirts of the West and from the dark continents beyond, from Russia and Ireland, from Africa and Asia and Latin America—Dostoevsky and Joyce, Chinua Achebe and Tanizaki, Cortázar and Borges—I saw another literature emerge, in a variety of times and places, to reclaim the plural sources of man's humanity and inhumanity.

Moreover, this newfound perspective freed Balzac from his sociological fetters and enabled me to see him as a visionary writer of the unending tragic struggle between the claims of imagination and the intractability of power; to see Proust less in the context of *La belle époque* than in the light of the tragic myth of Tantalus, forever reaching out to grasp the elusive fruits of memory; to deliver Dostoevsky from the remoteness of his Great Russian chauvinism and his faith in the Byzantine Legacy of the Third Rome, in Muscovy, and inscribe him in the circular calendar of the origins, the vast spiral in which the founding acts of man are reenacted through parables of guilt and innocence such as the bearing of the enemy conscience within each Raskolnikov and Stavrogin, and the reunion of the lonely ego with the communal Other in each Myshkin and each Alyosha. And I was the Napoleons of the nineteenth-century novels, the Sorels and Rastignacs and Pips, suddenly turned away from the aspirations they deemed identical to their existence and become shadows of the tragic Oedipus, who walks toward his destiny by walking toward his origin: his future shall resolve the enigma of his past, he will come full circle to the beginning: tragic catharsis as the restoration of the dawn of the human order. Napoleon versus Oedipus: the man who could only be a hero or a villain, a monarch or a prisoner, versus the man who can be, at once, king and prisoner, guilty and innocent, criminal and victim.

And from this perspective, I saw what Jacques Dérrida calls "l'écriture blanche," the illegal palimpsest of barren white writing on a white wall, become stained with the mud of the Irish and Polish fields, the ashes of the Jewish cemetery in Prague, the smoking incense of Zosima's monastery, and the dust of the thorny Mexican plateau. Perhaps *Babbit* and *Main Street* could only have been written by a perfectly determined North American writer born in Sauk Centre, Minnesota, in the year of grace 1885. But *Absalom, Absalom!*, *Light in August*, or *The Sound and the Fury* could, in their mythic essence, have been told by a wise savage in central Africa, an ancient guardian of memory in the Himalayas, an amnesiac demon, or a remorseful god. Yet it was from the deep South of the same central, optimistic, success-nurtured, pragmatic culture that emerged these Comptons and Sartorises and Benjys and Burdens and Joe Christmases to bestow the gift of tragedy on an epic civilization, to undermine the Puritan legacy of the elect and the damned, by the obscure, searching, potent certainty that there is no moral tragedy unless the struggle is between equally legitimate forces, forces that together represent a moral dilemma that can only be transcended by embracing the moral conflict of its antagonist. What makes the teller of Faulkner's tales identical to the tellers of the Yaqui or Arabian or Chinese tales is that he creates another time, a past that is a constant present in memory. Sinclair Lewis is yours, and as such, interesting and important to us. William Faulkner is both yours and ours, and as such, essential to us. For in him we see what has always lived with us and rarely with you: the haunting face of defeat.

Colored writing on a white wall. The development I have been sketching has led me to envision all eccentric writing as colored writing.

That James Joyce is indeed a black Irishman, wreaking a vengeance, even wilder than the IRA's, on the English language from within, invading the territory of its sanitary ego-presumptions with a flood of impure, dark languages flowing from the damned-up sources of collective speech, savagely drowning the ego of the traditional speaker and depositing the property of words in everybody, in the total human community of those who speak and have spoken and shall speak. And that Jean Genet is a red Frenchman, obsessed with the burning hole of flesh made mind and mind made flesh through which he can first violate the pure, reductivist perfection of Cartesian reason and create thereby a newborn, fiery, crimson consciousness, both inclusive and subversive. And that Octavio Paz is a green poet of Latin-American rebirth, fusing the triumphant and the defeated, the clamorous and the silent, the consecrated and the outlawed strains of our plural heritage: poetry is an offering of gold and excrement on the black volcanic tables of the Toltec pyramid. And, finally, that Jerzy Kosinski is a tatooed American on whose writing skin one can read the blue wounds of the Slavic world: the novel as a painted bird.

What is colorless writing is the well-made novel meant to be read on lazy weekends, the well-crafted play meant to be digested between the final curtain and the last suburban train, the mint-flavored poem-on-the-occasion-of, the bland milk diet of vicarious thrills, the white opera of the soapsuds; the sedative writings for drowsy readers eager to be reassured: mirror, mirror, on the page/ have you known a happier age?/ and deliver us from rage/ and keep tigers in their cage. The perfection of the white future was a white death: the death of a culture based on a central human nature, exclusive of all things that did not fit its optimism, its abolishment of the tragic sphere, its religion of progress, its disregard for both the fullness of the instant and the presentness of the past, its deliberate ignorance of the cultures foreign to its particular reason.

André Malraux has recently remarked that the era of Western supremacy, commencing in the Renaissance, ended the day that Nehru and Mao established the independence of the two most populous and ancient civilizations of the world. From my own point of view, I would say that the West's supreme confidence in its own universal future, born from the French Revolution and the rise of the bourgeoisie, ended in the decade that Proust and Joyce, Musil and Broch, Kafka and the Surrealists perceived the cracks in the facade and liberated literature by going beyond the crisis of the established order to the depths of the constant, truly universal language of literature: poetry, in its original significance of *poeisis*, the creative binder, the cement for the true unity of the diverse.

Poetry is the common home of writers: here, East is West. West is East, and the twain forever meet.

There William Golding's partial unitary truth of the West meets Akutagawa's partial multiple truth of the East; William Styron's myth of North American anguish meets Gabriel García Márquez's myth of South American solitude; Kurt Vonnegut's corrosive laughter of the future meets Witkiewicz's serene madness of the past; Virginia Woolf's shining instant meets Pablo Neruda's cascade of times, and all literature, perhaps, can be seen as the labor of one blind sage, Homer alias Milton alias Joyce alias Borges alias a sightless gaucho who sings nameless poems over an open fire in the night of the pampas.

So here we are today, so far from God, so near to Poland, to Mexico, to Russia, to the United States, wondering what makes our humanity tick, not in the frozen abstractions of a Godlike separateness, but in the infernal variety of our coming together, questioning the men who report from both deep within and far from us, who bring us our humanity from the forgotten frontiers of consciousness, from multiple times and far-off spaces and create, with us, the common ground where the denied can meet and tell each other the stories forbidden by the deniers, by the officials of negation who would have us believe that human life lives only here and not everywhere, that human truth is only this and not all these. I mean to say that all great writing has become eccentric to the central verities of modern society, that literature is the fiery ritual of introducing God to the Devil and seeing the angelic feathers cringe and singe, and of introducing the Devil to God and seeing the demonic horns become a halo.

For what has the typically modern writer become if not a Persian of the soul, a phantom risen from the outskirts of a privileged humanity to claim the humanity of the marginal, to extend the boundaries of all living flesh and living minds beyond the dogmas proclaimed throughout the world by the industrial technocracies, whether they are the self-appointed heirs to Adam Smith or to Karl Marx, whether they make buffoons or martyrs of the writers who turn their backs on the neon-lighted altars and gaze at the burning pit or the fathomless abyss, or the hungry jungle and the empty desert and proclaim: "This, too, is the land of man!"?

To people the wilderness that surrounds the exclusive oasis of self-satisfaction in every contemporary society; to give voice to the silent mutiny of the muted in New York or Mexico City, in New Delhi or Moscow, in Tokyo or Warsaw; to fill in the blank pages of history; to remind ourselves and our contemporaries that nowhere do we live in the best of all possible worlds. The writer's mission has always been to extend the limits of the real, to create with words another reality, for there will not be more human reality unless imagination fashions another reality. This is critically true today: either we prove ourselves capable of increasing the real and so offer other alternatives, other models of existence, or we will be left with no choice but the one imposed by the dual hegemony of the Eagle and the Bear.

Thus literature does make eccentrics of us all, and thus we live in Pascal's awesome circle, where the center is nowhere and the circumference everywhere. But if we are all marginal, then we are all central.

Let me now, having come full circle, return to the beginning. Poland and Mexico, Japan and India: history has made us all eccentric reaches of the West. And one of our problems has been that our two-pronged plugs do not exactly fit into the one-hole sockets of the West. Should we sacrifice one of our prongs so as to fit the Western socket? Frankly, I feel much better off knowing that both the Bible and the *Popol Vuh* belong to me. An Egyptian is far wealthier by owning the poetry of both Petrarch and Ibn Al Farid, as is the Japanese with access to both Marlowe and Matsuo Basho. Why should the *Aeneid* exclude the *Baghavad Gita*, or Flaubert's *L'education sentimental* Tsao Hsueh-Chin's *Dream of the Red Chamber*? Our two-holed sockets admit this double relationship: we can receive and we can give. Shouldn't the West adapt to our double current, instead of imposing a single source of light?

I am proposing to you that our real, creative role should be a double-edged one. First, to protect and offer to the West our own very rich and deep cultural experience. And, second, to rescue from the West what the West has sacrificed within itself. For, in reality, what Western socket are we speaking about? The socket of the victors of the West, or the socket of the defeated of the West? Parmenides or Heraclitus? St. Augustine or Pelagius? The Inquisition and John Calvin or Giordano Bruno? Descartes or Erasmus? Machiavelli or Campanella? Thomas Hobbes or Charles Fourier? John Locke or William Blake?

Let me put it to you that the role of the marginal cultures is that of the guardians of memory. A memory both of what the West sacrificed within its own culture and of what the West sacrificed in other cultures through its imperial expansion. Both aspects are intimately linked, for the West could only overpower the alien cultures of Mexico and Peru, Indochina and Dahomey, by sacrificing the Western values of Heraclitus and Pelagius, Bruno and Erasmus, More and Campanella: the values of openness to metamorphosis, of diversity set above uniformity, direct grace above intermediary salvation, community above power, utopia above topia, the furtherance of pleasure above the protection of property, the ironical praise of folly above the ironclad sufficiency of reason, understanding of the other above destruction of the strange.

As a Mexican, I am particularly sensitive to this argument: the aboriginal cultures of my land were the object of genocide and wholesale destruction in the name of the imperial *raison d'état* of Spain and of the univocal truth of the Christian religion as spelled out by the Church hierarchy. But behind the ships of the conquistadores, the Ship of Fools arrived in the New World; the *navis stultorum* of the Renaissance. Campanella was the navigator, Erasmus the cartographer, Thomas More the lookout, and the ghost of Hieronymus Bosch lurked somewhere in the hold.

In effect, the happiest community of the New World flowered for a time in the missions of Michoacán, where the friar Vasco de Quiroga, an avid reader of *The City of the Sun*, perfectly blended the teachings of Utopia with the Mexican Indian's tradition of communal life, universal sacrality, respect for the fabrication of objects both useful and singular, and consecration of the body as the living center of civilization. So, in one privileged moment, the best of the Indian values—the values that, in fact, had been oppressed by the fascist Aztec theocracy—and the best of the European values came together and flourished. The successors to Aztec tyranny, the Spanish viceroys, soon put an end to that: history as a probing myth was crushed by history as a conquering, self-justifying epic.

But in the deepest layers of my country's culture, the seed for this reunion of values continues to germinate, and it continues to offer a positive alternative, among others, to the delusion that the models of Western progress are worthy of uncritical imitation. We in Latin America have arrived at the threshold of modernity just at the time when the values of modernity are cracking up in their very places of origin. I believe that we can, with political and intellectual courage, extract from ourselves the elements for a more humane model of life: neither a return to the sacrificial pyramid of the Aztecs, nor a blind plunge into the fog of ecocide, loneliness, and the production of garbage, but a reconstitution of a harmonious society built on the best legacies of the Indian and Western cultures.

It is a great honor for me to address an audience drawn from the independent, creative, and open commonwealth of writers associated with American PEN. I have come here to say finally that you are not alone and that we are not alone: that the work you do here, and we do in Mexico, and everywhere that a PEN center, whether actually or potentially, exists, is linked by common purposes and a feeling of community that supersede our national boundaries yet thrive on the contributions of our particular cultures and individualities.

The present-day fetishism of interdependence tends to disguise, in the international arena, the submission of the weak to the strong, of the dependent many to the independent few: it is the screen of a détente between two major powers and their division of the world into tidy spheres of influence. The community of writers is more and more an international fact, and it proposes the true meaning of interdependence: only if all of us are independent can all of us be interdependent.

A writer's independence and interdependence depends on his language. For a writer embodies a terrible paradox. He works alone, but he works with the most socialized of tools: language. The fullness of the collective expression. He cannot exist as a writer without a collectively wrought, preexistent reality: the reality of language. But his work cannot die if he adds to that reality a significant voice that is actually a contribution to the life of a language that will outlive him. In this process he gives up his ego in order to feed that reality, and so writing is always a sacrificial act. But his language will endure because a people cannot be deprived of language, for language is like air: it belongs to all or to none, it cannot be caged, murdered, or stripped, no matter how many books are burned, forbidden, or persecuted: for language to die, the whole human race would have to perish along with it. Thus Thomas Mann outlives Hitler, Osip Mandelstam outlives Stalin, Pablo Neruda will outlive the Chilean junta. Meanwhile, the development of Philip Roth's language depends upon Milan Kundera's language.

A writer's task in relation to other writers—the impure and healthy mixing of our times, spaces, and cultures—prefigures a rich, diversified polycivilization that would constantly renew and reenact the struggles of living with death and dying for life: a struggle, in fact, against the dreary, uniform monocivilization promoted by the superpowers of the political world, who offer us life without death tomorrow, if we are willing to live without life today. This plural civilization of our hopes is also prefigured, concretely and actually, within organizations such as PEN.

I recall Dostoevsky's words: "We are all responsible to all and for all." This is the angelic and the demonic, the humble and the prideful sense of writing, and this is the sense of our association in PEN. We are responsible for the meaning of the written word, and we must maintain its living beauty, its violence, its risk. But we are also responsible to the silence of the world, to the absent, imprisoned, censored, forgotten words that could not be written—or else published—because of a tyrant's whim, a society's indifference, or a people's hunger.

I would simply like to add, as your Mexican guest, that there is more to Latin America than historical defeats, bananas growing in the jungle, and oppressive dictatorships: there are Pablo Neruda and Jorge Luis Borges and José Lezama Lima. And there is more to the United States than historical success, napalm raining from the sky, or political dirty tricks: there are Arthur Miller and Saul Bellow and Robert Lowell.

Bananas and napalm can only meet in enmity and despair.

You and I can only meet in friendship and hope.

MARIO VARGAS LLOSA
[1936–]

BORN IN AREQUIPA, Peru, to parents who were divorced before his birth, Vargas Llosa spent his early childhood in Bolivia, brought up by his mother and grandparents. When his parents reunited in 1946, the family moved to Lima where he attended Leoncio Prado Military Academy, the setting for his first novel, *La ciudad y los perros*, 1963 [*The Time of the Hero*, 1966]. While still in his teens, Vargas Llosa began working as a newspaper writer, a period of his life which inspired a later novel, *La tía Julia y el escribidor*, 1977 [*Aunt Julia and the Scriptwriter*, 1982].

After completing his college degree at San Marcos University in Lima, Vargas Llosa moved to Paris where he spent several years, later living in London, Barcelona, and again in Lima. He made his first visit to Cuba in 1965, as a judge for the Casa de las Américas Prize, but an early enthusiasm for the ideals of the Cuban Revolution gave way to disenchantment after the human-rights abuses of the 1970s. His novel of the Peruvian jungle—*La casa verde*, 1966 [*The Green House*, 1968]—was awarded the coveted Rómulo Gallegos Award for the best novel in Spanish during the previous five years, and it established his reputation as one of the Boom's most outstanding young authors. In his acceptance speech for that award, Vargas Llosa made his now-famous "literature is fire" statement in which he upheld the writer's function as a contributor to the founding of a new social order out of the ashes of old injustices.

His third novel, a critical portrait of Peru under the dictator Manuel Odria (1948–1956), was entitled *Conversación en la cate-*

dral, 1969 [*Conversation in the Cathedral*, 1975]. Its experimental narrative technique, referred to by Emir Rodríguez Monegal as a "diachronic collage of dialogues," contains echoes of Faulkner; indeed, that North American is one of the authors—along with Flaubert, Sartre, Camus, and Martorell—most admired by Vargas Llosa. Subsequent novels include *Pantaleón y las visitadoras*, 1973 [*Captain Pantoja and the Special Service*, 1978]; *La guerra del fin del mundo*, 1981 [*The War of the End of the World*, 1984]; *Historia de Mayta*, 1984 [*The Real Life of Alejandro Mayta*, 1986]; and *¿Quién mató a Palomino Molero?*, 1986 [*Who Killed Palomino Molero?* 1987]. Vargas Llosa has also published plays, numerous essays, and full-length studies of García Márquez and Flaubert.

The essay reproduced here was given as a lecture in English at the University of Oklahoma in March 1977, during a two-week stay as guest of honor in conjunction with the Puterbaugh Conference series; it was later published in *World Literature Today*, the literary quarterly of the university. In this characteristically dynamic and elegant presentation, Vargas Llosa addresses not only the issue of social commitment for the contemporary Latin American writer but also the fundamental problem of literature's relationship to history and politics. As in his recent novels, he focuses on the pitfalls of seeking "the truth" on either one side or the other. "Novels aren't written to recount life but to transform it by adding something to it," he has said. It is the reader, in the end, who must make his or her own truth in a world too complex to have one explanation.

Social Commitment and the Latin American Writer

Mario Vargas Llosa

The Peruvian novelist José María Arguedas killed himself on the second day of December 1969 in a classroom of La Molina Agricultural University in Lima. He was a very discreet man, and so as not to disturb his colleagues and the students with his suicide, he waited until everybody had left the place. Near his body was found a letter with very detailed instructions about his burial—where he should be mourned, who should pronounce the eulogies in the cemetery—and he asked too that an Indian musician friend of his play the *huaynos* and *mulizas* he was fond of. His will was respected, and Arguedas, who had been, when he was alive, a very modest and shy man, had a very spectacular burial.

But some days later other letters written by him appeared, little by little. They too were different aspects of his last will, and they were addressed to very different people: his publisher, friends, journalists, academics, politicians. The main subject of these letters was his death, of course, or better, the reasons for which he decided to kill himself. These reasons changed from letter to letter. In one of them he said that he had decided to commit suicide because he felt that he was finished as a writer, that he no longer had the impulse and the will to create. In another he gave moral, social and political reasons: he could no longer stand the misery and neglect of the Peruvian peasants, those people of the Indian communities among whom he had been raised; he lived oppressed and anguished by the crises of the cultural and educational life in the country; the low level and abject nature of the press and the caricature of liberty in Peru were too much for him, et cetera.

In these dramatic letters we follow, naturally, the personal crises that Arguedas had been going through, and they are the desperate call of a suffering man who, at the edge of the abyss, asks mankind for help and compassion. But they are not only that: a clinical testimony. At the same time, they are graphic evidence of the situation of the writer in Latin America, of the difficulties and pressures of all sorts that have surrounded and oriented and many times destroyed the literary vocation in our countries.

In the USA, in Western Europe, to be a writer means, generally, first (and usually only) to assume a personal responsibility. That is, the responsibility to achieve in the most rigorous and authentic way a work which, for its artistic values and originality, enriches the language and culture of one's country. In Peru, in Bolivia, in Nicaragua, et cetera, on the contrary, to be a writer means, at the same time, to assume a social responsibility: at the same time that you develop a personal literary work, you should serve, through your writing but also through your actions, as an active participant in the solution of the economic, political and cultural problems of your society. There is no way to escape this obligation. If you tried to do so, if you were to isolate yourself and concentrate exclusively on your own work, you would be severely censured and considered, in the best of cases, irresponsible and selfish, or at worst, even by omission, an accomplice to all the evils—illiteracy, misery, exploitation, injustice, prejudice—of your country and against which you have refused to fight. In the letters which he wrote once he had prepared the gun with which he was to kill himself, Arguedas was trying, in the last moments of his life, to fulfill this moral imposition that impels all Latin American writers to social and political commitment.

Why is it like this? Why cannot writers in Latin America, like their American and European colleagues, be artists, and only artists? Why must they also be reformers, politicians, revolutionaries, moralists? The answer lies in the social conditions of Latin America, the problems which face our countries. All countries have problems, of course, but in many parts of Latin America, both in the past and in the present, the problems which constitute the closest daily reality for people are not freely discussed and analyzed in public, but are usually denied and silenced. There are no means through which those problems can be presented and denounced, because the social and political establishment exercises a strict censorship of the media and over all the communications systems. For example, if today you hear Chilean broadcasts or see Argentine television, you won't hear a word about the political prisoners, about the exiles, about the torture, about the violations of human rights in those two countries that have outraged the conscience of the world. You will, however, be carefully informed, of course, about the iniquities of the communist countries. If you read the daily newspapers of my country, for instance— which have been confiscated by the government, which now controls them—you will not find a word about the continuous arrests of labor leaders or about the murderous inflation that affects everyone. You will read only about what a happy and prosperous country Peru is and how much we Peruvians love our military rulers.

What happens with the press, TV and radio happens too, most of the time, with the universities. The government persistently interferes with them; teachers and students considered subversive or hostile to the official system are expelled and the whole curriculum reorganized according to political considerations. As an indication of what extremes of absurdity this "cultural policy" can reach, you must remember, for instance, that in Argentina, in Chile and in Uruguay the departments of Sociology have been closed indefinitely, because the social sciences are considered subversive. Well, if academic institutions submit to this manipulation and censorship, it is improbable that contemporary political, social and economic problems of the country can be described and discussed freely. Academic knowledge in many Latin American countries is, like the press and the media, a victim of the deliberate turning away from what is actually happening in society. This vacuum has been filled by literature.

This is not a recent phenomenon. Even during the Colonial Period, though more especially since Independence (in which intellectuals and writers played an important role), all over Latin America novels, poems and plays were—as Stendhal once said he wanted the novel to be—the mirrors in which Latin Americans could truly see their faces and examine their sufferings. What was, for political reasons, repressed or distorted in the press and in the schools and universities, all the evils that were buried by the military and economic elite which ruled the countries, the evils which were never mentioned in the speeches of the politicians nor taught in the lecture halls nor criticized in the congresses nor discussed in magazines found a vehicle of expression in literature.

So, something curious and paradoxical occurred. The realm of imagination became in Latin America the kingdom of objective reality; fiction became a substitute for social science; our best teachers about reality were dreamers, the literary artists. And this is true not only for our great essayists—such as Sarmiento, Martí, González Prada, Rodó, Vasconcelos, José Carlos Mariátegui—whose books are indispensable for a thorough comprehension of the historical and social reality of their respective countries, but it is also valid for the writers who only practiced the creative literary genres: fiction, poetry and drama. We can say without exaggeration that the most representative and genuine description of the real problems of Latin America during the nineteenth century is to be found in literature, and that it was in the verses of the poets or the plots of the novelists that, for the first time, the social evils of Latin America were denounced.

We have a very illustrative case with what is called *indigenismo*, the literary current which, from the middle of the nineteenth century until the first decades of our century focused on the Indian peasant of the Andes and his problems as its main subject. The indigenist writers were the first people in Latin America to describe the terrible conditions in which the Indians were still living three centuries after the Spanish conquest, the impunity with which they were abused and exploited by the landed proprietors—the *latifundistas*, the *gamonales*—men who sometimes owned land areas as big as a European country, where they were absolute kings who treated their Indians worse and sold them cheaper than their cattle. The first indigenist writer was a woman, an energetic and enthusiastic reader of the French novelist Émile Zola and the positivist philosophers: Clorinda Matto de Turner (1854–1909). Her novel *Aves sin nido* opened a road of social commitment to the problems and aspects of Indian life that Latin American writers would follow, examining in detail and from all angles, denouncing injustices and praising and rediscovering the values and traditions of an Indian culture which until then, at once incredibly and ominously, had been systematically ignored by the official culture. There is no way to research and analyze the rural history of the continent and to understand the tragic destiny of the inhabitants of the Andes since the region ceased to be a colony without going through their [the indigenists'] books. These constitute the best—and sometimes the only—testimony to this aspect of our reality.

Am I saying, then, that because of the authors' moral and social commitment this literature is good literature? That because of their generous and courageous goals of breaking the silence about the real problems of society and of contributing to the solution of these problems, this literature was an artistic accomplishment? Not at all. What actually happened in many cases was the contrary. The pessimistic dictum of André Gide, who once said that with good sentiments one has bad literature, can be, alas, true. Indigenist literature is very important from a historical and social point of view, but only in exceptional cases is it of literary importance. These novels or poems written, in general, very quickly, impelled by the present situation, with militant passion, obsessed with the idea of denouncing a social evil, of correcting a wrong, lack most of what is essential in a work of art: richness of expression, technical originality. Because of the didactic intentions they become simplistic and superficial; because of their political partisanship they are sometimes demagogic and melodramatic; and because of their nationalist or regionalist scope they can be very provincial and quaint. We can say that many of these writers, in order to serve better moral and social needs, sacrificed their vocation on the altar of politics. Instead of artists, they chose to be moralists, reformers, politicians, revolutionaries.

You can judge from your own particular system of values whether this sacrifice is right or wrong, whether the immolation of art for social and political aims is worthwhile or not. I am not dealing at the moment with this problem. What I am trying to show is how the particular circumstances of Latin American life have traditionally oriented literature in this direction and how this has created for writers a very special situation. In one sense people—the real or potential readers of the writer—are accustomed to considering literature as something intimately associated with living and social problems, the activity through which all that is repressed or disfigured in society will be named, described and condemned. They expect novels, poems and plays to counterbalance the policy of disguising and deforming reality which is current in the official culture and to keep alive the hope and spirit of change and revolt among the victims of that policy. In another sense this confers on the writer, as a citizen, a kind of moral and spiritual leadership, and he must try, during his life as a writer, to act according to this image of the role he is expected to play. Of course he can reject it and refuse this task that society wants to impose on him; and declaring that he does not want to be either a politician or a moralist or a sociologist, but only an artist, he can seclude himself in his personal dreams. However, this will be considered (and in a way, it is) a political, a moral and a social choice. He will be considered by his real and potential readers a deserter and a traitor, and his poems, novels and plays will be endangered. To be an artist, only an artist, can become, in our countries, a kind of moral crime, a political sin. All our literature is marked by this fact, and if this is not taken into consideration, one cannot fully understand all the differences that exist between it and other literatures of the world.

No writer in Latin America is unaware of the pressure that is put on him pushing him to a social commitment. Some accept this because the external impulse coincides with their innermost feelings and personal convictions. These cases are, surely, the happy ones. The coincidence between the individual choice of the writer and the idea that society has of his vocation permits the novelist, poet or playwriter to create freely, without any pangs of conscience, knowing that he is supported and approved by his contemporaries. It is interesting to note that many Latin American men and women whose writing started out as totally uncommitted, indifferent or even hostile to social problems and politics, later—sometimes gradually, sometimes abruptly—oriented their writings in this direction. The reason for this change could be, of course, that they adopted new attitudes, acknowledging the terrible social problems of our countries, an intellectual discovery of the evils of society and the moral decision to fight them. But we cannot dismiss the possibility that in this change (conscious or unconscious) the psychological and practical trouble it means for a writer to resist the social pressure for political commitment also played a role, as did the psychological and practical advantages which led him to act and to write as society expects him to.

All this has given Latin American literature peculiar features. Social and political problems constitute a central subject for it, and they are present everywhere, even in works where, because of the theme and form, one would never expect to find them. Take the case, for example, of the "literature of fantasy" as opposed to "realist literature." This kind of literature, whose raw material is subjective fantasy, does not reflect, usually, the mechanisms of economic injustice in society nor the problems faced by urban and rural workers which make up the objective facts of reality; instead—as in Edgar Allan Poe or Villiers de L'Isle-Adam—this literature builds a new reality, essentially different from "objective reality," out of the most intimate obsessions of writers. But in Latin America (mostly in modern times, but also in the past) fantastic literature also has its roots in objective reality and is a vehicle for exposing social and political evils. So, fantastic literature becomes, in this way, symbolical literature in which, disguised with the prestigious clothes of dreams and unreal beings and facts, we recognize the characters and problems of contemporary life.

We have many examples among contemporary Latin American writers of this "realistic" utilization of unreality. The Venezuelan Salvador Garmendia has described, in short stories and novels of nightmarish obsessions and impossible deeds, the cruelty and violence of the streets of Caracas and the frustrations and sordid myths of the lower middle classes of that city. In the only novel of the Mexican Juan Rulfo, *Pedro Páramo* (1955)—all of whose characters, the reader discovers in the middle of the book, are dead people—fantasy and magic are not procedures to escape social reality; on the contrary, they are simply alternative means to represent the poverty and sadness of life for the peasants of a small Jalisco village.

Another interesting case is Julio Cortázar. In his first novels and short stories we enter a *fantastic* world, which is very mischievous because it is ontologically different from the world that we know by reason and experience yet has, at first approach, all the appearances—features—of real life. Anyway, in this world social problems and political statements do not exist; they are aspects of human experience that are omitted. But in his more recent books—and principally in the latest novel, *Libro de Manuel* (1973)—politics and social problems occupy a place as important as that of pure fantasy. The "fantastic" element is merged, in this novel, with statements and motifs which deal with underground militancy, terrorism, revolution and dictatorship.

What happens with prose also happens with poetry, and as among novelists, one finds this necessity for social commitment in all kinds of poets, even in those whom, because of the nature of their themes, one would expect not to be excessively concerned with militancy. This is what occurred, for instance, with religious poetry, which is, in general, very politicized in Latin America. And it is symptomatic that, since the death of Pablo Neruda, the most widely known poet—because of his political radicalism, his revolutionary lyricism, his colorful and schematic ideology—is a Nicaraguan priest, a former member of the American Trappist monastery of Gethsemane: Ernesto Cardenal.

It is worth noting too that the political commitment of writers and literature in Latin America is a result not only of the social abuse and economic exploitation of large sectors of the population by small minorities and brutal military dictatorships. There are also cultural reasons for this commitment, exigencies that the writer himself sees grow and take root in his conscious during and because of his artistic development. To be a writer, to discover this vocation and to choose to practice it pushes one inevitably, in our countries, to discover all the handicaps and miseries of underdevelopment. Inequities, injustice, exploitation, discrimination, abuse are not only the burden of peasants, workers, employees, minorities. They are also social obstacles for the development of a cultural life. How can literature exist in a society where the rates of illiteracy reach fifty or sixty percent of the population? How can literature exist in countries where there are no publishing houses, where there are no literary publications, where if you want to publish a book you must finance it yourself? How can a cultural and literary life develop in a society where the material conditions of life—lack of education, subsistence wages, et cetera—establish a kind of cultural apartheid, that is, prevent the majority of the inhabitants from buying and reading books? And if, besides all that, the political authorities have established a rigid censorship in the press, in the media and in the universities, that is, in those places through which literature would normally find encouragement and an audience, how could the Latin American writer remain indifferent to social and political problems? In the practice itself of his art—in the obstacles that he finds for this practice—the Latin American writer finds reasons to become politically conscious and to submit to the pressures of social commitment.

We can say that there are some positive aspects in this kind of situation for literature. Because of that commitment, literature is forced to keep in touch with living reality, with the experiences of people, and it is prevented from becoming—as unfortunately has happened in some developed societies—an esoteric and ritualistic experimentation in new forms of expression almost entirely dissociated from real experience. And because of social commitment, writers are obliged to be socially responsible for what they write and for what they do, because social pressure provides a firm barrier against the temptation of using words and imagination in order to play the game of moral irresponsibility, the game of the enfant terrible who (only at the level of words, of course) cheats, lies, exaggerates and proposes the worst options.

But this situtation has many dangers, too. The function and the practice of literature can be entirely distorted if the creative writings are seen only (or even mainly) as the materialization of social and political aims. What is to be, then, the borderline, the frontier between history, sociology and literature? Are we going to say that literature is only a degraded form (since its data are always dubious because of the place that fantasy occupies in it) of the social sciences? In fact, this is what literature becomes if its most praised value is considered to be the testimony it offers of objective reality, if it is judged principally as a true record of what happens in society.

On the other hand, this opens the door of literature to all kinds of opportunistic attitudes and intellectual blackmail. How can I condemn as an artistic failure a novel that explicitly protests against the oppressors of the masses without being considered an accomplice of the oppressor? How can I say that this poem which fulminates in assonant verses against the great corporations is a calamity without being considered an obsequious servant of imperialism? And we know how this kind of simplistic approach to literature can be utilized by dishonest intellectuals and imposed easily on uneducated audiences.

The exigency of social commitment can signify also the destruction of artistic vocations in that, because of the particular sensibility, experiences and temperament of a writer, he is unable to accomplish in his writings and actions what society expects of him. The realm of sensibility, of human experience and of imagination is wider than the realm of politics and social problems. A writer like Borges has built a great literary work of art in which this kind of problem is entirely ignored: metaphysics, philosophy, fantasy and literature are more important for him. (But he has been unable to keep himself from answering the social call for commitment, and one is tempted to see in his incredible statements on right-wing conservatism—statements that scare even the conservatives—just a strategy of political sacrilege in order not to be disturbed once and for all in his writings.) And many writers are not really prepared to deal with political and social problems. These are the unhappy cases. If they prefer their intimate calling and produce uncommitted work, they will have to face all kinds of misunderstanding and rejection. Incomprehension and hostility will be their constant reward. If they submit to social pressure and try to write about social and political themes, it is quite probable that they will fail as writers, that they will frustrate themselves as artists for not having acted as their feelings prompted them to do.

I think that José Mariá Arguedas experienced this terrible dilemma and that all his life and work bears the trace of it. He was born in the Andes, was raised among the Indian peasants (in spite of being the son of a lawyer) and, until his adolescence, was—in the language he spoke and in his vision of the world—an Indian. Later he was recaptured by his family and became a middle-class Spanish-speaking Peruvian white. He lived torn always between these two different cultures and societies. And literature meant for him, in his first short stories and novels (*Agua* [1935], *Yawar Fiesta* [1949], *Los ríos profundos* [1958]), a melancholic escape to the days and places of his childhood, the world of the little Indian villages—San Juan de Lucanas, Puquio—or towns of the Andes such as Abancay, whose landscapes and customs he described in a tender and poetic prose. But later he felt obliged to renounce this kind of lyric image to fill the social responsibilities that everybody expected of him. And he wrote a very ambitious book, *Todas las sangres* (1964), in which he tried, escaping from himself, to describe the social and political problems of his country. The novel is a total failure: the vision is simplistic and even a caricature. We find none of the great literary virtues that made his previous books genuine works of art. The book is the classic failure of an artistic talent due to the self-imposition of social commitment. The other books of Arguedas oscillate between those two sides of his personality, and it is probable that all this played a part in his suicide.

When he pressed the trigger of the gun, at the University of La Molina, on the second day of December in 1969, José María Arguedas was too, in a way, showing how difficult and daring it can be to be a writer in Latin America.

ELENA PONIATOWSKA
[1933–]

BORN IN PARIS, of Polish-Mexican background, Poniatowska was eight years old when her family immigrated to Mexico. She was later sent to the Convent of the Sacred Heart in Philadelphia for her secondary schooling. "I come from a family of nomads," she once wrote. "The only way I found not to feel afloat was to write."

Since the mid-1950s, when she began writing for newspapers in Mexico City as well as writing her own poetry and prose, Poniatowska has become an author identified with the voice of the Mexican people. This authentic, clear voice speaks through her work powerfully, whether in the testimonial novel based on interviews with the indomitable Jesusa Palancares—*Hasta no verte, Jesús mío*, 1969 [*Here's Looking at You, Jesus*, forthcoming]—or in the dramatic montage of first-person accounts of the 1968 student riots in *La noche de Tlatelolco*, 1973 [*Massacre in Mexico*, 1975]. By bringing history to life in individual portraits, Poniatowska forces her reader to reconsider the personal dimensions of otherwise distant events or situations. She is particularly adept at conveying the experiences of women; prime examples would be the paralyzed *Gaby Brimmer*, 1979, a woman of great courage and determination, or the artist Angelina Beloff in *Querido Diego, te abraza Quiela*, 1978 [*Dear Diego*, 1986], whom Diego Rivera spurned after having lived with her for ten years and fathering her son.

Poniatowska openly confesses the debt she owes as a person and a writer to those whom she admires. In a recent book of portraits of other Mexican writers, including Rosario Castellanos and Carlos Fuentes, she says: "I have lived in their surroundings and in that of their characters. Their substance has nourished me. They have given me life and strength. This isn't a settling of accounts nor is it literary criticism, nor even essays. Rather it's meant to be a gesture of love toward men and women who are part of my being." The same could be said about the very different, but equally moving tribute to Jesusa Palancares in the pages which follow.

This piece (not to be confused with her testimonial novel of a similar title) was originally published in the Mexican journal *Vuelta* in 1978 and is translated here for the first time. In this essay Poniatowska shares her experience of getting to know Jesusa, whose story was later told in *Hasta no verte, Jesus mío*. In the process of interviewing Jesusa over a period of several years—trying to fathom the complexity of this feisty, iconoclastic old woman of Mexico City's burgeoning slums—Poniatowska found more than she had anticipated. The following pages testify to the power of personal contact regardless of class distinctions.

AND HERE'S TO YOU, JESUSA

Elena Poniatowska
Translated by Gregory Kolovakos and Ronald Christ

Out there where Mexico grows scrubbier every day, where the streets
meander off and peter out and lie in greater disrepair every day, out
there is where Jesusa lives. Along those streets the squad car winds its
way, cruising slowly all through the day, the policemen drowsy with the
heat; and it parks at the corner for hours on end. The general store is
called "El Apenitas," The Just Barely. The cops get out for something to
drink, but by now the ice in the *Victoria* and *Superior* coolers is only a
pool of water where beers and sodas float. Women's hair sticks to the
napes of their necks, plastered down with sweat. The heat buzzes, just
as the flies buzz. How greasy and wringing wet the air coming from that
direction! People out there live in the same skillets in which they fry
their tortillas and their potato and squash-blossom quesadillas, that daily
bread the women pile up on rickety tables along the street. Some
squashes are being dried on the flat roofs.

Jesusa is dried out too. She keeps time with the century. She's sev-
enty-eight now, and the years have shrunk her the way they've shrunk
the houses, curving her spine. They say old people shrink so as to take
up as little space as possible on this earth. Little red veins show in her
weary eyes. Around the pupil, the iris is earthen, grey, and the coffee
pigment is slowly fading away. Her eyes no longer water, and the tear
ducts are blood red. There is no moisture under her skin either, and that
is why Jesusa is constantly repeating: "I'm shriveling away." Still, the skin
remains taut over her protruding cheekbones. "Every time I move, I shed
some scales." First, a front tooth fell out and she decided: "When another
one on the side falls out, I'll get myself a piece of gum, chew it real
good, and stick it back." She has lost her beautiful hair, that hair that
made the soldier boys call her "Queen Xochitl." What bothers her most
are her two stringy braids, and now when she goes to town for bread

139

or milk, she covers her head with a shawl. She walks along stooped, hugging the wall, bent over herself; nonetheless, I like her two graying, thin braids, the whisps of white hair curling at her temples over her wrinkled, cloth-covered brow. She also has those big spots on her hands. She says they come from her liver, but I think they come from time. With age, men and women become covered with mountain ranges and furrows, hills and deserts. Each day Jesusa looks more and more like the earth; she is a walking clod of soil, a little mountain of clay packed down by time and now dried out by the sun. "I've got four stumps left," and she raises her fingers, deformed by arthritis, to point to the gaps in her mouth.

Over the years, Jesusa has also tamed down. When I first knew her, she was gruff, remiss, not even saying "Come on in." Now, if you visit her, she offers you a seat.

"What brings you? What brings you here?"

"I'd like to chat with you."

"With me? Look, I work. If I don't work, I don't eat. I can't sit around gabbing."

Grudgingly, Jesusa agreed to my seeing her on the only day of the week she had free: Wednesday, from four to six. I began to live a little from Wednesday to Wednesday. Jesusa, on the other hand, did not give up her hostile attitude. When her neighbors let her know from the doorway that she should come tie up the dog so I could go in, she would mutter peevishly: "Oh, it's you." Tied to a very short chain, the black dog guarded the whole building. He was big and strong: a vicious dog. He blocked the way, narrow as it was, to all strangers. When I slipped past with a huge tape recorder, I was aware of his hot breath and his barking as surly as Jesusa's hostility. The building had a central corridor and was cut up into rented rooms on either side. The two "sanitary facilities," with no running water and always filled to the top, were at the back. Nobody kept an eye on them; there was a toilet to sit on but the dirty paper accumulated on the floor. The sun scarcely entered Jesusa's room, and oil fumes from the stove made your eyes water. The walls were decaying with saltpeter, and despite the corridor's being very narrow, half a dozen shoeless boys were playing there and peering in at the various neighbors. Jesusa asked them: "Want a taco, even if it's just with beans? No? Well, don't go begging from door to door then." Rats would peer in too.

In those years, Jesusa did not spend much time at home, because she left early for a printshop that still employed her. She'd leave her room locked up tight, her animals suffocating inside, along with her potted plants. At the printer's she cleaned, swept, picked up, mopped, washed the metal plates, and she brought home the overalls and, often, the workers' own clothes. The first time I asked her to tell me about her life (because I had overheard her talking at a laundry, and her language struck me as fearsome, especially the degree of her indignation), she responded: "I don't have time." She pointed to her work: the pile of overalls, the five chickens she had to take out in the sun, the dog and the cat to feed, the two caged birds that looked like sparrows, prisoners in a cage that grew smaller day by day. "See? Or are you going to give me a hand?" I said I would. "OK, then put the overalls in the gasoline." That's when I found out what overalls really are. I took hold of a hard object, shriveled with age, stiffened with grime, covered with large greasy stains, and I soaked it in a washtub. It was so stiff the water couldn't cover it; it was an island in the middle of the water, a rock. Jesusa ordered me: "While it's soaking, put the chickens out in the sun on the sidewalk."

So I did, but the chickens started cackling and scattering across the street. I got frightened and flew back inside. "A car's going to run them over."

"You mean you don't know how to sun chickens?" she asked me angrily. "Don't you see the cord? You have to tie them by the feet." In a second she had gotten the chickens back in, and she started scolding me again. "Who would think of putting chickens out like that?"

Remorsefully, I asked her: "How *can* I help you?"

"Well, put the chickens out in the sun on the roof, even if it's only for a little while."

Full of fear, I did it. The building was so low that from down on the ground I could see the hens flutter, fluff themselves, and happily peck out fleas. That pleased me, and I thought: "Well, I'm doing something right."

Jesusa yelled at me again: "All right, and what about the overalls?"

When I asked: "Where's the washing machine?" she pointed to a ribbed board scarcely ten or twelve inches wide and twenty long, saying "No washing machine, not even a pot to piss in! Scrub it yourself, on that!" She took a basin out from under the bed. She looked at me sarcastically: I wasn't able to scrub anything. The uniform was so stiff, it was difficult even to get hold of it. Then Jesusa exclaimed: "Just look what a waste you are! One of those stuck-up women too good to get their hands dirty." And she made me stand aside. Later she acknowledged that the overalls had to soak overnight in gasoline, and, shoving the full tub back under the bed, she commanded: "Now we have to go get food for the animals." I offered her my VW. "No, it's just down the corner."

She walked rapidly, change purse in hand, never looking at me. In contrast to the silence she had maintained with me on the way, she joked in the shop with the butcher, softsoaped him, and bought a miserable heap of scraps wrapped in tissue paper that immediately became soaked with blood. Back home, she flung the offal on the floor, and the cats, with their tails on end, electrified, pounced on it. The dogs were slower. The birds didn't even chirp.

I tried to plug in my tape recorder, nearly the size of a navy-blue coffin and with a speaker big enough for a dance hall, and Jesusa protested: "You're going to pay for my electricity, right? Don't you see you're stealing my current?" Later, she gave in. "Where are you going to put your beast? I'll have to move all this filth." And besides, the recorder was borrowed: "How come you go around with other people's things? Aren't you scared to?"

The following Wednesday I asked her the same questions again.

"Wait, didn't I tell you all that last week?"

'Yes, but it didn't record."

"Then that monster of yours doesn't work?"

"Sometimes I'm not aware whether it's recording or not."

"Then don't bring it anymore."

"It's just that I can't write quickly, and we'll waste a lot of time."

"That's just it. Better let's stop here, since neither of us is getting much out of this."

After that I started writing in a notebook, and Jesusa sneered at my handwriting: "So many years of study to come up with such a scrawl." That method helped me, though, because when I returned home at night I could reconstruct what she had told me. I was always afraid that on the least expected day she would "hang up" on our conversations. She didn't like the neighbors seeing me nor my greeting them. One day, when I asked after the smiling girls in the doorway, Jesusa, from inside her room, explained: "Don't call them girls, call them whores. Yes, little whores. That's what they are."

One Wednesday I found Jesusa lying on her bed, wrapped in a gaudy sarape—red, yellow, parakeet green, with big, loud stripes. She got up only to let me in, and went back to stretch out under the sarape, entirely covered from head to foot. I had always found her seated in the darkness in front of the radio, like a little bundle of age and loneliness, but listening, attentive, alert and critical. "They're telling complete lies in that box! They only say what suits them! When I hear them mention Carranza on the radio, I shout 'Damn Crook!' Every government boasts about what suits it. Now they call him the Baron of Four Marshes, and I think it's because his soul was all smeared with mud." Or: "So now they're going to put Villa's name up in gold letters on a church! How can they if he was a filthy killer, a cattle thief, a rapist? To me, those revolutionaries are like a kick in the . . . , well, that is, if I had balls. Nothing but thieves, highway robbers, protected by the law!" I looked at the unfamiliar sarape and sat down on a small chair at the foot of the bed to wait. Jesusa didn't utter a single word. Even the radio that was always playing while we talked was turned off. I waited for about half an hour in the darkness.

From time to time, I would ask: "Jesusa, are you feeling ill?"

She did not answer me.

"Jesusa, don't you feel like talking?"

She did not budge.

"Are you angry?"

Total silence. I chose to wait. Jesusa was often in a bad mood when our interviews began. After a while, she would compose herself but not lose her cranky, contemptuous attitude.

"Have you been sick? Haven't you gone to work?"

"No."

"Why not?"

"I haven't gone in more than two weeks."

Once again we fell into absolute silence. You couldn't even hear the chirping of her birds, who always made their presence known with a lament, a gentle, humble notice of here I am, under the rags covering the cage. Discouraged, I waited a long while and then launched another attack:

"Aren't you going to talk to me?"

She did not answer.

"Want me to go?"

Then she lowered her sarape down to her eyes, then to her mouth and spat out:

"Look. You've been coming here for two years and bugging me and bugging me and you don't understand a thing. So it's better if we put a stop to it right here and now."

I left hugging my notebook against my breast like a shield. In the car I thought to myself: "My God, what an old woman! She doesn't have anyone in her life. I'm the only person who visits her, and she's capable of telling me to go to hell." (On one occasion she had already said: "Go straight to hell!")

On the following Wednesday I was late (it was an unconscious slip), and I found her outside on the sidewalk. She grumbled: "Well, what happened to you? Don't you see I don't have the time? After you leave, I have to go to the barn for my milk, go for my bread. You annoy me when you leave me here waiting."

Then I went with her to the dairy, because in the poor districts the countryside comes right up to the city limits—or the other way around—even though nothing may smell like country and everything smacks of dust, garbage, swarms of people, and rot. "When we poor people drink milk, we drink it straight from the cow, not that junk in bottles and cartons you people drink." In the bakery Jesusa bought four rolls. "No pastry. That stuff doesn't fill you up, and costs more."

I came into contact with poverty, real poverty—the poverty of water drawn in pails and carried carefully so as not to spill a drop, of laundry done on the metal scrubbing board because there is no washing machine, of electricity stolen by rascals, of hens that lay eggs without shells ("just clear membrane") because the lack of sunlight never lets them harden. Jesusa belongs to the millions of men and women who do not live, who merely survive. Just getting through the day and making it to nighttime costs them so much effort that all their hours and energy are expended that way. How hard it is to stay afloat, to take one peaceful breath, even if only for a moment at dusk, when the chickens are no longer cackling behind their wire-mesh fence, and the cat is stretching out on the trampled ground.

Nevertheless, on Wednesday afternoons at sundown, in that little room almost always in shadow, in the midst of children's shrieks from the other rented rooms, the slamming of doors, the shouting, and the radio at full blast, another sort of life emerged, Jesusa's life, both her past and what she was reliving now in retelling it. Jesusa informed me that this was the third time she had come to earth and that if she suffered and was poor now that was because in her last incarnation she had been a queen. "I'm here on earth paying my debt, but my life is elsewhere. In reality, anybody alive on earth is here on loan. He's only passing through, and when his soul is freed from the sack of skin and bones we're all wrapped in, when he leaves his misery below ground, that's when he begins to live. We are the dead ones, turned inside out so we can see. We think we're alive, but we're not. We only came to earth in seeming flesh to fulfill one mission. We make our way encountering obstacles, and when He calls us to our final reckoning we die materially. The flesh dies and they bury it, but the soul returns to the place where it was released. We are reincarnated every thirty-three years after we die." Thus, between one death and another, between one coming to earth and another, Jesusa had invented a previous, interior life that made her present misery tolerable. "Now you see me in this dunghill, but I had my glorious garment, and Pierrot and Columbina carried my train because I was their sovereign, they my subjects."

Through Jesusa Palancares I learned of a doctrine that is widespread in Mexico: *spiritualism*. At the Government Ministry they informed me that in the Federal District alone there were more than 176 spiritualist churches, and I was able to visit various gathering places, meet mediums in Portales, Tepito, Luna Street, in the poor neighborhoods. The Catholic Church condemns spiritism and spiritualism equally, and yet this doctrine has much of Catholicism in it. Obviously it is a sect, and the faithful adopt it because they receive—just as in the banks—"more personalized attention." They refer to themselves as "Marist Trinitarians," alluding to the Virgin Mary and the Trinity, and they never completely break with the Roman Catholic Church although they stop attending it because they prefer the Spiritualist Opus.

The Spiritual Opus always seemed rather hazy to me, incomprehensible sometimes, and Jesusa got annoyed when I made her repeat some idea: "But didn't I already talk with you about that? How many times am I going to have to tell you?" She spoke of Allan Kardec, of her priest and protector Manuel Antonio Mesmer, and thus I discovered Franz Anton Mesmer, the founder of mesmerism and the famous *baquet magnetique*. Visiting a spiritist temple under the Nonoalco Bridge, the Midday Temple on Luna Street, I was introduced to a brotherhood and listened to a holy lecture on revelation and radiance that the priests and the "Guide" delivered to a reverent congregation who kept their eyes closed.

The United States anthropologist Isabel Kelly and the poet Sergio Mondragón point out that there is a difference between spiritism and spiritualism. The people interested in spiritism are educated and economically well off; many of them are politicians (Madero, for example, was a spiritist), and their interest focuses on appearances, ectoplasms, the effects of light and sound, levitation, and spiritual writing. They meet in private homes or in a rented space (in Gante, on the top floor of a building from the days of Porfirio Díaz, a select and elegant group of spiritists used to meet and was sometimes visited by Gutierre Tibón). They conduct their sessions in the dark. Joining hands in a circle that must not be broken, the power of their spirits vibrates out to the beyond, and the response is not long in coming: the dead descend to earth and make themselves known, the table moves, the curtain rises, the supernatural breaks through, communication begins.

On the other hand, poverty dominates spiritualism, and many inhabitants of the poorer neighborhoods search out spiritualist temples to receive treatment and cures, since the spiritual doctors usually charge between three and five pesos, and sometimes the operations are more effective than those in hospitals and, of course, have a much more uplifting effect: a shot of Coramine is hardly the same as a cleansing with a spray of seven herbs: hypericum, lavender, rue, sweet scabious, pepper tree, fennel, and clove. Twenty-two days of cleansings: seven cleansings with the bunch of herbs, seven of fire, and seven of vapors; a vigorous rubdown with Siete Machos lotion, and a massage that ends in ecstasy.

Men and women of all ages experience a sort of transport when they are spiritually possessed by their protectors: Mesmer, Adrian Carriel or Alan Cardel (possibly Allan Kardec), Light of the East, and many Mexican spirits, such as Pedrito Jaramillo, Rogelio Piel Roja, and others who obey Roque Rojas, that is, Father Elías. Roque Rojas is the founder of spiritualism, and in 1886 he was transformed into Father Elías. His photograph looks as though it had been taken from some volume of the Larousse. His eyes attempt to be penetrating. Alongside him and his prodigious miracles, Jesus Christ pales. Moreover, Roque possesses, he penetrates, his flock. When he enters them, after a violent trembling, women and men start speaking out loud in a trance, their eyes closed and their bodies agitated by spasms, and they unburden themselves: the conflicts, the frustrations, the husband's impotence, the fear of old age, the hatred for the woman next door all tumble out in a torrent. Afterward, the faithful return to their homes feeling very much relieved. And they return in a week and suddenly rise up and emerge from the gathering: rigid, with their eyes shut and their mouths covered with saliva, in expectation of divine possession, they sway back and forth because their protector rocks them as he massages them. And then! It happens: the floodgates open and the torrent of their misery pours out.

Most of these people are mestizos with very low wages. They are part of this monstrous city, part of its rootless, floating population composed of immigrants from the countryside and provinces who have traded their traditional culture for television and radio. For them, Catholicism is far less satisfactory than spiritualism, with its more powerful emotions that give them a sense of individuality. For example, at one time the Spiritual Opus was the only thing that gave meaning to the life of Jesusa Palancares, and she even went so far as to have herself baptized in it at a ceremony at "El Pocito," on the road to Pachuca, a ceremony that caused her to cry a great deal. Her protectress, the priestess Trinita Pérez de Soto, pressed a triangle of light on Jesusa, first on her forehead, then on her skull, ears, mouth, brain, feet, and on her hands with their palms turned up. This divine triangle prevents storms, winds, floods, whirlpools, and it also "calms the storms within one, the spiritual ravages, because it is a defense against all evils on earth." That day Jesusa saw a spiritual hand make a sign of the cross on the water of El Pocito, and she saw a "vision" that consoled her—three roses on the water: one white, one yellow, and one pink. From that moment on she spoke with her dead relatives, her parents and her brothers, whom she had rescued from darkness and who, thanks to her, no longer wandered lost in infinity, flying about with no one to remember what sort of life they had lead on earth. But Jesusa broke with the Spiritual Opus because other priestesses in white nylon gowns and with large, tightly woven sprays of amaranth scorned her, refused to yield her proper place to her, and demanded that she move away. As she herself relates it: "At the time when I was entering into ecstasy, and all of us were seated so the beings could take possession of us, they gave me an elbow: 'Sister, move someplace else, a little farther back.' " Until one day Jesusa became angry and shouted at them: "All right, there are your chairs, and you can go squash your rumps on them."

Listening to Jesusa, I imagined her young, swift, independent, rugged and I experienced along with her all her rages and pains, her legs that went numb with the snow from up north, her reddened feet. Seeing her act in her own story, capable of making her own decisions, my own lack of character made itself plain to me. I especially liked to imagine her in the ocean, facing out to sea, the wind on her face tugging her hair back, her naked feet on the sand, lapped by the water, her hands cupped to taste the sea, to discover its saltiness, its tang. "You know, there's a lot of ocean." I also saw her running, petticoats between her legs and glued to her firm body, her pretty head sometimes in a shawl, sometimes covered with a straw hat.

Imagining her haggle at the market with a stallkeeper was a thrill for me; imagining her traveling on the roof of a train was the best of movies. While she was talking, images sprang to mind, and they all filled me with joy. I felt strenghtened by everything I have not experienced. I would arrive home and tell them: "You know, something is being born inside me, something new that didn't exist before." But they did not respond at all. I wanted to tell them: "I feel stronger and stronger. I'm growing. Now, for sure, I'm going to be a woman." What was growing— or maybe what had been lying dormant there for years—was my Mexican self, the forging of me as a Mexican, the feeling that Mexico, identical to Jesusa's Mexico, lay within me, and that by the merest cracking of my shell it would emerge. I was no longer the eight-year-old girl who had arrived on *The Marquis of Comillas*, a boat carrying refugees. I was no longer the daughter of eternally absent parents, of transatlantic travelers, the daughter of ships and trains. Instead, Mexico was inside me; it was a beast (as Jesusa called my tape recorder) inside, a powerful, vigorous animal that grew larger until it filled the whole space. Discovering it was like suddenly holding a truth in your hands, a brightly lit lantern that casts its circle of light on the floor. I had only seen lamps float in the dark and then disappear: the kerosene lantern of the station chief or the switchman's, which sways to the rhythms of his steps only to vanish finally; but this solid, steady lamp gave me the security of a home. My grandparents and my great-grandparents used to use a pat phrase: "I don't belong." One night, before falling asleep and after identifying myself for a long time with Jesusa, reviewing all my images of her one by one, I was able to tell myself in a whisper: "I *do* belong."

For months, I would fall asleep thinking about Jesusa. Just one of her phrases, barely sensed, was enough to humiliate me and dash my hopes. I heard her within me just as when I was a child lying in bed, I had heard myself growing in the night. "I know I'm growing because I can hear my bones rumble ever so quietly." My mother had laughed. Jesusa laughed inside me, sometimes scornfully, and sometimes she hurt me. Always, always she made me feel more alive.

Bit by bit, a cautious, timid love developed between Jesusa and me. I used to arrive with my spoiled pet's burden of woe, and she would take me to task: "Woman, what's getting into you? Everybody, not just you, has his burden to bear here."

It was a healthy blow to my self-esteem and a way of minimizing the oldest problem in the world: either being in or out of love, heads or tails of the same coin. There we were, the two of us, afraid of hurting one another. That same afternoon she brewed a bitter tea for my biliousness and handed me her fifth hen: "Here, take it home to your mama so she can make broth for you." But I already had another image of hens; and when I saw the plucked, yellow chicken on the table at home, I was thinking about the five hens squabbling at her house in Cerro del Peñón and how they were already my friends. One Wednesday I got there and fell asleep on her bed, and she sacrificed her soap operas to let me sleep. And Jesusa *lives* for the radio! It's her means of communication with the outside, her only link to the world. She never turns it off, she never left it even to tell me the most intimate episodes of her life. Little by little the confidence between us was growing, the "fondness" as she says but which we never mentioned out loud nor even named. I think that Jesusa is the human being I most respect after Mane. . . . And she is going to die on me, just the way she wants to. That's why every Wednesday my heart skips a beat at the thought she might not be there. "Someday when you come, you're not going to find me anymore. You'll only bump into thin air." And, after her showing two legs dangling in coarse-ribbed cotton stockings and my hearing her soap opera, she lets me in. Grumbling and muttering, she greets me with her little hands knobby from so much washing, the yellow and brown spots on her face, her stringy braids, her sweaters fastened with a pin. And I beg God to let me take care of her right to the grave.

When I traveled to France, I wrote to her, especially postcards. The first replies, by return mail, were hers. She went to public letter writers in Santo Domingo Square, dictated her letters, and deposited them in the main post office. She related what she thought would interest me: the arrival in Mexico of the President of Czechoslovakia, the external debt, highway accidents; but in Mexico she and I never spoke about current events or newspapers. Jesusa always was unpredictable. One afternoon I found her seated, glued to the radio, a notebook on her lap, a pencil between her fingers. She wrote the letter "u" upside down and "n" with three descending strokes, and she did it with infinite slowness. She was taking a radio course in writing. Foolishly, I asked her: "And why do you want to learn that now?" And she answered me: "Because I want to die knowing how to read and write."

On different occasions I tried to get her to go out: "Jesusa, let's go to the movies."

"No, because I can't see good anymore . . . in the old days I used to enjoy the serials, movies with Lon Chaney."

"Then," I would propose, "let's go out for a walk."

"And what about the chores? It's easy to see you don't have any chores."

I suggested a trip to Tehuantepec Isthmus to see her home province again, something I thought would please her, until it dawned on me that the hope of something better upsets her, makes her aggressive. Jesusa is so used to her condition, so warped by her solitude and her poverty, that the possibility of a change seems like an affront to her:

"Get out of here. You-know-it-all. Get out, I tell you. Leave me in peace."

Then I realized that there comes a time when one has suffered so much that one can no longer cease to suffer. The only respite that Jesusa allowed herself was that single "Farito" she smoked slowly around six in the afternoon, with her radio always turned on even while she was speaking to me out loud. She unwrapped and rewrapped gifts very carefully. "So they're not mistreated." That was how I learned about her box of dolls, all new and untouched. "There're four. I bought them for myself. As a girl, I never had any."

Jesusa might have every justification for dying, but she does the impossible to stay alive. And to sleep. Sleeping is an adventure for her. Each night she awaits the sleep that will put her, once again, in contact with the beyond. She has revelations that reach the point of scenting the air as though the resin known as copal were being burnt. Sometimes her humble palace smells of citrus blossoms, at others of verbena, fruit, or musk, and the room is showered in a pale violet light.

Moreover, Jesusa is a woman who fends off men, not like some saint (because she herself admits to being a big drinker, a big dancer: "Lots of men fell in love with me, hear? A bunch of real men chased my skirts.") but as a whole person who respects herself. I see her as a temple, a temple in the sense we conceived of it as children when they told us that there is a sacred place inside us that we must never desecrate. I have always had that image of purity when thinking of Jesusa.

In writing *Hasta no verte, Jesús mío* [*Here's Looking at You, Jesus*], I faced a problem: the problem of nasty language. In an early version, Jesusa never talked that way, and it pleased me to think about her discretion, her reserve. The possibility of writing a story without bad words made me happy, but as the trust developed between us, and especially when I came back from almost a year in France, Jesusa let herself go. She opened up her world to me, no longer watching what she said; and she herself admonished me: "Don't be an ass. You're the only one who believes in people. You're the only one who thinks people are good." I had to look some of her words up in the dictionary of Mexicanisms, to trace others—like *hurgamaderas, bellaco*—back to the most archaic Spanish. She threw my absence in my face: "You and your self-centered interest! You'll keep coming to see me so long as you can get something out of me that benefits you, and afterwards not a trace, not even your taillights. That's how it always is: everybody's trying to milk the other person dry."

Like all old people, she recounted a long series of ailments and complaints: her weak ribs, the aching backs of her knees, how badly they drive trucks, the awful quality of food supplies, rent you can't afford any longer, neighbors who are lazy drunks. Tiresome, she returned time after time to the same subject, seated on her bed, her legs dangling over the edge since the bed was raised up on bricks on account of the water that came into the rooms, flooding them, especially during the rainy season when Doña Casimira, the owner, didn't bother to have the drain in the corridor opened.

Over a period of ten years, I saw her change houses three times, and each time she had to move farther away, because the city drives its poor people out, pushing them to the city limits, forcing them away, as it expands. Jesusa first lived close to Lecumberri, to the north, in Iguarán; later she moved to Cerro del Peñón. Now she has landed on the highway to Pachuca, near a few settlements named Aurora, Tablas de San Agustín, San Agustín Gardens, which use blue arrows pointed in the four cardinal directions to announce *drainage* (spelled with a "j"), *water* (with an "h"), and *electricity* (with an "s"). There is no drainaje, no whater, no electrisity. Nor is there a single tree on those untilled flatlands, nor a blade of grass, not even a bush, except for those carted in by the settlers in their Mobil Oil cans. The dust storms look like the Hiroshima mushroom itself, and they are no less deadly since they carry all the world's debris and swallow up even the people's souls.

Jesusa now lives in two small 12′ x 12′ rooms built for her by her adopted son Perico, and she observes: "Here everybody's from Oaxaca, so that's why we help each other out." The settlers huddle together according to state and, recognizing each other by their native region, they help each other or, at least, do not harm each other. Jesusa expresses it well: "When all's said and done, I don't have a country. I'm like the Hungarians—from nowhere. I don't feel like a Mexican, and I don't acknowledge Mexicans. The only thing here is pure convenience and self-interest. If I had money and possessions, I'd be Mexican; but since I'm less than trash, I'm nothing. I'm garbage the dog pisses on and then trots away. The wind comes up and carries it off, and that's the end of everything."

If previously when I went to see her I had had to cross stréets, when I visited her in her new home I drove across open tract after open tract, with nothing but the car's tires raising clouds of yellow dust. There was no highway, nothing, only the desert. Suddenly, far away, in the middle of an open stretch, I saw a little black dot, and, as I approached, this dot turned into a man squatting in the baking sun. I thought to myself: "What will happen to this poor man? He must be sick." I drove up close and asked him from the car window: "Don't you want . . . ?" I stopped dead. The squatting man was defecating. Annoyed, he looked at me. Starting up the car, I thought about the oddity of this man's walking who knows how far to defecate in the middle of the land, so to speak, on the cusp of the world. I told Jesusa about it, and, irritated, she spat out: "You're always making a jackass out of yourself."

To write the book about Jesusa I used a journalistic device: the interview. Two years earlier I had worked for a month and a half with the U.S. anthropologist Oscar Lewis, author of *The Children of Sánchez* and other books. Lewis asked if I would help him edit *Pedro Martínez, The Life of a Tepoztlán Peasant*. Lewis worked with a team that inquired into the facts and did a sort of topographical survey of poverty. His informants came to see him at his apartment in Gutenberg Street, where he turned on his tape recorder and asked questions. It was my job to revise and prune those stories, that is, to eliminate repetitions and useless digressions. Undoubtedly this experience left its mark on me in writing *Here's Looking at You, Jesus*; nevertheless, since I am not an anthropologist, my work may be viewed as a testimonial novel and not an anthropological or sociological document. I made use of the anecdotes, the ideas, and many of Jesusa Palancares's expressions, but I would never be able to assert that the narrative is a direct transcription of her life because she herself would reject that. I killed off the characters who got in my way, I eliminated as many spiritualist sessions as I could, I elaborated wherever it seemed necessary to me, I cut, I stitched together, I patched, I invented. After finishing, I had some feeling of having stayed on the surface; I had not brought the essential, the depths of Jesusa's character, to light. With time, however, I have come to think that if I did not do that it was because I was treading on what was most vital without really being conscious of it: I limited myself to *divining* Jesusa.

I collected incidents, I always got ahead of her, I did not know how to portray those moments when the two of us remained silent, alone, almost not thinking, waiting for the miracle. We were always a little feverish; we always yearned for the hallucination.

Since I could turn to the tape recorder only when she let me use it, I would reconstruct what she said each Wednesday in the evening. In her voice I heard the voice of the nanny who taught me Spanish, the voice of all the maids who passed through our house like drafts, with their expressions, their way of looking at life, if they looked at it at all, because they only lived in the cold light of day and had no reason to dream. These and other women's voices added their choir to the main one: Jesusa Palancares's voice; and that is why I think my book contains words, expressions, proverbs—many proverbs—not only from Oaxaca, Jesusa's home state, but from all over the Republic, from Jalisco, Guerrero, the Puebla mountains, the Federal Distict.

On some Wednesdays, Jesusa spoke only about her obsessions of the moment: the sealed drain in the corridor, for example; but in the marasmus of routine and the difficulties of living, there were moments when we cried together, very gently, because she had suffered and continues suffering quietly to this day; moments when happiness burst in from who knows where, and we took the hens out from behind their chicken wire and settled them comfortably on the bed as if they were our children; when we met at a corner, and from far away, with my heart beating fast, I saw her raised arm hailing me down, because she, who saw nothing, had been warned by Mesmer that I was going to come.

On Wednesday afternoons I went to see Jesusa, and in the evenings I accompanied my mother to some cocktail party at one embassy or another. I always tried to maintain a balance between the extreme poverty I shared in the afternoon and the glitter of the receptions. My socialism was two-faced. Climbing into my really hot bath, I recalled Jesusa's washtub, under her bed, in which she soaked the overalls and bathed herself on Saturdays. All I could think was: "I hope she never comes to know my house, never learns how I live!" When she did come to know it, she told me: "I'm never coming back. They're not going to think I'm a beggar." And yet our friendship persisted: the link had been forged, and Jesusa and I loved each other. She never stopped criticizing me, but she never offended me: "I've known for a long time that you put on airs." When I was in the hospital, she wanted to stay and sleep there: "I'll just stretch out, even if it's under your bed." I have never gotten so much from anyone; I have never felt more to blame. All I did was move over a little in the bed: "Come, Jesusa, there's room for both of us." But she did not want to. She said goodbye at 5 A.M., and I still said to her: "Oh, come on, since there's room!" And she answered: "The only bed with room enough for the two of us is mine, because it's a poor woman's bed."

When I had retyped the first version of her life, I brought it to her in a sky-blue binder. She said: "What do I want this for? Get this crap out of here! Don't you see I can't have anything else in the way?" I had thought she would like it for its bulk and because Ricardo Pozas had once told me that Juan Pérez Jolote had been disappointed with the second edition of his life story as published by the Fondo de Cultura Económica and yearned for the yellow binding of the Instituto Nacional Indigenista's edition: "That edition was two inches thick!" On the other hand, even if Jesusa did reject the typed version, I chose the image of the Infant of Atocha, who presided over the darkness of her room, for the cover of the printed book; and, as a matter of fact, when she saw it, she asked me for twenty copies, which she gave to the boys in the shop so they would know what her life had been like, the many rocky roads she had had to travel.

Her reactions always unsettled me. Right in front of me she ripped into a thousand pieces some photos that Hector García had taken of us one afternoon: "This shows a lack of respect! This is filth! What I wanted was one like this!" She did not like to see herself with an apron, standing in the middle of the entrance to her building. "I thought it was going to come out like this!" And she pointed to her large sepia portrait hanging in a wooden frame. "That's a Marcel wave, with three or five waves, according to the size." (The size of what? Her head?)

In 1968 she made her hatred of the students clear. "They're a bunch of troublemakers. Why aren't they studying instead of rioting? I despise them." She also hated unions. "Union dues and more union dues, and I ask you: what for? So the leaders can get rich, get fat on our money? I used to march on the first of May with the barbers' union and the woodworkers', until I saw Cárdenas up close, smothered in streamers; but when I realized it was a matter of out and out robbery, I shouted at them: 'Take your harp, I'm not playing your tune anymore.' " She also censured and rejected teachers, nuns, and priests: "Those nuns, I've watched them, and that's why I tell them right out: 'Hypocritical little daughters of Eve, stop playing the fool and let yourselves go, out in the open.' Besides, how ugly priests and nuns are, always chasing after each others' skirts." Oddly enough, she always accepted homosexuality: "Women are such pigs these days, a young man doesn't know who to lay anymore. . . ." Then she observes: "Don Lucho was a good sort, because queens are better than machos." And that is how she also justifies her friend Manuel the Cradlesnatcher: "Maybe women disgusted him because he got the clap or they cheated on him, and so he was better off devoting himself to boys. He had lots of fun with them and used to say that men are less expensive than women and much more amusing." And yet she always kept her own man under the wraps of great modesty.

This is her only reference to her love life: "When Pedro went on military duty, then he used me. I never took off my trousers, just dropped them when he used me, and that was that. We had to keep our trousers on so that when they sounded the trumpet: 'Fall in, everybody up!' we could go wherever. My husband wasn't a man for much petting, not at all. He was a very serious man. Nowadays I see kids over there necking and hugging in the doorways. It seems odd to me because my husband never went around making such foolish faces. He had what it took and he did it and that was it."

Jesusa is no more explicit about her puberty: "These days everybody blabs everything: they wave the flag of their filthiness and worse. Back in those days, if you bled, well, you bled, and that was that. If you had your period, then you did, and if not, not. They never told me anything about using rags or anything. I bathed two or three times a day and did so all my life. I never went around with such filthiness there, stinking like a dead dog. And I didn't get my clothes dirty. There was no reason to get dirty. I'd go, wash myself, change my clothes, hang them up to dry, and put them on again perfectly clean. But I never suffered, or thought about it; I never hurt or said anything to anyone."

As for Mexican politics, her reaction was one of anger and disillusionment, and it aroused totally Buñuelian images in my mind: "So many banquets! So many banquets! And why doesn't the president invite the hordes of beggars walking the streets? Come on, why not? A real revolutionary s.o.b. With each passing day we are trampled on more and more, and everything that comes along gnaws away at us, leaves us toothless, crippled, maimed, and they build their mansions out of our bits and pieces." Nor do other people console her: "This not dying on time is really tough. When I'm sick, I don't open my door all day long; I spend entire days locked inside. I just boil tea or corn-meal mush or something I make for myself. But I don't go outside to quarrel with anybody, and nobody stops at my door. The day I'm stuck here dying like an animal, my door will be bolted. . . . Otherwise, the neighbors poke their heads in to see that you're dying, that you're grimacing, since most people come to laugh at a person in their death throes. That's life. You die so others can laugh. They mock your visions. You're left with your legs spread, bent in two, twisted, with your lips swollen, mouth open, and your eyes popping out. Tell me if this life's not hard, to die in such a way. That's why I bolt my door. They'll drag me out of here, stinking, but come here to look at me and say this or that—no, nobody, . . . nobody . . . only God and me."

Ultimately, I would have liked to place Jesusa Palancares within Mexican literature, to speak of her role as a follower of the troops during the Revolution, of her ancestors, to say that she is a heroine in the cast of those spontaneous fighters, the women who went on strike, who did not "give in," either in her life or her work, but I felt that it was out of place, pedantic. I tried to emphasize Jesusa's personal qualities, to stress what distinguishes her from the traditional figure of the Mexican woman: her rebelliousness, her independence: "In the end, the more you give the more they drive you into the ground. I think that right in Hell there must be a place for all the women who gave in. Well, let 'em get shafted!" Her combativeness: "Before they land one on me, it'll be because I landed two on them." I came to the conclusion that it was not up to me to analyze her character historically. To what end? What I can indeed assure you, however, is that Jesusa continues to live in me, in other women, in my daughter, in other girls who will come along, in the daughters of Guayaba. She is not a militant member of any party, she is not political, she does not attend any demonstrations—nor does she invade countries. I cannot set her to standing guard beneath any red/black flag or to march in the ranks of the unions. She's seen it all. While I am on my way there, she's already come back.

"You can pull the wool over my eyes once; twice, never." If I were to transform her into a neighborhood Zapata, I would betray all those hours we had together. I seem to see Jesusa in the sky, on the earth, and everywhere in Mexico—like that, as God once was, Him, the masculine one.

LÊDO IVO
[1924–]

LÊDO IVO WAS BORN in Maceió, Alagoas, in Brazil. He began his literary activities in Recife before moving to Rio where he continued to pursue a career in journalism as well as creative writing. His first book of poetry, *As imaginações*, 1944 ["Imaginings"], was linked to the so-called 45 Generation, and thereafter followed a steady output of verse. His subsequent collections include *Ode e elegia*, 1945 ["Ode and Elegy"]; *Acontecimiento do soneto*, 1948 ["The Birth of the Sonnet"]; *Cántico*, 1951 ["Canticle"]; *Um brasileiro em Paris*, 1955 ["A Brazilian in Paris"]; *Magias*, 1960 ["Sorceries"]; and *Finisterra*, 1972 ["Finisterre"]. The last of these books won a number of prizes including that of the PEN Club of Brazil. All his poems, with the exception of *Finisterra*, have appeared in a single volume entitled *O sinal semafórico* ["The Semaphoric Symbol"], published in 1974.

In addition to his poetry and journalism, Ivo has written a handful of novels and some critical essays. His novel *As alianças*, 1947 ["The Alliances"], won the Graca Aranha Prize, and a much more recent novel, *Ninho de cobras*, 1973 [*The Snake's Nest or a Tale Badly Told*, 1981], was awarded the Walmap National Prize. Critical essays include *O universo poético de Raul Pompeia*, 1963 ["The Poetic Universe of Raul Pompeia"]; *Poesia observada*, 1967 ["Poetry Observed"], *Teoria e celebrão*, 1976 ["Theory and Celebration"]; and *Confissões de um poeta*, 1979 ["Confessions of a Poet"], from which the following selection is taken.

The author has recently been elected to the Brazilian Academy of Letters.

To Write Is Not to Live

by Lêdo Ivo
Translated by Giovanni Pontiero

I am a poet and a writer. I live by writing. How I sometimes envy people who live their lives remote from art, distanced from the words and materials that engender the creation of poetry: people who are simply absorbed by the very pattern of life!

My sympathy lies with those human beings who dispense with the use of language in order to declare what they are, or what they judge or imagine themselves to be—since a glow of pretense illumines everyone's existence. Creatures bereft of language, who use silence like a shield raised against love, boredom and death, how I envy you!

My voids fill me. My blank spaces are part of the intellectual writing that narrates me. They are also one of the many languages in which they try to recite me.

And suppose I were to express nothing in my books? I ponder the effectiveness of a language that might extol nothingness with majesty and transparency.

Poetry ended up imposing itself on me like a verbal process destined to conceal my private life, and generating a peculiar mythology that replaces the futile truth of existence.

I increasingly feel that my writing creates me. I am the invention of my own words. The myth-maker in me speaks the truth. And one of the eternal mysteries of creative writing is that readers should seek in a novel, in a poem, in a painting or musical composition—that is to say, in inventions and myths—some proof of reality.

To you, dear reader, I can only offer my inventions. If for you they become the truth, that is your affair. What is involved is a creative process, which transforms every reader into an invisible author.

My momentary flashes of inspiration illumine my imaginary precursors—poets and writers who emerge from the shadow and oblivion and, having become my contemporaries thanks to a certain accentuation, they form a capricious language into which I insert myself, wherein I might become dissolved tomorrow and be reinvented by time. A poet's genuine tradition is rooted in this relationship that the academic eye rarely perceives.

Contemplate the poetry of this nightfall, in the narrow street of an old provincial town that still holds so many secrets. There is a sign-plate: "Pensão Avelaneda. Refeições *avulças*"* [Pension Avelaneda. Meals served upon request]. The unexpected *ç* gives that word, which has been worn out and eroded by usage, a new dignity, a magical touch that lights up the evening sky crammed between the rooftops of old houses and the flickering glass of skyscrapers.

Such is poetry: the apparent cedilla of an error in the debased body of existence.

The concisions and incisions of prose, the white lights that illumine the consonants in their metaphorical cocoons, the prosodic night of the text, starred like a dahlia, the juices of fruits that flow from vowels and resemble metaphysical coagulations, transgressions and breaches converted into law, a style that has transformed its entire weight and gravity into leaps and bounds, the commas lurking among the sentences like insects in the dense hedgerow, words that light up and are extinguished like the semiotic system of airports, the fauna and flowers of words, a verbal richness that jests about economy and amuses itself in the evergreen grass of language, the everlasting stylistic feast of those who love words as if they were nudes, the semantic compartments of the graphic wardrobe that stores dreams and memories, vacillations and obscurities, certainties and doubts, the hieratic letters that spy on us amidst the humming syllables, the paragraphs of stone and water in the day enlarged by the heat of hyperbole, the syntax of the absolute . . .

Ever since childhood, M. has been in the habit of dreaming that he is dead and about to be buried. The moment they throw the first spadeful of earth over his coffin, M. raises one hand to protect his face, and wakes up.

In time, this final gesture became mechanical. On dreaming, M. already knows beforehand that he is about to raise his hand and wake up, thus saving himself from death.

A golf club. Moving across the undulating green landscape, the players plagiarize a scene from an English novel. But the caddies are black urchins dressed in tatters.

One of the main features of the so-called mass culture (on radio,

---

*The correct spelling in Portuguese is *avulsas* (literal meaning in this context: *separate*). [*Trans.*]

television, screen, and in the press) is that it strives to make people laugh. Laughter is now the opium of the people.

In a crowded street in the city center, I see a mangy dog. In the dog's eyes, which are almost blind and streaked with blood, I detect passiveness mingled with irritation, as if something inside that dog were rebelling against those offending wounds.

Some days later, while visiting an acquaintance, I see an old blind dog colliding with furniture and walls, incapable of understanding the curse that has befallen it.

The god of dogs is as merciless as the god of men.

The frontier is not a boundary but an invitation to cross.

I look at a friend for the last time as he lies in his coffin. On his face I see no sign of composure, only the humiliation of being dead.

It is more difficult to be a writer than a great writer.

As for the endless conflict of interests that arises between the writer and the publisher—especially in the case of the writer who has little or no aptitude for business, and who only succeeds in building up a readership in slow stages as in my own case—I recall the observation made by G. K. Chesterton, in a letter to his literary agent, about the peculiar nature of the literary market. He wrote: "There are perfectly sensible reasons why a man who writes books should not be the best person to negotiate them." Someone selling a house can advertise its attractions, the wonderful views of the surrounding countryside, the comfort and amenities of the property—but what author is able to announce to any prospective publisher that his novel is one of the most brilliant and witty that has ever been written, or that his poem is a sublime epic?

Perhaps the best solution in this impasse (which also has its moral aspect) when trying to sell one's books (although there are authors who are sufficiently simple-minded or astute not even to consider it) would be to have recourse to a literary agent. But where does one find this literary agent if the agent in question has been generated by a stifling cultural system that puts a price on creative writing, which must be sustained on the one hand by a reading public that is attracted by novelty and on the other by the whims of financial speculation?

May death only claim me when I have become drained of myself.

I implore the god of poets and writers: deliver me from perfection. I am afraid of perfection. I often think that perfection is the melodious voice leading me to the edge of the abyss.

May perfection keep its distance, may it get out from under my skin and leave me free to wander in the direction of fruitful errors, felicitous lapses, indulgences that become a gateway to wonder and discovery; to wander in the direction of hazardous experiments with form, of texts dignified by a message that is both revealing and disturbing.

If there is something that a poet or writer should fear, it is perfection, this radiant burial of any tomorrow. Let my writing have the imperfections of the earth—let it be the incomplete domain of man and of life, the discourse of the world.

In that small provincial city, swept by sea breezes, nothing ever happened, apart from murders, suicides, adultery, and the boredom that eroded human lives.

My reality erodes me.

On leaving the cinema, Teseu do Carmo saw the Stranger, who transfixed him with eyes of steel. Teseu do Carmo decided to follow him. The Stranger walked ahead impassively. Seagulls were flying around the War Memorial. He slowly crossed the deserted esplanade, entered the airport through a side entrance and made his way towards his machine, a great camellia settled on the lawn. Teseu do Carmo saw him disappear, in vertical flight, into the sky which was still blue.

We were no longer alone. As night advanced, the Earth was systematically being occupied by inhabitants from other planets. The human monopoly had come to an end.

If I were to write a science-fiction novel, I would borrow a phrase from Pascal as my epigraph: *"Que de royaumes nous ignorent!"* ["How many kingdoms don't know about us!"]

Nightfall. That inverted dawn is the world's most beautiful moment as it simultaneously becomes light and dark. It is still day with its clarity, and it is already night with its darkness.

Nightfall has the radiant majesty of things fulfilled and complex. Let night come—I have already lived my day. Let death arrive—I have already lived my life.

Like the universe, I also want to turn day to night, to feel within myself that tussle between light and darkness.

A room with bare walls (with a small arched window from where you can view the sea or countryside), a bed and a table—behold man's real castle.

The spirit dances—then it is awakened.

A wall made of what I am, my individual reality protects me from other realities.

Within my dreams and words, I feel myself impenetrable and secure. My own silence defends me, as if it were a shield. And language conceals me.

My dreams are the prefaces of reality.

On the hill stands the white lighthouse, and before it the blue sea and the ships. This is the first scene I witnessed as a child, and it will certainly be the last thing I shall contemplate at the hour of death.

The beginning is always in the end.

Pact? Transgression?
In your poetic art
everything is constellation.

The crab disappears into the black, slimy mud of the swamp and conceals itself in the deep night that protects and guards everything the crab possesses.

Dreams are poetic creations. The artifices and figures of reality merge with inventions and improbabilities and cause the imaginative aspect of life to impose its intangible truth.

Once again, I dream about places where I have never been and that I shall never find in books. They are fictions that are impenetrably mine, private edifices constructed in my sleep, semantic constellations, gothic cities, water from the dam that opens in my soul, when fast asleep. I entrust myself to the laws of repose and freedom.

The protagonist of those fables woven with what in me is both excess and poverty, similitude and contrast, ambiguity or repression, and therein I discover the flavor of a contemporaneity or of an urgency which increasingly incites and intrigues me.

Compared with those strange eyes that swarm in my dreams, the frequently extenuated ego of my wakeful existence is the mere invention of everyday life, imposed by the collective patterns of the reality of others.

Dreams are poems without words, as if the latter had already recognized the unnecessity of attaining the level of images and visions.

And the rhetoric of the Night provides the laws regulating those dreams, and support the changeable and precarious edifice of a universe intent upon reconstituting with the remains of real life, that truer reality pursued by poets.

Stendhal wrote in his *Histoire de la Peinture en Italie*: "J'aime mieux un ennemi qu'un ennuyeux" ["I prefer an enemy to a bore"].

From death to birth is the same path.
The past is the future: it lies before us.

To give meaning to life and form to reality—these are the two essential duties of the poet.

The intention of Machado de Assis when he wrote *Dom Casmurro* was to produce an open work, endowed with ambiguity. So from an aesthetic point of view, the question about the guilt or innocence of Capitu is irrelevant.

As a reader, I hold the view that she committed adultery with Escobar; but that clandestine love bore no fruit, and Ezequiel is the son of Bentinho.

OCTAVIO PAZ
[1914–]

A NATIVE OF Mexico, Octavio Paz is his country's most respected poet and essayist. Not only have his works delved into the complexities of the Mexican psyche, but they have also addressed universal themes such as alienation and reintegration through spiritual and ethical awareness. Influenced as a young man by Surrealism and by his personal experience with Oriental cultures, Paz portrays the artist as exile and visionary seeking liberty through the reinvention of language and communion with the senses. Since his writings in such diverse fields as art, literature, anthropology, politics, and sociology are often intellectually dense, his work is better known to scholars than to the general public. Yet Paz's reputation as a man of letters is internationally recognized.

Paz's most famous work, *El laberinto de la soledad*, 1950 [*The Labyrinth of Solitude*, 1961], is a book of essays on Mexican history and culture, now considered a Latin American classic. Among his many other publications, those available in English include *El arco y la lira*, 1956 [*The Bow and the Lyre*, 1973]; *Piedra de sol*, 1967 [*Sun Stone*, 1963]; *Claude Levi-Strauss o el nuevo festín de Esopo*, 1967 [*Claude Levi-Strauss: An Introduction*, 1970]; *Corriente alterna*, 1967 [*Alternating Current*, 1973]; *Postdata*, 1970 [*The Other Mexico: Critique of the Pyramid*, 1972]; and, soon to be published in English, *Sor Juana Inés de la Cruz o las trampas de la fe*, 1982 ["Sor Juana Inés de la Cruz or The Traps of Faith"], called by one eminent critic "one of the most exciting books to have appeared in the Spanish language in this century: a true intellectual feast."

Paz joined the Mexican diplomatic corps in the 1930s and was Mexico's ambassador to India from 1962 to 1968. Of his political affiliation, he has said simply, "disillusioned leftist." He has taught regularly at universities in the United States and has been awarded numerous international literary prizes.

This essay, written in 1976, from the collection *El ogro filantrópico*, 1979 ["The Philanthropic Ogre"], is included in Paz's latest book of essays in English, *One Earth, Four or Five Worlds*, 1985. Its assessment of the Mexican experience vis-à-vis the United States bears comparison to Fuentes' essay in this anthology; both authors recognize—as do many contemporary Latin American intellectuals—that the experience of "otherness" is fundamental to understanding the complexities of the U.S.–Latin American relationship. Cleverly reflecting in its title the author's plea for a "re-vision" of the different shapes of U.S. and Latin American history and culture, this essay is proof that the "telltale mirror" of literature can also reveal to U.S. readers the image of alternative values.

THE TELLTALE MIRROR

Octavio Paz
Translated by Helen Lane

Before becoming a reality, the United States was an image to me. That is not surprising: we Mexicans begin as children to see that country as the *other*, an *other* that is inseparable from us and that at the same time is radically and essentially alien. In the north of Mexico the expression "the other side" is used to mean the United States. The other side is geographical: the frontier; cultural: another civilization; linguistic: another language; historical: another time (the United States is running after the future while we are still tied to our past); metaphorical: it is the image of everything that we are not. It is foreignness itself. Yet we are condemned to live with this foreignness: the other side is right next to us. The United States is always present among us, even when it ignores us or turns its back on us: its shadow covers the entire continent. It is the shadow of a giant. To us this giant is the same one that appears in fairy tales and legends—a big overgrown fellow and something of a simpleton, an ingenuous sort who doesn't know his own strength and who can be fooled, though his wrath can destroy us. The image of the good-hearted, doltish giant is juxtaposed with that of the shrewd and blood-thirsty cyclops. A childish image and a licentious one: the ogre that eats children up alive in Perrault, and the ogre of Sade, Minsk, at whose orgies the libertines eat smoking platefuls of human flesh, using the seared corpses as tables and chairs. Saint Christopher and Polyphemus. And Prometheus as well—the fire of industry and of war. The two faces of progress: the automobile and the bomb.

The United States is the negation of what we were in the sixteenth, seventeenth, and eighteenth centuries and of what, since the nineteenth century, many among us would prefer us to be. Like all countries, Mexico has been born several times: the first time in the seventeenth century, a hundred years after the Conquest; the second at the beginning of the nineteenth century: Independence. But perhaps it is not correct to say that Mexico has been born twice; what we are really doing is calling several quite different historical entities by the same name (Mexico). The first of these entities is the old indigenous society composed of city-states, ruled by military theocracies, that were the creators of complex religions and no less complex artistic works. Rather than another society, this world is seen as another civilization. Later, after the great cleft of the Conquest and Evangelization, around the middle of the seventeenth century, another society appears: New Spain. This society was not really a colony, in the strict sense of the word, but a kingdom subject to the crown of Spain like the others making up the Spanish Empire: Castile, Aragon, Navarre, Sicily, Andalusia, Asturias.

From the very beginning, the offspring of the Spaniards born in Mexico, the so-called *criollos*, felt different from Europeans, and their feeling of difference grew stronger from the seventeenth century on. Their awareness—initially dim and confused—of their own social and historical uniqueness found expression, slowly but powerfully, in the course of the seventeenth and eighteenth centuries. The originality of the Creole genius was particularly notable in three domains: sensibility, aesthetics, and religion. As early as the end of the seventeenth century, there was what we may speak of as Creole *character*—a manner of being in which a whole series of vital attitudes have developed, ways of confronting this world and the other, sex and death, leisure and work, oneself and others (above all those who were *others* by aatonomasia: the European Spaniards). In the realm of the arts, the Creoles expressed themselves with great felicity; I need hardly mention Baroque architecture—both in its erudite and in its popular form—or the figure of Sor Juana Inés de la Cruz. This woman was not only a great poet but also the intellectual conscience of her society and, in certain respects, of our own society today. But the great creations of New Spain were above all in the sphere of religious beliefs and myths. And the greatest of all of these was the Virgin of Guadalupe.

Though Creole society has had separatist aspirations ever since its birth, these did not manifest themselves openly until the last years of the eighteenth century. The embryonic, confused nature of the Creoles' political sentiments stands in sharp contrast to the richness, complexity, and originality of their artistic and religious creations and expressions. When the Creoles began to think in political terms, they were inspired by the Jesuits. The Society of Jesus had made itself not only the educator of the leading Creole class but also its moral and political conscience. At the very time when the revelation of their uniqueness was coming to political consciousness, certain Creoles realized that their tradition—monarchism and Neo-Thomism—had not only lost almost all its vitality but also did not offer a broad enough base to serve as the solid underpinning of their aspirations and enable them to articulate these in a program of political action. Of course, the Creoles and their Jesuit mentors did have in mind a vague project for an Empire of South America. This idea, whose origins go back to the last third of the seventeenth century, lingered on in the Mexican Conservative Party until the middle of the nineteenth century.

More than a political idea, the Mexican Empire was an image. As an image, it attracted many outstanding minds; as an idea, it revealed certain inconsistencies. The first and gravest of these was that, since it was a simple extension of the Spanish system, it did not offer the basic elements and concepts needed to draw up a truly national program. In truth, New Spain was a social reality much vaster than the Creoles and comprised social and ethnic groups, Indians and mestizos, whose hearts could not be stirred by the idea of empire. Apart from being a mere extension of the Spanish system, the idea of a Mexican Empire was a project that ran counter to the general current of that era. In those years the idea of a nation, which was the foundation of independence, had become inseparable from the idea of popular sovereignty, which was, in turn, the foundation of the new republics. Finally, there was in the as- piration to independence an element that did not appear in the imperial project: the eagerness for modernity. Or, as people put it in those days: the eagerness for progress. In Mexico and in the rest of Hispanic Amer- ica, "independence," "republic," and "democracy" were words synony- mous with "progress" and "modernity."

The expulsion of the Jesuits precipitated the intellectual crisis of the Creoles: not only were they left without teachers but also without a philosophical system to justify their existence. Many of them then turned to the other tradition, the enemy of the tradition that had founded New Spain. At that moment the radical difference between the two Americas became visible and palpable. One, the English-speaking one, is the heir of the tradition that has founded the modern world: the Reformation, with its social and political consequences, democracy and capitalism; the other, ours, the Portuguese- and Spanish-speaking one, is the heir of the universal Catholic monarchy and the Counter-Reformation. The Mexican Creoles could not found their separatist project on their own political and religious tradition: They *adopted*, though without *adapting* them, the ideas of the other tradition. This was the moment of the second birth of Mexico; more precisely, it was the moment when New Spain, in order to consummate its separation from Spain, denied itself. That negation was its death and the birth of another society: Mexico.

The United States enters our history during this second moment, making its appearance not as a foreign power that must be fought, but as a model that must be imitated. This was the beginning of a fascination that, despite having changed form during the last 150 years, is still as intense as ever. The history of that fascination goes hand in hand with the history of the groups of intellectuals who, since Independence, have drawn up all those programs of social and political reform aimed at transforming the country into a modern nation. Above and beyond their differences, there is a shared idea that inspires liberals, positivists, and socialists alike: the project of modernizing Mexico. Since early in the nineteenth century this project has always been defined vis-à-vis—whether for or against—the United States. The passion of our intellectuals for U.S. civilization ranges from love to bitter rancor and from adoration to horror. These are contradictory but coincident forms of ignorance: at one extreme, the liberal Lorenzo de Zavala, who did not hesitate to side with the Texans in their war against Mexico; at the other, the contemporary Marxist-Leninists and their allies, the "liberation theologians," who have made of materialist dialectic a hypostasis of the Holy Spirit and of American imperialism the prefiguration of the Antichrist.

The "intelligentsia" is not the only class to have experienced contrary feelings toward the United States. On the morrow of Independence and up until the middle of the nineteenth century, the well-to-do classes were resolutely against it; later on they became its allies, and in almost every case, its servants and accomplices. Nonetheless, since in the final analysis they are heirs of the hierarchical society that was New Spain, our rich have never really wholeheartedly adopted the liberal and democratic ideology; they are friends of the United States for reasons of interest, but their real moral and intellectual affinities lie with authoritarian regimes. Hence their sympathy for Germany during the two world wars of this century. The same evolution can be seen in the political and military castes: General Miramón, a conservative, was an enemy of the United States, but General Porfirio Díaz, a liberal, was his proconsul. It may be concluded, insofar as it is possible to venture generalizations in so contradictory a domain, that during the nineteenth century the liberals were the friends and the allies of the United States (the outstanding example is Juárez) and the conservatives its adversaries (Lucas Alamán is the most notable case), whereas in the twentieth century these roles have been reversed. But in both centuries the enemies of the Americans have had to seek allies and protectors outside the continent: in the nineteenth century, a Miramón looked toward France; in the twentieth, a Fidel Castro looks toward the Soviet Union.

Brazil did not repudiate Portugal; in Hispanic America, on the other hand, the liberals were anti-Spanish. The anti-Hispanolism of our liberals may appear to be absurd and irrational, and in fact it is. But it is explainable: the democratic ideas adopted by the liberals were the negation of everything that New Spain had been. The Revolution of Independence, in Mexico and in all of Spanish America, was simultaneously an affirmation of the Hispano-American nations and a negation of the tradition that had founded these nations—a self-negation. Here there appears another difference from the United States. On declaring their independence from England, the Americans did not break with their past; on the contrary, they affirmed what they had been and what they wanted to be. The Independence of Mexico was the negation of what we had been since the sixteenth century; it was not the institution of a national project but the adoption of a universal ideology foreign to the whole of our past.

Between puritanism, democracy, and capitalism there was not opposition but affinity; the past and the future of the United States are reflected without contradiction in these three words. Between republican ideology and the Catholic world of the Mexican viceroyalty, a mosaic of pre-Columbian survivals and Baroque forms, there was a sharp break: Mexico denied its past. Like all negations, ours contained an affirmation—that of a future—except that we did not work out our idea of the future using elements and concepts drawn from our own tradition; instead we took over ready-made the image of the future invented by Europeans and Americans. Ever since the seventeenth century our history, a fragment of Spain's, has been an impassioned negation of the modernity being born: the Reformation, the Enlightenment, and all the rest. As the twentieth century dawned, we decided that we would be what the United States already was: a modern nation. The entry into the Modern Age demanded a sacrifice—of ourselves—and the result of this sacrifice is well known: we are still not modern, but we have been searching for ourselves ever since.

The first seeds of democracy on this continent appeared among the dissident communities and sects of New England. It is true that the Spanish established in the countries of the Conquest the institution of the *ayuntamiento*, the municipal council, founded on the principle of self-government of cities and towns. But the existence of the *ayuntamientos* was always precarious, strangled as they were by a vast, complex network of bureaucratic, nobiliary, ecclesiastic, and economic jurisdictions and privileges. New Spain was always a hierarchical society, without representative government and dominated by the dual power of the viceroy and the archbishop.

Max Weber divided premodern regimes into two great categories: the feudal system and the patrimonial. In the first, the prince governs with—or at times against—his equals by birth and rank: the barons. In the second, the prince rules the nation as though it were his patrimony and his household; his ministers are his family and his servants. The

Spanish monarchy is an example of a patrimonialist regime. So were (and are) its successors, the "democratic republics" of Latin America, forever wavering between the Caudillo and the Demagogue, the despotic Father and the rebellious Sons.

From their very beginning, the religious communities of New England jealously declared their autonomy with respect to the State. Inspired by the example of the Christian churches of the first centuries, these groups were always hostile to the authoritarian and bureaucratic tradition of the Catholic Church. Since Constantine, Christianity had lived in symbiosis with political power; for more than a thousand years the Church had followed the imperial-bureaucratic model of Rome and Byzantium. The Reformation marked the rupture of this tradition, a rupture that the religious communities of New England, in their turn, carried to its limits, emphasizing the egalitarian features and the tendency toward self-government of the Protestant groups of the Low Countries.

In New Spain the Church was first and foremost a hierarchy and an administration—that is, a bureaucracy of clerics that in certain respects is reminiscent of the institution of the mandarins of the old Chinese Empire. Hence the admiration of the Jesuits when, in the eighteenth century, they were confronted with the regime of K'ang-hsi, in which they at last saw the concrete realization of their idea of what a hierarchical and harmonious society could be—a society that was stable but not static, like a watch that keeps perfect time and doesn't run down. In the English colonies the Church was not a hierarchy of clerics who were the exclusive repositories of knowledge, but the free community of the faithful. The Church was plural and from the beginning it was made up of a network of associations of believers, a true prefiguration of the political society of democracy.

The religious basis of American democracy is not visible today, but it is not any the less powerful in consequence. More than a foundation, it is a buried taproot; the day it dries up, so will that country. If we do not take this religious element into account, it is impossible to understand either the history of the United States or the meaning of the crisis that it is undergoing today. The presence of the Protestant religious ethic transforms an incident such as Watergate into a conflict that shakes the very foundations of American democracy. These foundations are not only political—the social compact between men—but religious: the covenant of men with God. In all societies politics and morality exist side by side, but unlike what happens in a secular democracy such as that of France, in the United States it is almost impossible to separate morality and religion. In France democracy was born of the criticism of the two institutions that the *ancien régime* represented: the Throne and the Altar. The consequence of the criticism of religion was the rigorous separation between religious morality, a private domain, and political morality. In the United States, on the other hand, democracy is the direct offspring of the Reformation—that is, of a *religious* critique of religion.

The fusion between morality and religion is characteristic of the Protestant tradition. In Reformed sects, rites and sacraments yield their cardinal place to morality and soul-searching. Other eras and other civilizations had known theocracies of warrior-monks and empires ruled by priestly bureaucracies; the union of theology and power, dogma and authority, was a frequent phenomenon, not a rarity. It was the modern age, the age that made the critique of the kingdom of heaven and its ministers on earth, that undertook to invert the terms of the age-old, impure alliance between religion and politics. American democracy lacks dogma and theology, but its foundations are no less religious than the covenant that unites Jews and Jehovah.

Because of its religious origins and also because of the political philosophies that later shaped it, American democracy tends to strengthen society and the individual vis-à-vis the State. From the very beginning, we find in U.S. history a twofold aspiration, toward egalitarianism and toward individualism. Seeds of life, but at the same time seeds that are contradictory. In recent days, American intellectuals, on the occasion of the Bicentennial of Independence and in the face of the crisis that has shaken the very pillars of the nation, have again posed the question that divided the Founding Fathers: freedom or equality? The controversy risks becoming a Scholastic disputation: from the moment they lose their concrete historical dimensions, freedom and equality become entelechies. Freedom is defined in terms of its limits and the obstacles that confront it; the same thing happens with equality. In the case of the United States, freedom was defined in contradistinction to the hierarchical inequality of European society, so that its content was egalitarian; the desire for equality, in turn, was manifested as concerted action against the oppression of economic privileges—that is, as self-determination and freedom. Both freedom and equality were subversive values, but that was because they had previously been religious values. Freedom and equality were dimensions of the life beyond: they were gifts of God, appearing mysteriously as expressions of divine will. Just as in Greek tragedy the freedom of heroes is a dimension of Destiny, so in Calvinist theology freedom is closely linked to predestination. Hence the religious revolution of the Reformation anticipated the political revolution of democracy.

In Latin America, exactly the contrary occurred: the State fought the Church, not to strengthen individuals but to replace the clergy as the power controlling consciences and wills. In our America there was no religious revolution to pave the way for political revolution; nor was there, as in eighteenth-century France, a philosophical movement to take on the criticism of religion and the Church. The political revolution in Latin America—I am referring to Independence and the struggles between liberals and conservatives that drenched our nineteenth century in blood—was merely a manifestation, yet another, of Hispano-Arabic patrimonialism: it did battle with the Church as with a rival whose place must be taken over; it fortified the authoritarian State, and the liberal *caudillos* were no more benign than the conservatives; it accentuated centralism, though beneath the cloak of federalism; and, finally, it made an endemic disease of the exceptional regime that has ruled in our lands since Independence: *caudillismo.**

Independence was a false beginning: it freed us from Madrid, but not from our past. To the evils we had inherited we added others that were all our own. As our dreams of modernization faded, the fascination exerted on us by the United States grew. The war of aggression of 1847 turned it into an obsession. An ambivalent fascination: at one and the same time, the titan was the enemy of our identity and the unacknowledged model of what we would most like to be. In addition to being a political and social ideal, the United States was an interventionist power, an aggressor. This double image, which corresponded then and still corresponds today to a reality—the United States is both a democracy and an empire—lingered throughout the nineteenth century and was one of the basic themes of the bitter polemic between liberals and conservatives. In order to understand the attitude of the liberals, it suffices to recall what the attitude of thousands of "progressivist intellectuals" has been toward the Soviet Union: they close their eyes to the reality of the vast Soviet bureaucracy, its omnipresent and omnipotent police, its concentration camps, and the imperialist policy of Moscow, seeing only their mental image of a free, peaceful, beatific socialist fatherland. Though liberals were less credulous, in their case, too, ideology was more real than reality itself.

The liberals were enemies of the Mexican past, which they denounced as a foreign imposition, a Spanish intrusion. Thus they said that Mexico had "regained" its Independence, as though the nation had existed before the arrival of the Spaniards. What they celebrated by contrast to the inauthentic past of the viceroyalty was not the pre-Columbian past—which they had almost no knowledge of and which many of them scorned: Juárez, an Indian, was not an *indigenista***—but, rather, the

---

*Rule by *caudillos*: military leaders, often of irregular forces, and, by extension, strongmen, political bosses. [*Trans.*]

**In this context, a defender of native Indian peoples and their rights. The term is also used for writers and scholars dealing with Indian themes and ways of life. [*Trans.*]

future of liberal democracy. In the face of the two eccentricities (from the modern Western point of view) that had made us what we were, the Spanish past and the Indian past, the liberals postulated an abstract universality, derived from the progressivist ideologies of the day. The United States was the immediate example of this universality: in its present we could see a vision of our future. A telltale mirror: like the stepmother's mirror in the fairy tale, each time we asked it to show us our image, it showed us that of the *other*.

Conservatives thought that the United States, far from being a model, was a threat to our sovereignty and our identity. The ideological contagion seemed no less dangerous to them than the physical aggression: it was a complementary form of penetration. If the future that the liberals proposed to us was an alienation, the defense of our own present demanded, for the same complementary reason, that of our past. The conservatives' reasoning was only apparently irreproachable: the past that they were so stubbornly defending and, not without reason, identifying with the present, was a past in the process of disappearing. I have already pointed out that the tradition of New Spain—an admirable tradition, which modern Mexicans have had the stupidity to ignore and even to scorn—offered no elements or principles that could serve to resolve the twofold problem confronting the nation: that of independent life and that of modernization. The first had to do with finding the political form and the social organization that an independent Mexico should adopt; the second, with working out a viable program that, without too many upheavals, would permit the country to enter upon that modernity to which, until then, the Spanish Empire had barred the way. Like all of Spanish America, Mexico was condemned to be free and to be modern, but its tradition had always rejected freedom and modernity.

Independence was not so much a consequence of the triumph of liberal ideas—adopted only by a minority—as of two circumstances that to date have received very little attention. The first was the disintegration of the Spanish Empire. It must here be repeated once again, even though the statement may cause more than one reader to raise an eyebrow, that the Independence of Spanish America was achieved not only because of the action of the insurgents but also, and most significantly, because of the inertia and paralysis of the mother country. The continent of Hispanic America was young and rebellious, but healthy: Spain was a soul fast asleep in a body drained of its life's blood. This image accounts for the phenomenon of Independence with greater economy and no less exactitude than ideological explanations. The second crucial circumstance was the existence of a social contradiction in New Spain. This contradiction, which was insoluble within the presuppositions underlying the social order of New Spain (and was not without certain analogies to that faced by the United States today with respect to its ethnic minorities), lay in the opposition between Creoles and mestizos. The leading class of Creoles postulated an abstract universalism, but the mestizos—the new historical reality—had no place outside of a metaphorical one in this universalism. The heirs of the twofold Hispanic universalism (the Empire and the Church), the Creoles, under the influence of the Jesuits, had dreamed in the eighteenth century of a Mexican Empire: New Spain would be the other Spain. Independence fulfilled the separatist ambitions of the Creoles, except that it was not they who were the real winners, but, rather, the mestizos, who thus far had been a marginal group within the society of New Spain. Mexico was not an empire but a republic, and the ideology that nourished its governing caste was not that of a Catholic empire but bourgeois nationalism.

The episode of Maximilian is a cruel illustration of the illusory nature of the conservatives' project. Calling upon a European prince to found a Latin empire that would check the expansion of the Yankee republic was a solution that was not at all preposterous in 1820 but had become an anachronism by 1860. The monarchical solution had ceased to be viable, because the monarchy was identified with the situation prior to Independence. The perceived difference between Creoles and Spaniards had been the decisive cause of the separatist movement. From the very outbreak of hostilities, mestizos and many Indians—that is to say, the dispossessed classes—had participated in the battles for Independence. It was only natural that once Independence had been attained, these groups should have no interest in reconstituting the monarchical system—not out of republicanism, but because monarchy represented the legitimization and consecration of the existing social hierarchies. The mestizos, who were the most energetic and dynamic sector of society, were seeking their place in the sun, socially, economically, and politically. The democratic republic opened doors to their aspirations and ambitions, even though these latter had little to do with either republicanism or democracy.

The liberal ideology was not a real solution. The nationalism of the republicans was a superficial imitation of French nationalism: its federalism—a copy of the American—was a disguised *caciquismo**; its democracy, the façade of dictatorship (instead of monarchs we had dictators). Nor did the shift in ideology lead to a change in social structures, and still less to a change in psychic structures. Laws changed, but not men or the relations of ownership and domination. During the civil and foreign wars of the nineteenth century, the Creole aristocracy was forced

---

*Rule by *caciques*, petty Indian chiefs. (Like *caudillismo*, the term, by extension, has come to mean political bossism.) [*Trans.*]

out of its seats of power by mestizo groups. The army was the school for the new groups of leaders. Backed by military force, the regime sought and obtained the protection of foreign powers, especially of the United States. In its first phase, during the second half of the nineteenth century, the imperial career of the Republic of the United States coincided with its backing of the liberal regime in Mexico, which soon became a dictatorship. This phenomenon, *mutatis mutandis*, has been repeated throughout Latin America. The liberal revolution, begun at Independence, did not result in the implantation of true democracy, or in the birth of a national capitalism, but in a military dictatorship and in an economic regime characterized by *latifundismo** and concessions to foreign companies and consortiums, particularly U.S. ones. It was a barren liberalism and produced nothing comparable to pre-Columbian creations or those of New Spain: neither pyramids nor convents, neither cosmogonic myths nor poems of Sor Juana Inés de la Cruz.

Mexico went on being what it had been, but it no longer believed in what it was. The old values fell to pieces, but not the old realities, which were soon cloaked by the new progressivist and liberal values. These masked realities marked the beginning of inauthenticity and lies, endemic ills of Latin American countries. By the beginning of the twentieth century, pseudo-modernity was in full swing: railways and *latifundismo*, a democratic constitution and a *caudillo* within the best Hispano-Arabic tradition, positivist philosophers and pre-Columbian *caciques*, Symbolist poetry and illiteracy. The adoption of the U.S. model contributed to the disintegration of traditional values; the political and economic action of U.S. imperialism shored up the archaic social and political structures. This contradiction revealed that the ambivalence of the giant was not imaginary but real: the country of Thoreau was also the country of Roosevelt-Nebuchadnezzar.

The Mexican Revolution was an attempt to recover our past and to conceive a national project that would not be the negation of what we had been. But I am doing something worse than being inaccurate—I am oversimplifying when I speak of the Mexican Revolution as though it were *one*. From the very beginning it was broken up into a number of contradictory movements, which rather than representing ideological programs and political philosophies, were popular reactions, spontaneous uprisings around a leader. The word "Revolt" would be more appropriate than "Revolution."

Among the revolutionary groups was one that, instinctively, was aimed at correcting the course adopted by our groups of leaders since

---

*The holding of large landed estates (*latifundios*) by individuals. [*Trans.*]

Independence: the peasant movement headed by Emiliano Zapata. What the Zapatistas demanded and really wanted was a return to origins, to a type of precapitalist agrarian society: the self-sufficient village, characterized by communal ownership of the land and a social, economic, and spiritual organization in which the basic unit was not the individual but the family. The Zapatistas bore as their standard an image of the Virgin of Guadalupe, the same standard around which the barefoot peasants who had fought for Independence had rallied. The image of the Virgin admirably symbolized not the march toward progress and "modernity," but the return to roots. "Giving the land back to the villages": this phrase, the heart of Zapata's program, points to the real meaning of his movement; it aimed at returning to a situation—in part a historical reality and in part a millenarian myth—that was the very negation of the program of "modernization" of liberalism and its heir, the regime of Porfirio Díaz. The other revolutionary tendencies, by contrast, were determined to continue the work of "modernization" of the liberals and positivists, though with different methods.

The winning faction drew up a program that endeavored to harmonize the various aspirations of the revolutionaries. More than a synthesis, it was a compromise. Civic altars were erected to Zapata—Mexico is, par excellence, the land of official and bureaucratic art—but the program of "modernization," under various names, was made the central dogma of the regime that has governed us for more than fifty years. What happened later on is a familiar story: the Mexican Revolution was taken over by a political bureaucracy not without similarities to the communist bureaucracies of Eastern Europe, and by a capitalist class made in the image and likeness of U.S. capitalism and dependent upon it. In contemporary Mexico, beyond a few of us eccentrics who mistrust "development" and would like to see a change of orientation of our society, both the factions on the right and those on the left, though irreconcilable, are fellow members of the suicide cult of progress.

For a Mexican, to travel through the United States is to enter the giant's castle and visit its chambers of horrors and marvels. But there is one difference: the ogre's castle leaves us wonderstruck by its archaism, the United States by its novelty. Our present is always just a little behind the real present, whereas its present is a little bit ahead. Its present is one in which the future is already written; ours is still tied to the past. I am wrong to use the singular when I speak of our past: we have any number of them; all of them are alive and all continually at war with one another within us. Aztecs, Mayas, Otomis, Castilians, Moors, Phoenicians, Galicians: a jungle of roots and branches that suffocates us. How to live with all of them without being their prisoner? This is the question we keep asking ourselves endlessly, without having yet arrived at any definite answer. We have not found a way to accept our past, but neither have we found a way to criticize it. The difficulty Americans have had is precisely the opposite: their nation was born as a categorical criticism of the past. This act of criticism was a no less categorical affirmation of the values of modernity, such as they had been defined first by the Reformation and later by the Enlightenment. It is not that Americans do not have a past but that their past was oriented toward the future.

The conquest of the future is the United States' tradition, therefore a tradition of change, whereas the Hispanic tradition is one of resistance to change. Spain and its works: lasting constructions and eternal, timeless meanings. To us, "valuable" is a synonym for "enduring." The pre-Columbian heritage accentuates this inclination: the pyramid is the very image of immutability. The polar opposites that exist between Americans and Mexicans are epitomized in our attitudes toward change. To us the secret lies not in getting ahead but in managing to stay where we already are. It is the opposition between the wind and the rock. I am not speaking of ideas and philosophies but of beliefs and unconscious mental structures; whatever our ideology, even if it is progressivist, we instinctively relate the present to the past, whereas Americans relate it to the future. Mexican workers who emigrate to the United States have shown a notable capacity for *not* adapting to American society, a capacity that has its roots in an insensitivity to the future. In them the past is alive. It is the same past that has preserved the Chicanos, the minority group in the United States that seems to have been able to keep its identity. In Mexico it has not been the professionals of anti-imperialism who have put up the strongest resistance, but the humble folk who make pilgrimages to the Sanctuary of the Virgin of Guadalupe. Our country survives thanks to its traditionalism.

The tradition that founded Mexico and the other countries of Spanish America began to reveal its insufficiencies and its limitations as far back as the eighteenth century. Because the Spanish Empire was not able to change, it broke up into so many fragments. Today the tradition that the United States represents is threatened with the same fate. The ideas that for more than two hundred years have constituted modernity and what may be called the *tradition of the future* have lost a large part of their universal prestige; indeed, there are many who question their self-consistency and their value. Progress was an idea no less mysterious than the will of Allah to Moslems or the Trinity to Catholics, yet it stirred souls and wills for two centuries. Today we ask ourselves: progress toward what and for what?

It is pointless to deal at greater length with the symptoms of what has been called, for almost fifty years now, "the crisis of Western civilization." During the last decade this crisis has manifested itself in an acute form in the richest, most prosperous, and most powerful nation in our world, the United States. It is not, essentially or basically, an economic or military crisis—although it affects the economy and the global strategy of the United States—but a political and moral crisis. It is a doubt as to the path that the nation has taken, as to its goals and the methods of reaching them; it is a critique of the ability and the honesty of the men and the parties that administer the system; and finally, more than a questioning, it is a passing of judgment on principles that have been the base and the justification of U.S. society.

Many of the problems confronting the United States, though far from insignificant, are more symptoms than causes of the ills that it is suffering. Such is the case, to cite a notable recent example, of the rebellion of young people in the sixties. The racial problem, on the other hand, affects the life of the country in a more profound and permanent way; it is a festering wound, a permanent focus of infection. The United States is faced with a dilemma: either the perpetuation of civil strife, or the construction of a multiracial society. It is not mere wishful thinking to predict that the United States will choose the latter alternative. In point of fact, this alternative has already been chosen, and American society is heading that way, though not without many setbacks and much sidetracking. Other oppositions, present since the birth of the nation, are basic ones. All societies have within them a life principle that at the same time is a death principle, a principle necessarily dual in nature; at moments of crisis it assumes the form of a contradiction. This principle involves questions of life or death, such as wars and rivalries between cities were for the Greek *polis*, or finding a policy to deal with Christianity and the Gnostic sects was to the Roman emperors of the third and fourth centuries. The contradiction of the United States—what gave it life and may cause its death—can be summed up in a pair of terms: it is at once a plutocratic democracy and an imperial republic.

The first contradiction affects the two notions that were the axis of the political thought of the "Founding Fathers." Plutocracy provokes and accentuates inequality; inequality in turn makes political freedoms and individual rights nothing more than illusions. Here Marx's criticism went straight to the heart of the matter. Since U.S. plutocracy, unlike the Roman, admittedly creates abundance, it is able to lessen and lighten the burden of unjust differences between individuals and classes. But it has done so by shifting the most scandalous inequalities from the national scene to the international: the underdeveloped countries. There are those who think that this international inequality could also be, if not entirely eliminated, at least reduced to a minimum. Recent history, however, argues against this hypothesis. But even if it were to turn out to be true, an essential point is being forgotten: money not only oppresses; it also corrupts. And it corrupts rich and poor alike. On this score the moralists of antiquity, especially the Stoics and the Epicureans, knew more than we do. U.S. democracy has been corrupted by money.

The second contradiction, intimately linked to the first, stems from the difference between what the United States is domestically—a democracy—and what its actions abroad make it—an empire. Freedom and oppression are the opposite and complementary faces of its national being. In the same way that plutocracy begins by giving rise to inequality and ends up manacling freedom, the arms that the imperial State brandishes against its enemies abroad are, by an imperceptible process which it took the Watergate scandal to bring to light, inevitably turned into instruments that the political bureaucracy uses against the country's independent-minded citizens. The needs of empire create a bureaucracy whose specialty is espionage and other methods of intelligence used in the international power struggle; this bureaucracy in turn threatens national democracy. The first contradiction put an end to the republican institutions of ancient Rome; the second, an end to the very life of ancient Athens as an independent city.

But I am not pronouncing a death sentence upon U.S. democracy. Besides being presumptuous, that would be ridiculous. Historical analogies are useful as rhetorical tropes; they are not historical laws, but metaphors. Any and every reflection on the crisis of the republic of the United States must end in a question mark. In the first place, there is no such thing as historical determinisms. Or, rather, if such determinisms exist, we do not know what they are, nor is it likely that we ever will, since they are far too vast and complex. In the second place, societies die not from their contradictions but from their inability to resolve them. When this happens, a sort of paralysis immobilizes the social body—the thinking and deliberating centers first, then the executive arms. The paralysis is a society's response to questions to which its tradition and the assumptions of history offer no answer but silence. This was what happened in the case of the Spanish Empire. All the misfortunes of the Hispano-American peoples are distant effects of this stupor, the end product of the stubbornness, pride, and blindness that overcame the Hapsburg monarchy in the middle of the seventeenth century. The United States is faced with an entirely different situation. In the very principles on which it was founded lies, if not the answer, the method for finding it. This method is none other than that employed by the Puritans to scrutinize the will of God in their own consciences: soul-searching, expiation, propitiation, and the action that reconciles us with ourselves and with others.

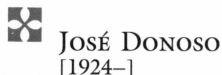

José Donoso
[1924–]

A NATIVE OF Santiago, Chile, and a graduate of Princeton University, José Donoso worked for a time as a shepherd in Patagonia. He has also been a journalist and has taught English in Chile as well as creative writing at the Iowa Writers' Workshop in the mid-1960s.

Primarily a writer of novels and short stories, Donoso's work includes *Coronación*, 1957 [*Coronation*, 1965]—for which he won the William Faulkner Foundation Prize; *El Charleston*, 1960 [*Charleston and Other Stories*, 1977]; and his best-known novel, *El obsceno pájaro de la noche*, 1970 [*The Obscene Bird of Night*, 1973], praised as "a dense and energetic book, full of terrible risk-taking." Also published in English are *Historia personal del "Boom,"* 1972 [*The Boom in Spanish American Literature: A Personal History*, 1977]; *Tres novelitas burguesas*, 1973 [translated as *Sacred Families*, 1977]; and a recent novel, *Casa de campo*, 1978 [*A House in the Country*, 1984].

Donoso has recounted the travails of becoming recognized as a writer in Chile. His first collection of short stories was published in 1975 only after he guaranteed the sale of one hundred copies, whereupon he enlisted friends to help sell copies on Santiago streetcorners. Today he is Chile's most acclaimed writer, known for his critical visions of Chilean bourgeoisie and his insistence upon the nightmarish qualities of a disintegrating social order.

His *Historia personal del "Boom"* is an entertaining literary memoir highlighting the decade 1961 to 1971, when Latin American literature achieved worldwide attention for its innovative and vigorous expression. Anecdotal and witty, this extended essay offers insight into the friendships among writers of the Boom (such as Fuentes, García Márquez, Vargas Llosa, and the author) and the political events (notably the Cuban Revolution and the Padilla affair) which originally united them and later separated them. It is a literary testimony of the sort the present volume endeavors to bring together in English translation.

As early as 1965, even before the 1973 military coup that overthrew Salvador Allende and established the authoritarian regime of Augusto Pinochet, Donoso spent most of his time abroad, living in Barcelona, and returning to Chile only temporarily. The following essay, originally presented in English at Barnard College in February 1980 as part of the Jacob C. Saposnekow Memorial Lectures, depicts the dilemma experienced by many authors who choose—or are forced—to live outside their native countries, particularly with regard to the problem of language.

Recently, Donoso has moved back to Santiago.

ITHACA: THE IMPOSSIBLE RETURN

José Donoso

To be here at all, facing an audience that is sure to expect a learned argumentation in favor of or against solid intellectual convictions and theories, makes me feel slightly uneasy. I possess little or no academic learning beyond the kind that a gentleman of my years with a college education naturally has: I'm a writer who has "small Latin and less Greek." Mine is a scrappy, unorganized mind, wholly subjective, completely arbitrary, a kind of warehouse that happily stores all sorts of apparently useless odds and ends, and rejects what it shouldn't reject. Ideologies and cosmogonies are alien to me: they can be amusing, even challenging, but their life is too short and they are too soon proved wrong, their place immediately taken by another explanation of the world. I read a lot, mostly novels, memoirs, literary biographies, but I don't know how to crack a book open with those formidable instruments that are the works of critics. I know their names, of course, Lacan and Chomsky, Barthes and Dérrida, and a little of what they have to say, but I prefer to leave their use in the hands of scholars who can surely do this sort of thing with much more flair than I could ever hope to achieve. I'm more interested in the *how* than in the *why*, that tyrannical demand for explanations which reduces phenomena to the rational. Like Nietzsche, I believe that the question *why* is the seed of all conflict and nihilism, and that Socrates, who gave that question the currency in the spell of which we still abide, was really the first decadent. No real, unequivocal history exists. What we believe to be history is no more than an accumulation of conflicting interpretations; the power of the rational lies in its nonrational sources. I'd rather read Klee and the letters of Gauguin on art, or Flaubert and Virginia Woolf on the *how* of the literary endeavor: the thing itself, and the how of the thing—not the consequences or the meaning of the thing—are, to me, what is really exciting, rather than all-encompassing explanations. Thus, my convictions, political, aesthetic, and philosophical, never achieve the status of convictions since they waver so, and tend to be contradictory.

Yet I do possess one kind of knowledge which scholars can come by only secondhand: the knowledge that springs from the experience of writing books. I'm a novelist, only tenuously an intellectual, though I couldn't be farther from the coy anti-intellectualism of the guts and muscle, and slice-of-life literary persuasion, still so prestigious in Spanish and Latin American writing. I can claim that, as an inventor of fiction, I live primarily within the world of metaphor, a world which is never wholly transparent though it can be so radiant that it causes blisters. I think of the world of literature as the open world of the tentative, of hesitation, rarely one of assertion, and believe that the universe of literature is not one of meaning but of being. I thus cringe from formulating general ideas in connection with literature—let me be specific and say *novels*, which is what I know most about—because novels to me are, if anything, the art of the particular: if they are literature at all they will never unveil the secret of themselves as metaphor, no matter how much you tease them with theory. For metaphor exists first and foremost in and of itself, an object whose essence is placed outside the world of meaning, not a sign to be substituted for another kind of notation. (Such as it appears in fiction, metaphor is like a palimpsest of meanings. Isn't it?)

Yet it seems useless to pretend there are no wires electrically connecting these metaphors among themselves and to other phenomena, thus tempting us to place them in some kind of order. Things literary perversely happen with a symmetry, or a regularity, facing which one has to look at least twice. Certain intervals appear which are difficult to ignore. For at least a while, certain forms in certain places share tone, diction, theme, scope: schools sprout. Then they wither. And periods of drought set in, inviting hypotheses to explain them. Metaphor, then, no matter how irritated one can become by theory overpowering the created object, is not an isolated occurrence, but a shared experience glittering with many, often contradictory, facets.

Exile—and I shall use this word, perhaps inappropriately, meaning both political and voluntary absence from one's own country—exile, then, is one of those knots of live-wires, a shared, a collective experience, from which I think the greater part of Latin American contemporary fiction derives its strength. It is sure to become the great theme of the novel of the eighties, once all this pain and rage is hopefully remembered in tranquility: but not yet. We're too busy surviving, being confused and beset by doubts, to undertake that task just yet and metabolize it into metaphor. But living isolated, as an expatriate in Spain in the sixties and seventies, remote from the shattering experiences of those who stayed behind in my country—or in my continent, for that matter—, is the strongest collective experience I have undergone, no matter how paradoxical this may seem. I have lived away from Chile for seventeen years now, and gone back only twice, for a month each time—I must hasten to add, lest I'm taken for a hero, that I could have returned any day I wished to, since neither persons nor ideologies banned me—with the result that the greater part of my work has been written in Spain, a country I feel few cultural bonds with. What really surprises me once I come to think of it, is that I'm far from being an exception. Looking around me at the major Latin American novelists of my generation, I find that every single one of them has written the most important part of his *oeuvre* away from his country. Cortázar wrote *Rayuela, Los premios* and his best short stories in Paris. García Márquez wrote *Cien años de soledad* not in his native Colombia, but in Mexico. Vargas Llosa wrote *La ciudad y los perros* in Paris, *Pantaleón* in Barcelona, *La case verde* in England, large chunks of *Conversación en la catedral* in Barcelona and elsewhere, and I hear he's recently been writing in Brazil. Roa Bastos wrote practically everything in political exile in Buenos Aires. Carlos Fuentes has lived abroad for so long and in so many different places that it is impossible to chart the itinerary of his books. Cabrera Infante has written everything either in Brussels or in London: he's also a political exile. As regards Manuel Puig, he wrote his first three novels in Buenos Aires, but after that I believe all his other novels were written abroad. Speaking for myself, I wrote my first two collections of short stories and my first novel in Chile. My next two novels were written in Mexico, and all the rest of my books in Spain.

Are we, then, a generation of cosmopolites, of expatriates, rooted into new soil? I think the contrary is true. On the one hand, we are evidently wanderers: I belong to a floating community of Latin American rootless novelists, all of them ailing of this infirmity which is our strange relationship with our own countries: our inability to live or write there. This certitude provided the only feeling of community I have experienced for a long while. The advent of Salvador Allende, first, and then the irruption of General Pinochet on the scene, reversed things in my mind, and made me realize there was still another level to the idea of community. I found that the old bond, which I had thought dead, was still alive. On the other hand, although we have lived abroad for such extended periods, the Latin American novelists of my generation all obsessively write about our own countries, or of countries of the imagination closely resembling those we grew up in. If the Latin American living abroad becomes an expatriate, his literature never does. As Gertrude Stein said of another distinguished generation of writers living abroad: "It all happened in Paris, but it was an American experience."

Latin American literature, especially the novel now in its maturity, no matter how cosmopolitan the writer, always stays pretty close to the motherland. In many ways it's an Oedipal literature, guilty, dependent, an ambivalent literature of love and of accusation, yearning and damning at the same time. It is in fact probable that in most cases this very acceptance of ambivalence has given the contemporary Latin American novel its stature. The novelists who stayed home did not recognize the guilt of incest and accepted it without questioning the nature and consequences of this love. Plato talks of the artist who is only able to render the "sensory appearances of the material world," as contrasted to those who go beyond that: we made the voyage and went beyond sensory appearances. Those who stayed behind mostly reported only the given truth.

How have we gone beyond it, these contemporary wanderers of the Latin American novel? We refuse to live at home. We reject the idea of writing about the contingent problems of our countries in the present day. We are critical. Sometimes unkind. We accept foreign influences. We become involved in things not national. We do not write about the countries we now live in, or about the circumstances of our exile.

Yet something quite strange happens to the writing of these wanderers: we obsessively write about our homelands. It is as if we were substituting imaginary maps of our countries, within which we *can* live without guilt, for our actual countries, where we can't live. The details of the past, transformed into an imaginary present, flood the mind and cover·pages. In my opinion, this establishes what I want, for the time being, to call the novel of *absence*, which I would like to propose as one of the defining elements of the Latin American novel of my generation.

Sometimes, it is true, Latin American novelists don't go back to their countries for political reasons. But one must accept the fact that the political radicalism—now, in any case, notoriously in abeyance—which is supposed to keep most Latin American novelists away, is a position taken after, not before, they become expatriates by choice. Cabrera Infante and Roa Bastos are two exceptions. Some left their native Ithacas, like Odysseus, with the purpose of fighting in the great ideological wars of the world and thus transcend the meagre experiences they found within their own boundaries. Most of us left because our little island offered paltry intellectual stimulation. All of us, in any case, left in order to do, in one way or another, what Cavafy advises his traveler to do:

Stop at Phoenician markets,
and purchase fine merchandise,
mother of pearl and corals, amber and ebony,

and pleasurable perfumes of all kinds.
Buy as many voluptuous perfumes as you can;
visit hosts of Egyptian cities,
to learn and learn from those who have knowledge.

Yet it turns out that no matter how long we stay away from our countries—ten, twenty years—the only "voluptuous good" we acquire during absences which become no longer voluntary, but which habit makes compulsive, is the *guilt of absence*. Our roots do not sink deep into foreign soil. What we learn from Egyptian sages is mostly academic, worldly, never "voluptuous," that is to say, never related to pleasure and pain and love, which would shoot these experiences into the mainstream of our lives and thus find their way into our books. We write as if from a no man's land, rejecting the obligations of home, rejecting the voluptuousness of abroad, rooted more than anything in an absence that is not nostalgic. Unlike Odysseus in Calypso's island, we do not *"weep by the shore where so oft, consumed with tears, sighs and pains he fixed his gaze upon the sterile sea, weeping bitterly."*

What is it, then, that we do if we don't weep by the shore? One must acknowledge that the attitude of Odysseus was not an enlightened one. He wanted to go back to his Ithaca, barren and un-beautiful, and to his no longer young wife, while nymphs and princesses vied for his favors. T. E. Lawrence, in his Translator's note to his *Odyssey*, after saying of it: *"Crafty, exquisite, homogeneous ... whatever great art may be, these are not its attributes,"* concedes that *"it is the oldest book worth reading for its story and the first novel of Europe."* He calls Odysseus *"that cold-blooded egotist"* and adds that *"it is sorrowful to believe that these were really Homer's heroes and exemplars."* I would add that there was a side to Odysseus which was very much "the common man with commonplace aspirations": a wily man of action, not a reflective man for whom the experience of the voyage, the first and still the definitive voyage of our literature, would have been fine material and the best solace.

Yet, far from our countries, not wanting to go back, or to relinquish the experience of a voyage which, although it has become a habit, we do not allude to it in our books, we never write under the spell of feeling of loss, sighing to be in England now that April's there, so to speak. Nor do we bewail the more general loss of Keats:

The day is gone and all its sweets are gone
sweet voice, sweet lips, soft hand and softer breast.
Warm breath, light whisper, tender semi-tone ...

You will never find this note of nostalgia in our writing. For the point is that we are aware that we have lost our capacity to return home, no matter how much we write about our countries. We know it is advisable to stay away; our Ithacas are stifling and provincial. We know that within their bounds literary vanity and/or jealousy can kill. Above all we realize that the demand for public action is such that it can imperil and destroy our identities by making us "public" and our writing "useful."

Little of our international experience, however, occupies any space in our work. We have not recorded exile in any of its forms. No one, like Henry James in England, has given up his national identity as a writer, although I hear that Cortázar has become a French citizen and Cabrera Infante a British subject. However French, however English the Latin American writer, we all, without exception, in our major work, obsessively write about our own Ithacas using the detritus of our different vernaculars still floating in our memories: in order to keep our Ithacas at a safe distance we recycle them into metaphors. There is no foreign locale, no use of a foreign language or of a different vernacular, no creation of the international literary Latin American Spanish . . . nothing to be equated with the importance of French in Beckett, say, or of places like Spain in Hemingway, or Paris in Gertrude Stein. Cavafy warned us, "*Always keep Ithaca fixed in your mind.*"

We do, obsessively, and I'd say, guiltily. Our literature is not "committed" to the struggles of our countries. It was the past generation of Latin American novelists, those who never became expatriates, that wrote the useful novels, the didactic novels, immersed in struggle.

How is it that we don't? All interviewers ask the same question. Why do we not take part in the social and political struggles of our countries? In the Argentine, the police ferrets out writers and persecutes and imprisons those who refuse to play up the military. In Uruguay, a whole generation of writers was wiped out. In Chile, when Pinochet came along, a huge exodus of *literati* took place: the terror of those first years was not only the terror of being killed, it was also the problem of being intolerant of an intolerable situation. Things have changed, they say, in Chile. Writers, even some known to have been communists, are now returning with permission from the Junta, as the cases of Alfonso Alcalde and Gonzalo Rojas have recently proved. But if Cavafy tells his traveler to " . . . *pray that the road is long* . . .," he also reminds him that "*to arrive there is your ultimate goal.*" How can this be done? How to keep away from collective action in Chile? How can a writer continue writing within his own limitations, those which define him, when tyrannized by the immediate need for action on any front, with any weapons? Better to keep away for the time being. Not a heroic attitude, although most of us share it to some extent. But who said that writers were supposed to be exemplary human beings?

What we have tried to avoid by not going back is not action itself, but writing as action. This may be difficult for a contemporary American to grasp as an "obligation" since it is not an American tradition. There's evidently no "public" side in the writing of Cheever, or Updike, or Truman Capote, and no guilt because there isn't. But there is an exceedingly long tradition in Latin America of the writer considered "serious" only if there is a public, useful, didactic, civic side to his writing, and if he leads an exemplary life of action. Our tradition of the President-poet, of the diplomat-man-of-letters, of the politician-novelist is a much respected one even today.

There is yet another tradition, the one of exile: Andrés Bello, the Venezuelan man of letters living in exile in Chile and in London, wrote his *Silva on the Agriculture of the Torrid Zone* to delve into the prosaic realities of the New America. The Argentinian José Mármol, living in political exile in Montevideo, wrote his novel *Amalia* as a tract against his enemy, the dictator Rosas. The Chilean Blest-Gana wrote *Martín Rivas* as a diplomat in Paris, where he eventually died, as a study of the rising middle class of his country. Miguel Angel Asturias wrote his diatribe against dictators while in exile in Paris.

I feel that our dependence for our source-material and our diction derives so compulsively from our own countries due more than anything to an overriding feeling of guilt for not being connected with action. This is a romantic tradition. Lord Byron wrote to Lady Melbourne: "I prefer the talents of action—of war, of the senate, even of science—to all the speculations of our mere dreams . . ." The exile of the English Romantic poets stood for many things: their stance flaunted conventionality and stood for the liberal ideas of the times. There was even something exemplary about them all dying abroad: Keats in Rome, Byron in Missolonghi, Shelley in the Gulf of La Spezia—when he put out to sea in a storm aboard his yacht the *Ariel*, and Trelawney went out to look for his body in Byron's yacht called, in an uncanny way which seems to tie all these themes together, the *Bolivar*.

I'd venture to say that it was in order to escape that tyrannical superego demanding exemplary lives linked to action through literature, to write useful books pointing to exemplary public lives, to be concerned with the immediate and put it down on paper, that most of us took abode in countries abroad, from where we could manage our perspectives and be as private as we chose. I think it is this lack of the immediacy of the pressing public reality, this perspective, the time and the void for the imagination to grow in and to preen and prattle and prance, to be free and subjective, that has given the novel of my generation, written in un-useful and un-heroic style, its character and its stature.

In the previous generation it was the poets who fled and made Latin American poetry internationally renowned, not being respected at home until they came back with their heads wreathed in foreign laurels. When I went to teach in Iowa in the mid-sixties and suggested a seminar on contemporary Latin American fiction in translation, they made the counterproposal that I give one on Latin American poetry: it was so much more distinguished. Rubén Darío, Gabriela Mistral, Octavio Paz, Pablo Neruda, César Vallejo, Vicente Huidobro, were all invoked. It was, indeed, a most brilliant galaxy of writers.

All of them lived abroad for extended periods of their lives and were defined by that fact. Rubén Darío fled Nicaragua and became as European as Henry James became English. In Chile, the tradition of the expatriate poets is a legend. Vicente Huidobro not only lived in France, but wrote in French, publishing in such *avant-garde* magazines as *Nord-Sud*, side by side with Apollinaire and Tristan Tzara. Gabriela Mistral led as wandering an existence abroad as Rilke's. Their language was their only homeland.

The case of Neruda is slightly different. No writer ever professed to be more attached to his Ithaca than he. His first books were grey in tone, subjective and personal, in a way defined by the circumstances and size of Chile in the early twenties. Then he left for Ceylon, Burma, Indonesia, where his perspective shifted abruptly and he wrote *Residencia en la tierra*: in this shift, we can at once perceive the meaning of "the voyage," because it was then that Neruda gained an altitude and a speed of flight which he thereafter never lost. This wise traveler returned to Ithaca laden with beautiful objects. He stayed home only six months. Then he left again, this time for Buenos Aires, thence to the Spain of the Civil War, thence to the Mexico of the great muralists. I believe, however, that it was after his return to Chile, many years later, when for political reasons he had to live incognito, an exile in his own country until he was forced to escape for another five years, that he came to full fruition: in political exile, this time, all his previous absences seem to have *set*, so to speak, once and for all, into the monumental metaphor of the *Canto general*. It is an impassioned reconstruction in *absence*, of Ithaca. In *absence*, he does not weep by the shore, like Odysseus: out of the void in time and space grows that huge metaphor that he substitutes for the lost world and fills his absence with it.

If I compare the semantic field of the word *absence*, in English, to that of the word *ausencia*, in Spanish, which is what I mean, I discover that both semantic fields do not coincide. Absence, in English, carries, I think, little or no connotation of sorrow or loss: I'd say it is an emotionally inert word. In Spanish, however, its equivalent, *ausencia*, carries with it an almost elegiac semantic field. It is an emotionally charged word, rich with connotations of dreaminess, of guilt and punishment, of sleep, of recall, even of madness. I must hasten to correct myself, then, and explain that I'm speaking of the contemporary Latin American novel as a novel of *ausencia*, not of absence. I also detect in the Spanish word a sort of *will to stay away*, a determination taken, pulling the word out of shape, then to one side. But it also suggests a sorrow for staying away, pulling it out of shape to the other side: it establishes a conflict, and contains an implicit desire to return, and an implicit acknowledgment that it is impossible to return. This tension pulls the word apart in such a way as to leave a sort of void in the middle of it, filled with our guilt for not returning to be diplomat-poets, politician-novelists, senator-men-of-letters, President-translators of Dante, engaged in useful and admirable struggles, thrust into prison, tortured, persecuted, impoverished. There-fore, in that void, we reconstruct countries of the imagination where in *ausencia* we can live as we are, without guilt. It is from this unresolved ambivalence of guilt that the best novels of my generation spring.

What language should we use to write the novel of *ausencia*? None of us has turned into a Nabokov or a Beckett. To illustrate this all-important point of language let me talk a little about Guillermo Cabrera Infante's recent *La Havana para un infante difunto*. This novel of *ausencia* does not possess the literary glory of *Cien años de soledad*, or of *Rayuela*, or even Cabrera's earlier *Tres tristes tigres*, where the vernacular of each country—recalled and recreated abroad—undergoes the mystical trans-mutation of becoming the metaphor itself. In these novels the vernacular simply *is*, it cannot and need not to be explained in order to be the flesh of the metaphor: its semantic field either reaches you or it doesn't. *La Havana para un infante difunto* is a long monotonous narrative dealing with the amours of the young author with a seemingly endless parade of Cuban females who barely achieve identity. The spontaneous Cuban vernacular of *Tres tristes tigres* is very far in the past. If language is a form of action, the writer must continuously limber up for it, if he doesn't want to loose his power to handle it. Cabrera seems no longer fit in that sense. The vernacular is no longer the star, the novel itself. But he obsessively reconstructs an autobiographical Havana detained in the past, packed with minutiae. A void of time is placed between the period of the narrative and the late seventies, *when* he is writing. That void in time becomes equated with the void in space separating Havana and London, *where* he is writing. He can't go back to Ithaca because the angry, bearded Poseidon banished him from his island. This space–time void is filled with a strange silence. It is the sad silence of the lost ver-nacular, the absence of a valid Cuban Spanish which made *Tres tristes tigres* what it is. This Cuban Spanish of a certain class and a certain age was the marrow and the nerve itself of the novel, the code in which it was written. In *La Havana para un infante difunto* something quite dif-ferent happens: it is written mostly in flat, colorless Spanish, punctured by Cabrera's usual puns. When he does use the vernacular, it is either in dialogue, or more interestingly, seen *from the outside*: Cabrera has to account for it and explain it, using it as in between inverted commas. These inverted commas define the territory of Cabrera's *ausencia*. As an example, he carefully explains what the Cuban idiom *amor trompero* means: "Amor trompero, cuantas veo, cuantas quiero. Hace tiempo que no lo oigo pero no he olvidado lo que quiere decir." The whole of *La Havana para un infante difunto* is the anecdote of "amor trompero," but not the metaphor for it, since the vernacular is lacking, and it and everything becomes explained from the outside. The homeland of a writer is not really a place, but a language. Not even a language, but a certain section, a fraction of that language with which one identifies. The return voyage to Ithaca is an effort to regain one's vernacular, which the intervening silence of years and space has rendered powerless, and plug into it again, even when one lives abroad.

It seems to me that much of the power of the Latin American novel of my generation, written in *ausencia*, comes from the monumental effort of reconstructing and regaining one's vernacular, or inventing a vernacular that will take its place and possess a charged semantic field. Words *are* time and space if they are to be timeless. When used in *ausencia*, that time and that space placed in an order or perspective provided by distance become alive, and they form that structure which we call fiction.

The case of Manuel Puig may clarify things further. His is an artificial form of the vernacular. He claims to have always been an exile from reality, living in the fantasy world of films. Puig's Argentinian Spanish is not an Argentinian of *his* personal reality. It grows out of the subculture of the old films, out of fashion magazines, out of soap operas. Puig, as an individual, does not share this language. He stands at a distance from its mindlessness. He has lived away from his country for a long time. Yet he cannot use anything but what I'd call an artificial vernacular— not a "natural" one as in the case of Cabrera, or a "cultural" one as in the case of Cortázar's *Rayuela*—with artifical origins: this language is Puig's metaphor. Without its avowed artificiality, a certain world of the mind—and of an Argentinian reality of a space and time now vanished— could not be conveyed. I'd venture to say that even when he is not being Argentinian, this world of the mind is conveyed by means of the artificial Argentinian vernacular that he has invented, which defines a space and time. In Puig's *ausencia*, Ithaca is reached by means of an ironic code that is not the writer's own language, not one that embodies his own values: it is what I'd call a language of *disguise*. I'd venture to say that all of Puig's fiction is created by means of disguise. He pretends that it is all true, that it is the only language possible, but we know this is not true for him, and furthermore, the whole point is that we must be aware that it is not. Heidegger said when he was writing about Nietzsche: "The greatness of a thinker is measured in terms of what he did not know he was putting into his work." I wonder if Puig knows how much compassion he puts into his novels by means of using this disguise of an artificial vernacular. And compassion is important since it is a rare commodity in the pyrotechnical display of Latin American fiction: in Puig, the time–space void can be equated with the vernacular that is pure disguise, and disguise is a metaphor for indefinite *ausencia*. Puig can go on writing novels indefinitely by means of the false vernacular he has invented. He is, however, not the only one: Mario Vargas Llosa, in *Pantaleón* and in *La tía Julia y el escribidor*, wrote two novels of disguise with a somewhat different result. These two authors seem to me oddly symmetrical in their literary endeavors.

To wind up, let me talk a little about my own experience during these long seventeen years of *ausencia*. To quote Cavafy again:

Ithaca has given you a beautiful voyage.
Without her you would have never taken the road.
But she has nothing more to give you,

And if you find her poor, Ithaca has not cheated you.
With the great wisdom you have gained, with so much experience,
You must surely by then have understood what Ithaca means.

The stanzas are moving. The reasoning excellent, as always in Cavafy. As always, he points to intellectual pleasure, besides sensual pleasure— he tends to equate the two—as the greatest of gains. The voyage has made it possible—and that is the reason why it is not important if Ithaca is found to be poor—for us to understand not only our own Ithaca but, more important, the meaning of all Ithacas, which is what the traveler ostensibly in quest of voluptuous goods was really after.

The most important thing about the voyage, then—in other words about *ausencia*—is acquiring not a limited experience, but an experience that can be expanded into knowledge by means of a return to Ithaca, which will make the meaning of all Ithacas accessible. I myself, as a Latin American writer who stays away although he could go back, have to accept that one's essential knowledge is to be limited to the singular case of our own Ithaca, in contrast to the universal Ithaca of the completed return. I must begin by accepting the ambivalence: the return is stifling— I will find it poor—, but it will give me full knowledge of all Ithacas. The acceptance of return, of the particular *experience* of my own historical circumstances, is also the recuperation of a vernacular.

Return would be easy in my case if I felt a moral, social, or political obligation. But not feeling those urges is a limitation of my personality which I cannot ignore. I can do nothing more effective for my community than writing, and writing about my own limited universe. Now that seventeen years have gone by in *ausencia*, I find that I'm asking myself whether I can keep away from my country any longer, and yearning, in other words, for my lost vernacular. My first two volumes of stories and my first novel were written in Chile in a "natural" realistic language that never questioned its validity. Then, for years, I became entangled with a huge novel, a *summa* of my Chilean experience, getting right to the bottom of my language: but no matter how much I worked I couldn't place things in perspective and the novel was throttling me. I thus spent years in Chile accomplishing nothing at all. Then I left Chile. The year following my flight, in Mexico, I wrote two novels, *El lugar sin límites* and *Este domingo*: Chilean locale, Chilean characters, Chilean language: none of it questioned, but the sudden, and much needed experience of *ausencia* enabled me to write. In a way, though, both novels fall into the tradition of serious, useful realistic fiction: they are true, they stuck to the examination of class distinctions, there was an easy code to crack. But the years were going by and I was still obsessively at work at my labyrinthine *El obsceno pájaro de la noche*. I did not finish it until 1969, six years after leaving Chile. I think that novel both embodied all of my Chilean experience, and exhausted it. It is my contribution to the novel of *ausencia*.

After *El obsceno pájaro de la noche*, something quite odd began to happen. I began to become unable to use the unquestioned, "natural" Chilean-Spanish vernacular which, no matter how literary it became, I had used without qualms up until then. Chilean diction, tone, vocabulary, syntax, words, and turns of phrases that expressed experiences alien to me, especially those which were being formed during the Unidad Popular, seemed so odd that I, indeed, felt *ausente*. Even the use of the old vernacular I had grown up with, and perhaps even helped to create, seemed, now that so much time had gone by, unmanageable on the written page. I was living in Spain. But academic Spanish, or even the Spanish of the streets and everyday life—the Spanish that my very young daughter spoke to me, in fact—was just as foreign, just as unmanageable for me as was Chilean Spanish. I was living, then, within the silent limbo of *ausencia*. So I wrote *Historia personal del "Boom"* which, being a memoir, did not require anything more committed than a clear style.

There was, then, no language for me to write in. What I did was to try the language of disguise: I wrote *Tres novelitas burguesas*, in pseudo-Catalan Spanish, about Catalan people similar to the people I knew all over the world.

What to do next? *El obsceno pájaro de la noche* was inscribed in the group of large *summas* written by novelists from all over Latin America, who, each using his own vernacular, in *ausencia*, created whole countries of the imagination: its size, moreover, pointed to a certain period in time, now completely over. What I had to do was to get out of the linguistic limbo I was trapped in. I applied to the Guggenheim Foundation for a grant to return to Allende's Chile for a year in order to verify how bad my relations with Chilean Spanish were, and what I could do about them. I wanted to write a musical comedy about the Bavarian Romantic painter Rugendas who painted and lived in Chile at the beginning of the nineteenth century, and recorded all the popular *types* of the recently born nation. After that, and as part of my project, I meant to write a novel about what it was like to produce a musical comedy about Rugendas in Chile during Allende's time. It was an ambitious and interesting project, and I was given the grant. But then along came Pinochet, so I naturally gave up my trip to Chile and stayed in Spain. It was during this most horrifying period of *ausencia*, in the anguish of those first years, that *Casa de campo* began to grow out of what was by now a huge time–space void resulting in a sort of linguistic schizophrenia. The new novel could not, of course, be written *about* experience that not only I had not undergone, but that I was separated from for so many years. But at least on some levels the new novel could touch upon ideas and emotions that I had a right to feel and think, even though I had been neither a victim nor a witness of the terror. I could not use Chilean characters because I no longer knew what they were like. Or Chilean locales, which I'd lost the *bouquet* of. Or Chilean vernacular, which, by now, had become foreign to me without my acquiring a new one. From the desperate void of my *ausencia* sprang the whole travesty of *disguise* in *Casa de campo*. Diction in disguise, locale in disguise, characters in disguise, problems in disguise. It became the only way to solve the problem of writing a novel about my feeling for what had happened during my *ausencia*. This is what I think I did. But there is much in that novel—and some say they are the best parts—which, as Heidegger said, I did not know I was putting in. The imagination was let loose by means of its many fancy dresses, and the metaphor was created.

Fancy dress or not, on one level it would be a return to Ithaca: a useful, committed novel, a novel to teach and discuss, a novel with a "public face" within the old Latin American tradition. Yet not only that. I blush to confess that I hoped to make the problem of a tragic Chile in fancy dress a metaphor for all our Ithacas, and thus, for the first time in my life, I consciously chose to be an exemplary writer. A little bit absurd to my mind, but I realized it underwrote the guilt of my long years abroad, and gave my *ausencia* some sort of meaning. Besides, it did something else for me: it helped me to avoid the existential problem of what to do with my life-language, with my language-life, which was solved in that book.

Now I am again in a linguistic limbo. *Casa de campo* was published during the last month of 1978. This is early 1980. What have I been up to in the meantime? Could I wait it out in Madrid, with its penetrating idiomatic Spanish eroding the credibility of the remnants of my Chilean Spanish? I did use my Chilean vernacular, with a vengeance, in my spoken Spanish. But on paper it was impossible: it was blank, bereft of connotations, a semantic field lying, by now, in waste.

I am now on my way to Chile to see how things look there. I want to verify which of the conflicting tales are true. But also, and for me a much more important thing, to find out whether I can feel that the Chilean language is not a kind of *fancy dress*, as unfortunately I feel now. I feel it as totally alien as I feel Academic Spanish, another disguise, as *madrileño* street-Spanish is a disguise. I don't want to spend the rest of my life caught in linguistic travesty.

Meanwhile, in this quandary, having for the present soothed my conscience with the knowledge that, whatever *Casa de campo* is, and I hope it may be many things, at least it grew out of an emotion that was fully committed to an experience. I began to cast about for what to do next, since I'm of the persuasion that one doesn't write a book in order to say something, but to find out what one has to say. I have assumed, for the moment, disguise as a necessity while I solve other matters. I am writing a series of novellas which, collected, are to be called *Four Traditional Experiments*. They are four short, unrelated novels, written each in a different form that I've never tried before and for which I feel no particular concern or preference: an erotic novel, a political novel, a thriller, and a science fiction novella.

I tried my hand, first of all, with the erotic novella. Immediately, without even being conscious of what I was doing, all the disguises urged themselves upon me. I remembered an old collection of Spanish magazines which I had spent all one summer reading, while my wife looked down on me because she was absorbed in Marcuse. But the far away memory of those magazines suddenly sprang to my rescue: the new novella was to take place in Madrid, in the 1920s; it was not to be straight erotica but tongue-in-cheek, following a tradition of popular *madrileño* fiction, now completely forgotten, but which is nevertheless interesting and atmospheric; Felipe Trigo, Caballero Audaz, Pedro Mata, Alberto Insúa. In about two months I wrote *La misteriosa desaparición de la marquesita de Loria*, which will be published when I return to Spain in April, with all the news from Ithaca. The next novella will be about how Lenin, in 1908 in Paris, got money to publish one of his many clandestine papers and will also be comic. I can't predict what the result will be. I know, from writing *La misteriosa desaparición de la marquesita de Loria*, that comedy is necessary because it is another protective layer of disguise.

Tarántula, this Lenin novel, will require a lot of historical research, but the idea is enticing because I'll write about a historical reality different from my own, thus using another layer of fancy dress which at this point I find necessary to be able to write. But what shall I do for the actual language of *Tarántula*? I don't really know. I don't want to live for the rest of my life in *fancy dress*. I'd like to feel under my feet the secure soil of a vernacular in which to write. Even if I do go back to live in Chile, will I be able to assume the language I left in a completely different stage of its evolution, so many years ago? I don't know. I do know that the novel of *ausencia*, written in voluntary or political exile, which was the experience of my generation, has evolved into something else that I can't yet figure out. I know that it was at least as enthralling as the poetry of *ausencia*, a generation before. There are hordes of Argentinians in exile in Europe, lawyers washing dishes, professors of philosophy from Uruguay tending bars, long queues to get working permits, marriages broken up, Chileans like me who have lost or are in danger of losing their identity, architects making *empanadas* to sell, or little, unattractive bead necklaces no longer in fashion, *batik*, toys, pictures, anything. I know the political uncertainty, the terror that suddenly strikes when news of more killing suddenly arrives, and the ambivalent guilt of the few who have been able to make a go of it at their own thing, the lack of security, of faith in everything but especially in words, the frustration of being considered fifth-class citizens in France, of hating Swedish weather notwithstanding the security offered, the gradual loss of everything . . . yes, I've known this sorry crowd in Eastern and Western Europe alike.

I've begun to wonder, though I'm no political exile and can go back to Chile whenever I choose, whether this rootless community is not the only community I really belong to now . . . whether it is not my new Ithaca. But the language, the swear-words, the love-words that carry pictures and memories with them, which one didn't put there on purpose, what is its language, besides that of rage and frustration? I don't know.

But eventually I will perhaps find out. Just as it was necessary, at one point, to leave Chile, and introduce a distance, an *ausencia*, a linguistic silence so I could write—an experience shared with so many novelists of my generation—I may have to go back to the first Ithaca I came from in order to write about the uprooted and lonely people, younger than I, to whose breed, with its debilitated national identity and lost national vernacular, I now seem to belong. Yes, absent from the experience itself of being adrift, tucked away in Ithaca, I may be able to find the language to write out their, our story, and write about my long voyage without the need of disguise.

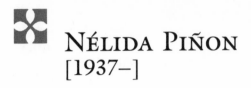

NÉLIDA PIÑON
[1937–]

NÉLIDA PIÑON WAS BORN in Rio de Janeiro of Spanish parents. Educated and trained as a journalist, she has also taught creative writing and has traveled widely in Europe and the United States. She emerged as a successful young author in the 1960s.

Her first novel, *Guía-mapa de Gabriel Arcanjo*, 1961 ["Guide-Map of the Archangel Gabriel"], was followed by another novel and a book of short stories, then two prize-winning novels, *A casa de paixão*, 1972 [*The House of Passion*, 1976] and *Tebas do meu coração*, 1974 ["My Beloved Thebes"], and a collection of stories that gained her much reknown, *Sala de armas*, 1973 ["Fencing Room"]. The experimental quality of her prose and her preference for mythic themes result in stories in which basic human values are closely scrutinized in metaphoric terms. Piñon's more recent publications include *A força de destino*, 1977 ["The Force of Destiny"], a novel; *O calor das coisas*, 1980 ["The Heat of Things"], a collection of short stories; and her novel, *A república dos sonhos*, 1984 [*The Republic of Dreams*], scheduled for English publication in 1987; in addition, several of her short stories have appeared in English-language anthologies. Piñon has won Brazil's most coveted literary prizes, and her works have been translated into many languages.

The accompanying essay was written for this collection in 1985 and is translated here for the first time. In this piece, Piñon conveys her sense of the writer's participation in the mythic dimensions of life through the medium of language. The wealth of expression of Brazilian Portuguese, in all its collective history, reinforces the author's feeling that she is a part of ancient rituals of creation that transcend the limitations of the human condition.*

*Portuguese usage does not require that pronouns be articulated as frequently as in English. Therefore the use of "he," "his," and "himself," when referring to "the writer" is far more pronounced in the English translation than in Piñon's original essay. Rather than include the feminine alternative in each case and thereby interrupt the flow of the prose, the translator has chosen to use the traditional generic "he." Similar problems arise in translations from Spanish into English. [Ed.]

THE MYTH OF CREATION

Nélida Piñon
Translated by Giovanni Pontiero

Creation pursues a difficult route, which is often imperceptible, its traces and origins scarcely visible. Any creative act is fundamentally united with life, with language, with one's own country, one's life history, with collective memory, and with time past and present.

Whenever you discuss this enigmatic and insatiable act of creation, you cannot exclude the table, the bed, the battles and the gestures of everyday existence.

My life, like that of every other writer, is probably built into the text, embedded like a lance. I can only speak about my life and writing in purely relative terms. I discovered from my grandfather Daniel, who disembarked in the Praça Mauá some ninety years ago on arriving from Spain, that long before I was born and pledged myself to this singular land, Brazil, he had initiated on my behalf a journey that I was to follow from the moment I was prepared for the realms of imagination, of uncertainty and doubt.

Even as a child, I came to know that Sinbad, that admirable and ever-changing myth, had not journeyed with the idea of narrating in every port the events he had experienced in the previous chapter. On the contrary, from the time of his birth and long before leaving *terra firma*, Sinbad had been endowed with a talent for invention and deceit, legitimate opposites capable of reflecting the truth. This talent for invention and deceit gave him a narrative power that vehemently refused to summarize the human adventure in a few brief sentences. In Sinbad's hands, history would begin without the perspective of ever ending.

Convinced, therefore, that one can even travel through the archipelagos of language itself, I understood at once that simply to appropriate the plot of collective memory authorizes us to become part of it. And that the street where one lives is very often the entire universe. The land one inhabits is sufficient once one knows how to embroider it with human needles and threads, personages, artful intrigues, and sustained metaphors—elements, in a word, which neutralize and, at the same time, illuminate the unlimited powers of anyone who feels he knows how to tell a story.

But, as proof that I weave quite differently from Penelope, who unraveled her own history by night (unlike the egoistic Ulysses, who gathered his entire history for himself), I only became a writer by slow degrees. I slowly penetrated the art of writing, without immediately recognizing the nature of the materials with which I was grappling, and without measuring its limitations. This is because any awareness of the moral responsibilities inherent in writing is only acquired with time, and with the assistance of passion, that combustible matter capable of conveying what lucid thoughts often fail to explain.

I know perfectly well that the goal of creation is the text. And that everything is achieved around this goal. But I am unable to grapple with the intricate details of the text and of the myth revolving around itself, without first announcing the presence of language, which is the physical form of our soul.

All of us hold language in our hands and in our hearts. Language is omnipresent, language is what we are, and what we make of it—notwithstanding our Portuguese heritage, which we violated in order to make our own history, and to create a new language, which might be truly representative of Brazil, this young nation with less than five hundred years of existence.

Guided by language and its historical process, the Brazilian writer must learn that mythologies and intrigues were created in such abundance in this country that they can never be exhausted or diminished.

The Portuguese language is at our disposal. It is young and African, like we Brazilians. Plangent and impassioned and ever-insistent that we should transcend ourselves, for only in this way can we fathom its true emotions. And, because our language is young and eager to assert its existence, it draws on every available source, on every concept that might be considered representative and explanatory.

This language of ours, which was once anchored in the River Tagus, started to become rejuvenated, perhaps even to be born, the moment the first navigators set sail from Europe, with the Lusitanian language tucked under their arms and impregnated with sweat and grammatical rigor. They had scarcely navigated the Atlantic when their taste for adventure began to influence their linguistic foundations. The land they came in search of almost immediately gave a new dimension to their language: it acquired a different syntax and began to shed obsolete words in favor of the neologisms that started to spring up.

Brazil, even before allowing itself to be discovered, or offering the navigators the first geographical location that might correspond to their dreams, exacted a language from them which, besides defining Brazil, would also meet its future needs. It exacted, above all, from the navigators and colonizers, a new form of narrative, for the world that blossomed here was so remarkable, so exuberant and ambivalent, that only an instrument suited to the purpose could portray it with any authenticity.

Brazil demanded from those navigators a liberal and multifaceted language, wherein the entire history of Brazil's future might be faithfully expressed. Brazil also demanded that this new language should be porous so that all the events which might follow could be accurately narrated.

To the existing vocabulary, the Brazilians added new words. They gave names to trees, to rivers, and to the feelings aroused by the sight of those rivers and trees. And everything they saw or divined was given a name which could readily be absorbed by existing categories, while contributing to the national language.

Nothing went unbaptized. Each name was transformed into a recognizable entity once it had been described and brought into use. There was a growing awareness that the more names we accumulated, the more we would have to create, justify, and defend. The nation exceeded us in everything, so that the history of our invention would always be the history of our existence, of our ability to control and subvert all realities. Everyone was summoned to participate in this struggle which precedes the fable of any nation. Those who wrote down their experiences as well as those who told their tales around the campfire. There was every opportunity for self-expression. Each narrator in his own fashion made strenuous efforts to reinforce the national heritage. Some achieved glory and a national monument. The majority, however, remained anonymous. Their names could not be rescued from obscurity so that they might be honored.

They simply narrated without the benefit of the quill. The voice was the only instrument with which they engaged their audience. But, wherever they might be, whether in some wilderness or in some parlor, those anonymous voices strengthened the process of language and the mysterious evolution of a nation. Their ephemeral stories entertained friends and neighbors. Those men and women were the nonexistent books on the shelves of an emerging nation. They were the books that remained to be written. What they narrated lacked any authority or sense of direction. On the other hand, their stories exuded an air of freedom which one does not find in written narration. And because they were skilled raconteurs, the stories they read aloud spoke of extraordinary events and achievements which every listener dreamed of experiencing and emulating.

No sooner had these storytellers woven their narratives than they themselves faded from sight. All that remained of them were the echoes of their words and the certainty that life renews itself each day. Above all, because they did not know how to finish a narrative which might expel both the creator and the created at the same time, they emended one book with another, until they all became invisible. Until they themselves were replaced in the business of invention. For with the passing of the years they had to face inevitable death.

Succession, in those cases, always came about in a natural way. Those who succeeded them caught the last phrase released into the air and began perfecting a technique capable of exhausting the greatest number of realities. And because the reality of their everyday existence still haunted them, they all went in pursuit of the word lodged in the human heart, and which hitherto had been its secret and mystery.

This magical investigation of life and language has continued without a moment's interruption right up to the present day, so that the writer may never doubt that the product of his creation is of collective origin and manufacture. And that without the provision of such anonymous and fleeting testimonies, existence as a whole would elude him, and his text would not exist. For the writer only emerges in harmony with the rhythm of this dispersed language in accordance with the legends, dreams, fantasies, and sorrows that humanity creates in a common desire to resist any system that might threaten this common patrimony. The formation of a world through which the writer might reach humanity's primordial artery and probe the myth that is subtracted and reconquered day by day. To probe the sacred and the profane and to mediate between them. To describe them as if the writer was capable of arresting them, of bestowing credibility on them and reaching their origins. So that the writer might ultimately embrace that most painful of myths, which never ceases to haunt his house, namely, the myth of creation. To recognize that to create represents a violent assault on one's senses. And that the upheavals of such an act fully justify the mystery of its genesis: that every version resulting from this genesis is a myth which every writer portrays in his own way and not necessarily in harmony with the versions accepted by friends, readers, and other writers.

The writer, meantime, is anxious to define himself; to clarify the mythical seeds that reverberate inside him and that are sufficiently sensitive to reverberate in others who, in their turn, are capable of describing them. The writer feigns to be completely in control of his resources, while obsessively restoring his fount of inspiration, lest he should exhaust those waters which often come to him in floods. In these probings, he forgets the precedence of the text, which was established before his *ars poetica*. A text intent upon contradicting the versions and descriptions which are based on it, and ever ready to strip away the writer's masks and disguises.

This is a poetic process whereby the writer constantly reappraises his verbal conscience and becomes convinced that to create is both the written manifestation of his obsessions and the precondition of the language he is about to exploit. For the act of creation is an eternal confrontation between the text and the author, each portraying respectively what permits itself to be described and what the author chooses to express—he aspires to attain all the states and appearances which he proposes to represent, but which resist his apprehension.

The attempt then to fix the text, to encounter something that has no verbal appearance and is still on the point of assuming form, even though foreseen, is, for the writer, a consequence of himself. Above all, because to achieve physical form is one of the enticements in writing the text.

Starting, therefore, from the initial process of writing, the author's contradictions become all too apparent. Once he is obliged to choose from a chaotic abundance of material what he judges to be indispensable for his narrative, the simple act of selection constitutes a moral option. And once all the moral freedoms have been guaranteed—for the text emerges from invented forms—to fill the void between the text conceived and the text being elaborated is one of the most compromising versions that the author possesses of his own book.

But, while the text is being elaborated, the writer's true vocation is to expel the other text that exists within him. As if within a book there existed another book which the author combines in a single volume in order to warrant readings destined to various authors. For, despite the immutable appearance of the book, the text is related to itself and to all that is proximate to it, as it gradually becomes an entity and a concept. Even the language of this entity and concept. For to write becomes an act of identification with any kind of reality. The writer's task is to look beyond the possibilities of subsidized reality in pursuit of a reality open to criticism.

Meantime, there exists a natural adjustment between the reality of the text and the reality that engendered it. And although the writer must express himself in concrete terms, the text itself harbors certain obscurities that contribute an element of poetry. Such obscurities betray the presence of language beneath the surface, whose function is to preserve a precious residue of mystery. An essence that must come to the luminous surface of the words so that nothing is lost of the initial concept.

Reality, however, is not opposed to language. Nor is language an abstraction of reality. On the contrary, because language is a social and socializing instrument, by means of language the writer bonds reality in his need to define emotions. He offers reality in a written form. A poetic representation of what was previously latent. The writer narrates the evolution of language. He studies its organic structure, its state of health and emotion, by means of a system of appropriations and expropriations, since nothing has a master or a name. Only what withstands time and the voracity of our emotions and imagination will have a name.

But, putting the instinct of his writing on a parallel with the popular instinct that reinforces the repertory of language, the writer confesses to the inadequacy of his own history, and to what extent the language he exploits imposes the collective plot upon him *a priori*. Mobile and modular by nature, the narrative is everywhere as it painfully assumes form. The narrative anticipates the writer, while the latter, intent upon revealing successive forms of life, strives to gather in time the furrows, suffering, and destiny imprinted on the human face.

The writer's struggle is to invent in order to tell the truth. And to this end, he is dependent on the fabric of words which will deny him their hidden resources unless he finds the courage to destructure himself permanently and obey the intuition to bury his dagger in the heart of language and life, which is the heart of humanity.

This is a difficult struggle, for the writer cannot be certain that he is not trespassing on occupied territory. Once he has achieved something new—that state eagerly pursued by the writer—it becomes transparent that only what is new determines itself, only the new allows itself to reflect. Undoubtedly, the new is a project that the future will or will not warrant.

Whether it be by writing or by listening, through narrow channels, the writer's destiny is to make the reader believe in the life he has created and unwittingly lives, his senses numbed by everyday reality at the service of power. This denunciation of life trapped within itself does not obstruct the revelation of a noble harvest which protects the best of human sentiments.

And because the writer's creatures, who are guided to the text, suffer from the rapid passage of time, from language that is implacably logical and rational, and from restrictions that inaugurate or even conclude his text, the writer projects false backdrops and doors whose entrances are not always indicated by painted markings. And he devotes himself, as the author, to intuition, which is more real than knowledge. And without which, for the sake of his profession, he would not integrate himself into a narrative which, however unyielding, derives its greatest inspiration from an uninterrupted sequence of emotions, rituals, and evocations.

And thus the writer operates, because his role is an essential one. And were he not to dedicate himself to narration, human bonds would probably be severed, language would lose its unparalleled power of combining everything bound to it with all that may be achieved in its name. Then we might finish up confusing invention with straightforward biography. Were it not for the contribution made by writers, we might fail to recognize that behind history there exists another history, and behind that other history yet another, and so on and so on, going all the way back to the origins of the world. Human life is preserved along the unending chain of narration. Along those acquittances on which we depend in order to know our own forms, the words uttered by chance, our common interests, our omissions, what we are in the end.

Were it not for literature registering the rise and decline of the most harsh, inhospitable, and ambiguous sentiments, and especially for the author's corroboration in warranting certain moments in life, we might believe ourselves to be the first to have experienced the assault of passion, the torment of uncertainty, and the misery of injustice.

There you have the writer who forever carries the myth and the word in his hands. For the myth and the word are intent upon transcending the frontiers of any possible reality in order to penetrate that imaginary reality, which is the collective dream. This is when history becomes that narrative so long awaited by the community so that it, too, might narrate and thus become the rightful custodian of a fable that will correspond to its need for self-expression.

A language directed once more toward the myth that engendered and activated it. So that inhabited by aspirations both sacred and profane, it might be magically absorbed into an indissoluble *corpus*, into a field mined by innumerable combinations. A language prepared to overcome any prejudice or censure that might restrict or limit its use.

The writer who is bound to the word, the myth, and imagination, draws upon life and makes it pulsate in his text. There, in this center, we all allow ourselves to be used in our expectancy of some profound revelation, in our certainty that human history is *a priori* and that all of us coincide in time. We shall all be subject to the same painful exile if we lose our memory and allow ourselves to be robbed of language, of myths, and of our rooted capacity for re-creating them.

ERNESTO CARDENAL
[1925-]

NICARAGUAN POET, MARXIST revolutionary, and Catholic priest, Ernesto Cardenal fuses his creative and political energies in his writing and his responsibility as Nicaraguan Minister of Culture—a post he has held since the Sandinista overthrow of Somoza in 1979.

Cardenal, who was born in Nicaragua and educated in Mexico and New York, studied with Thomas Merton at the Trappist abbey in Kentucky. He was ordained in 1965, initially espousing Merton's philosophy of nonviolence—a philosophy that was among the guiding principles of a religious commune he founded on an island in the larger of Nicaragua's two lakes, Lake Nicaragua. But by 1970, Cardenal—an admirer of Fidel Castro—shifted to a militant stance, convinced that it was the only means to social revolution in his country; thus, the one-time disciple of nonviolence joined the Sandinista rebel forces.

His published works include *La hora O*, 1956 [published with related poems as *Zero Hour and Other Documentary Poems*, 1980]; *Oración por Marilyn Monroe y otros poemas*, 1965 [*Marilyn Monroe and Other Poems*, 1975]; *Salmos*, 1967 [*The Psalms of Struggle and Liberation*, 1971]; *Homenaje a los indios americanos*, 1969 [*Homage to the American Indians*, 1974]; *En Cuba*, 1972 [*In Cuba*, 1974]; *El evangelio en Solentiname*, 1975 [*The Gospel in Solentiname*, 1976]; and numerous other collections of poetry and prose.

Often compared to Pablo Neruda in his epic verse and commitment to radical political and social change, Cardenal is less emotional and more documentary in his approach. He wants his readers to see the facts for themselves, and, to Cardenal, the facts are an incontrovertible argument against capitalistic imperialism. As a voice of "liberation theology" in Central America, Cardenal is a powerful figure in Nicaragua's effort to transform traditional Latin American society.

This speech was originally delivered in Nicaragua on September 7, 1981, at the Meeting of Intellectuals for the Sovereignty of the Peoples of America and was published in the Cuban literary journal, *Casa de las Américas*. It appears here for the first time in English.

CLOSING ADDRESS

Ernesto Cardenal
Translated by Cynthia Ventura

It's difficult to be the last to speak at an event where so much has been said by such important personalities, beginning with the inaugural speech by Comrade Minister Hart. At an event where not only so much has been said, but—I would say—everything has been said. Comrade Minister Hart has entrusted me with the closing words, but I suppose that he doesn't expect of me—nor would any of you—new words after all that's been said here. There's nothing I can do but repeat, but that's what we all must do when we leave here, repeat and repeat.

In the first place, it's my responsibility to repeat once again the importance of this event. Its importance, first of all, for being in Cuba. Everything in Cuba is of importance to Latin American and the world. The single word "Cuba" says everything. It was the first country in the New World that truly became independent. The one that has unleashed movements of absolute independence on the Continent. It began with twelve men in the Sierra Maestra, who changed the destiny of Cuba and Latin America and who changed history.

This event is also important because of the ominous international circumstance, rather the preapocalyptic circumstance we live in. It's a movie in which the cowboy aims at the Indian with his pistol, but it's a movie that's reality.

To refer just to the case of we the Nicaraguan people, we're threatened in every way: with economic strangulation, with blockade, we're denied loans, we were denied wheat, Somoza's ex-guards are being trained in Miami and in many other places in the United States.

I've come from a trip to Libya where I went as part of a delegation headed by Commander Daniel Ortega, Coordinator of the Governing Junta of Nicaragua, for the twelfth anniversary celebration of the triumph of the Libyan Revolution. Shortly before leaving, the Governing Junta of Nicaragua received a message from Washington saying that it would be looked upon with disapproval if Commander Daniel Ortega traveled to Libya, and that if he went, to expect the consequences. Commander Daniel Ortega went to Libya and, furthermore, he related Washington's message in a public speech, which demonstrates our determination to be independent, whatever the consequences, and to struggle in defense of this independence to the very end.

And this event is also important because of the importance of so many intellectuals gathered here. It's something that has never occurred in the history of Latin America.

Roberto Fernández Retamar once said that in Cuba the intellectual avant-garde wasn't on a par with the political avant-garde, it had lagged behind. However, I think that now, in Latin America, intellectuals are also avant-garde on a par with the political avant-garde, and the proof is in this meeting.

This demands sacrifices from us—some may perhaps have to stop writing—which isn't the best, but to die isn't the best either and we may also have to die for liberation.

Comrade Armando Hart evoked the large number of intellectual martyrs incorporated into the enormous legion of martyrs from Latin America and those who suffer or have suffered in prison and those who are in exile. No one has ever seen such political commitment in writers and artists in our America. And this is characteristic of Latin America, because Europe, in general, continues with art for art's sake.

In the United States there's also an important current of socially and politically committed intellectuals, and they're our allies. I'm going to plagiarize here a North American writer, Richard Peck. One could say quote him, but I think that intellectual borrowing is as legitimate as borrowing from banks. What I've borrowed from him is the following:

In a prologue to an anthology in which he presents some interesting protest poetry, he says that poetry previously had very narrow limits— for example, on gravestones or in a love letter—but that now there aren't any limits to themes in poetry. The subject of an eight-column cover story in a newspaper can inspire a poem, moreover, the poem can be more real than a newspaper cover story. This is a new development in contemporary poetry, which deals with contemporary themes, the same themes as in newspapers. And it wasn't so before. It wasn't so in China, it wasn't so in Europe during the Middle Ages, partly because there weren't any newspapers. But poetry wasn't supposed to deal with social and economic problems, with the exception of some like Dante. And this can be said also of all contemporary literature and the arts. And it can be said also of theologians. It's interesting that theologians were invited here to this meeting.

I think it's very clear that the participation of Christians in the Revolution is of great importance, but it goes beyond that. In Latin America we have numerous Christians integrated into Marxism, but there's also going to be a union of revolutionary Christians and revolutionary Moslems, which will constitute a union of the Arab and the Latin American worlds as well. Christianity and Islam, which for centuries fought against one another in holy wars, will unite revolutionary Christians and revolutionary Moslems for a holy war against imperialism. The same can be said of Buddhism. And that union will be of Christians, Moslems, and Buddhists with Marxism.

This is in order to defend the world. Those of us who have met here are all the heirs of visionaries, philosophers, mystics, poets, and sages who throughout the centuries have wanted to change the world. We're the builders of the future, with a nostalgia for the future, a nostalgia for paradise, which isn't in the past but in the future. We're the realizers of dreams, and we should defend this dream-come-true in Cuba and Nicaragua, and the dream which is being fought for in El Salvador and Guatemala, the dreams of the southern cone, now in the darkness, and of all the liberation movements in Latin America. It's the defense of culture, which is the same as saying the defense of sovereignty. There's no complete culture without complete sovereignty.

In Nicaragua, with the triumph of the Revolution, we've experienced an enormous cultural renaissance. Now laborers, artisans, members of the armed forces, the army and the police, write poetry—very good, modern poetry. We have many peasant and worker theater groups, and this began even before the triumph of the Revolution; it began with the insurrection in the barricades: many times the hand that brandished a gun was also the hand that strummed a guitar. And now in El Salvador many songs are being heard which are a prelude to victory. It's like hearing roosters sing in the darkness. But they're killing the young people there—simply for being young—as used to happen in Nicaragua; and the bodies appear with the eyes pulled out, the tongue cut out, the genitals torn off, as used to happen in Nicaragua; and the peasants, too, killed, simply for being peasants. And Guatemala under the rule of death squads. And all of this being done by imperialism so that El Salvador and Guatemala won't become like Nicaragua is now. But there's something worse: imperialism is doing this against Nicaragua, too, because imperialists want again what once existed in Nicaragua and now exists in El Salvador and Guatemala. Another crime of imperialism is that we're being divided in Central America, the small brother countries. And speaking of crime, the death of that great statesman and revolutionary—and also an intellectual and, for me, a poet—Omar Torrijos, is clearly a crime, yes a crime, and he's one more martyr in the liberation of Latin America.

In Nicaragua we know very well that we're simply a re-won trench, a liberated territory. But there is only one Revolution and we're only one people in all Latin America, with more unity than in the Arab world—and we also include the Latin America inside the United States, as our Chicano brothers and sisters have shown us here.

The Indians gathered around the fire at night say in a poem: "What shall we do with these thoughts?" That's what we should say here: "What shall we do with these thoughts?"

Concretize ideas, go from words to action. What has happened here is something that has scarcely begun and that from now on will continue. The Second Meeting of Intellectuals for the Sovereignty of the Peoples of Our America may take place in Nicaragua.

All of this began, I say, with twelve men who, after being defeated, entered the Sierra Maestra. They say that Fidel said there: "Batista has been screwed." And not only Batista, but imperialism.

We now have Roque Dalton's tiny country, which is an example of how the smallest countries can confront the most armed one on earth. Grenada is a small island, with some two hundred thousand inhabitants, almost the size of an island in Lake Nicaragua, a small island, alone, in the middle of the ocean, defying the power of the United States.

And we have all of the Third World. We must populate the world—as Vallejo would say—with powerful, weak people. Revolutions are breaking out everywhere. In Libya, where I've just been, Khadafy threatened to bomb any ship loaded with nuclear weapons that approached the coasts of Libya and to burn the petroleum in Saudi Arabia and then Libya itself, and he declared that Libya would be the center of operations against imperialism being carried out throughout the world.

The struggle, then, is more than regional, it's worldwide. The Ayatollah Khomeini told me that all revolutions are only one and that when the whole world was liberated, then all men, women, and children of the world would march hand in hand.

We know very little about the atom and even less about stars, but between microcosm and macrocosm we have a role to fulfill. We have a role in the cosmos. The Bible as well as Marxism give us the reassurance that we're headed toward a perfect universe; if not, the universe wouldn't make any sense; if not, the Cuban Revolution wouldn't make any sense, and we well know that it does. Although to completely achieve what Marx called the attack on the sky, I'd say that we may perhaps need as much time as has passed from the *Homo abilis* to us.

But we intellectuals must work as hard as the most spirited of the *Homo abilis*. It's a matter of defending Latin America and it's also a matter of defending the human species; it's a matter of defending all the species of living beings on the planet, of defending the planet itself. Defense is peace.

ROSARIO FERRÉ
[1942–]

A NATIVE OF Ponce, Puerto Rico, Rosario Ferré was
educated on the island and in the States, receiving a bachelor's
degree from Manhattanville College and a master's from the University of Puerto Rico. Her literary career began in the early
1970s: she was the editor of the magazine *Zona de carga*, which
published her first story, "La muñeca menor" ["The Youngest
Doll"], later translated by Gregory Rabassa. Known for her in-
cisive and often ironic portrayal of Puerto Rican society, Ferré has
become one of Puerto Rico's most respected authors. She has also
traveled and lectured widely in the United States where her work
has appeared in various literary magazines. She has recently completed work on a doctoral degree in Spanish and Latin American
literature at the University of Maryland.

Ferré's published works include a collection of short stories
and verse entitled *Papeles de Pandora*, 1976 ["Pandora's Papers"];
a book of poetry, *Fábulas de la garza desangrada*, 1982 ["Fables
of the Bled Heron"]; a collection of essays on feminist themes,
Sitio a Eros, 1980 ["Eros Beseiged"]; a novel, *Maldito amor*, 1986
["Damned Love"]; and several books of children's stories. Of *Papeles de Pandora* one critic has said: "The book is a constant tearing
apart of memory, imagination and word—impossible to read with
indifference."

The daughter of a former governor of Puerto Rico, Ferré was
raised in a traditional upper-class household with the kind of cultural myths and taboos familiar to women in all of Latin America.
The following essay is a personal manifesto of female creative au-

tonomy yet it speaks for a whole generation of Latin American women—daughters-in-spirit of earlier feminists such as Alfonsina Storni, Teresa de la Parra, Victoria Ocampo, and Rosario Castellanos, to name just a few. An earlier version of this essay was delivered as a talk at several Latin American literary conferences and later published in their proceedings. It also appeared in the second edition (1986) of *Sitio a Eros*. Slightly revised by the author, it was translated into English for this collection.

THE WRITER'S KITCHEN

Rosario Ferré
Translated by Diana L. Vélez

I

HOW TO LET YOURSELF FALL FROM THE FRYING PAN INTO THE FIRE

Throughout time, women narrators have written for many reasons: Emily Brontë wrote to prove the revolutionary nature of passion; Virginia Woolf wrote to exorcise her terror of madness and death; Joan Didion writes to discover what and how she thinks; Clarice Lispector discovered in her writing a reason to love and be loved. In my case, writing is simultaneously a constructive and a destructive urge, a possibility for growth and change. I write to build myself word by word, to banish my terror of silence; I write as a speaking, human mask. With respect to words, I have much for which to be grateful. Words have allowed me to forge for myself a unique identity, one that owes its existence only to my efforts. For this reason, I place more trust in the words I use than perhaps I ever did in my natural mother. When all else fails, when life becomes an absurd theater, I know words are there, ready to return my confidence to me. This need to reconstruct which moves me to write is closely tied to my need for love: I write so as to reinvent myself, to convince myself that what I love will endure.

But my urge to write is also destructive, an attempt to annihilate myself and the world. Words are infinitely wise and, like all mothers, they know when to destroy what is worn out or corrupt so that life may be rebuilt on new foundations. To the degree that I take part in the corruption of the world, I turn my instrument against myself. I write because I am poorly adjusted to reality; because the deep disillusionment within me has given rise to a need to re-create life, to replace it with a

214

more compassionate, tolerable reality. I carry within me a utopian person, a utopian world.

This destructive urge that moves me to write is tied to my need for hate, my need for vengeance. I write so as to avenge myself against reality and against myself; I write to give permanence to what hurts me and to what tempts me. I believe that deep wounds and harsh insults might someday release within me all the creative forces available to human expression, a belief that implies, after all, that I love the word passionately.

Now I would like to address these constructive and destructive forces with relation to my work. The day I finally sat down at my typewriter to write my first story, I knew from experience how hard it was for a woman to obtain her own room with a lock on the door, as well as those metaphorical five hundred pounds a year that assure her independence. I had gotten divorced and had suffered many changes because of love, or because of what I had then thought was love: the renouncing of my own intellectual and spiritual space for the sake of the relationship with the one I loved. What made me turn against myself was the determination to become the perfect wife. I wanted to be as they were telling me I should be, so I had ceased to exist; I had renounced my soul's private obligations. It has always seemed to me that living intensely was the most important of these obligations. I did not like the protected existence I had led until then in the sanctuary of my home, free from all danger but also from any responsibilities. I wanted to live, to enjoy firsthand knowledge, art, adventure, danger, without waiting for someone else to tell me about them. In fact, what I wanted was to dispel my fear of death. We all fear death, but I had a special terror of it, the terror of those who have not lived. Life tears us apart, making us become partners to its pleasures and terrors, yet in the end it consoles us; it teaches us to accept death as a necessary and natural end. But to see myself forced to face death without having known life—without passing through its apprenticeship—seemed to me unforgivable cruelty. I would tell myself that that was why children who die without having lived, without having to account for their own acts, all went to Limbo. I was convinced that Heaven was for the good, and Hell for the evil, for those men who had arduously earned either salvation or damnation. But in Limbo there were only women and children, unaware of how we had gotten there.

The day of my debut as a writer, I sat at my typewriter for a long time, mulling over these thoughts. Inevitably, writing my first story meant taking my first step toward Heaven or Hell, and that made me vacillate between a state of euphoria and a state of depression. It was as if I were about to be born, peering timidly through the doors of Limbo. If my voice rings false or my will fails me, I said to myself, all my sacrifices will have been in vain. I will have foolishly given up the protection that despite its disadvantages, at least allowed me to be a good wife and mother, and I will have justly fallen from the frying pan into the fire.

In those days, Virginia Woolf and Simone de Beauvoir were my mentors; I wanted them to show me how to write well, or at least how not to write poorly. I would read everything they had written like a person who takes several spoonfuls of a health potion nightly before retiring. The potion would prevent death from a host of plagues and ills that had killed off the majority of women writers before them, as well as some of their contemporaries. I must admit that those readings didn't do much to strengthen my as yet newborn and fragile identity as a writer. My hand's instinctive reflex was still to hold the frying pan patiently over the fire—not to blandish my pen aggressively through the flames—and Simone and Virginia, while recognizing the achievements that women writers had attained up to that time, criticized them quite severely. Simone was of the opinion that women too frequently insisted on themes traditionally considered feminine, the preoccupation with love, for example, or the denunciation of training and customs that had irreparably limited their existence. Justifiable though these themes were, to reduce oneself to them meant that the capacity for freedom had not been adequately internalized. "Art, literature, and philosophy," Simone would say to me, "are attempts to base the world on a new human freedom, the freedom of the individual creator, and to achieve this goal a woman must, above all, assume the status of a being who already has freedom."

In her opinion, a woman should be constructive in her literature, not of interior realities, but of exterior realities, principally of those of a historical and social nature. For Simone, the intuitive capacity, the contact with irrational forces, the capacity for emotion, were all important talents, but they were also of secondary importance. "The functioning of the world, the order of political and social events which determine the course of our lives, are in the hands of those who make their decisions in the light of knowledge and reason," Simone would say to me, "and not in the light of intuition and emotion," and it was with those themes that women should henceforth occupy themselves in their literature.

Virginia Woolf, for her part, was obsessed with the need for an objectivity and distance which, she thought, had seldom been found in the writings of women. Of the writers of the past, Virginia excluded only Jane Austen and Emily Brontë, because only they had managed to write, like Shakespeare, "with a mind incandescent, unimpeded." "It is deadly for a writer to think about his or her gender," Virginia would say to me, and "it is deadly for a woman to register a complaint, however mild, to advocate a cause, however justifiably"—deadly then, to speak consciously as a woman. In Virginia's opinion, the books of a woman writer who doesn't free herself from rage will contain distortions, deviations. She will write with anger instead of with sensitivity. She will speak of herself, instead of about her characters. At war with her fate, how can she avoid dying young, frustrated, always at odds with the world? Clearly, for Virginia, women's literature should never be destructive or irate, but rather harmonious and translucid as was her own.

I had, then, chosen my subject—nothing less than the world—as well as my style—nothing less than an absolutely neutral and serene language, which could let the truth of the material emerge, exactly as Simone and Virginia had advised. Now I had only to find my starting point, that most personal window, from among the thousands that Henry James says fiction possesses, through which I would gain access to my theme, the window to my story. I thought it best to select a historical anecdote, perhaps something related to how our Puerto Rican bourgeois culture changed from an agrarian one based on sugar cane and ruled by a rural oligarchy to an urban or industrial one ruled by a new professional class, an anecdote that would convey how this change brought about a shift in values at the turn of the century—the abandonment of the land and the replacement of a patriarchal code of behavior, based on exploitation but also on certain ethical principles and on Christian charity, with a new utilitarian code that came to us from the United States.

A story centered on this series of events seemed excellent to me in every way. There was no possibility whatever that I might be accused of useless constructions or destructions; there was nothing further from the boring feminine conflicts than that kind of plot. With the context of my plot finally chosen, I raised by hands to the typewriter, ready to begin writing. Under my fingers, ready to leap to the fore, trembled the twenty-six letters of the Latin alphabet, like the chords of a powerful instrument. An hour passed, two, then three, without a single idea crossing the frighteningly limpid horizon of my mind. There was so much information, so many writable events in that moment of our historical becoming, that I had not the faintest idea where to begin. Everything seemed worthy, not just of the clumsy and amateurish story I might write, but of a dozen novels yet to be written.

I decided to be patient and not to despair, to spend the whole night keeping vigil if necessary. Maturity is everything, I told myself, and this was, after all, my first story. If I concentrated hard enough, I would at last find the starting point of my story. It was dawn and a purple light washed over my study windows. Surrounded by full ashtrays and abandoned cups of cold coffee, I fell into a deep sleep, draped over my typewriter's silent keyboard.

Fortunately, I have since learned that the setbacks we must face don't matter, for life keeps right on living us. That night's defeat, after all, had nothing to do with my love for short stories. If I couldn't write stories I could at least listen to them, and in daily life I have always been an avid listener of stories. Verbal tales, the ones people tell me in the street, are the ones that always interest me the most, and I marvel at the fact that those who tell them tend to be unaware that what they are telling me is a story. Something like this took place a few days later, when I was invited to lunch at my aunt's house.

Sitting at the head of the table, dropping a slow spoonful of honey into her tea, my aunt began to tell a story while I listened. It had taken place at a sugarcane plantation some distance away, at the beginning of the century, she said, and its heroine was a distant cousin of hers who made dolls filled with honey. The strange woman had been the victim of her husband, a ne'er-do-well and a drunkard who had wasted away her fortune, kicked her out of the house, and taken up with another woman. My aunt's family, out of respect for the customs of the time, had offered her room and board, despite the fact that by that time the cane plantation on which they lived was on the verge of ruin. To reciprocate for their generosity she had dedicated herself to making honey-filled dolls for the girls in the family.

Soon after her arrival at the plantation, my aunt's cousin, who was still young and beautiful, had developed a strange ailment: her right leg began to swell with no apparent cause, and her relatives sent for the doctor from the nearby town so he could examine her. The doctor, an unscrupulous young man recently graduated from a university in the United States, made the young woman fall in love with him, then falsely diagnosed her ailment as being incurable. Applying plasters like a quack, he condemned her to live like an invalid in an armchair while he dispassionately relieved her of the little money the unfortunate woman had managed to save from her marriage. The doctor's behavior seemed reprehensible to me, of course, but what moved me most about the story were not his despicable acts but the absolute resignation with which, in the name of love, that woman had let herself be exploited for twenty years.

I am not going to repeat here the rest of the story my aunt told me that afternoon because it appears in "La muñeca menor," my first story. True, I didn't tell it with the words my aunt used, nor did I repeat her naive praises to a world fortunately gone by, a world in which day-laborers in the cane fields died of malnutrition while the daughters of plantation owners played with honey-filled dolls. But the story I listened to, in its broad outlines, fulfilled the requirements I had imposed on myself: it dealt with the ruin of one social class and its replacement by another, with the metamorphosis of a value system based on the concept of family into one based on profit and personal gain, a value system implanted among us by strangers from the United States.

The flame was lit. That very afternoon I locked myself in my study and didn't stop until the spark that danced before my eyes stopped right at the heart of what I wanted to say. With my story finished, I leaned back in my chair to read the whole thing, sure of having written a story with an objective theme, a story absolutely free of feminine conflicts, a story with transcendence. Then I realized that all my care had been in vain. That strange relative, victim of a love that subjected her twice to exploitation by her loved one, had appropriated my story; she reigned over it like a tragic, implacable vestal. My theme, while framed in the historical and sociopolitical context I had outlined, was still love, complaint, and—oh! I had to admit it—even vengeance. The image of that woman, hovering for years on end at the edge of the cane field with her broken heart, had touched me deeply. It was she who had finally opened the window for me, the window that had been so hermetically sealed, the window to my story.

I had betrayed Simone, writing once again about the interior reality of women; and I had betrayed Virginia, letting myself get carried away by my anger, by the fury the story produced in me. I confess that I was on the verge of throwing my story into the trash so as to rid myself of the evidence that, in the opinion of my mentors, identified me with all the women writers past and present who had tragically wasted themselves. Luckily I didn't do it; I kept it in a desk drawer to await better times, to await a day when I would perhaps arrive at a better understanding of myself.

Ten years have passed since I wrote "La muñeca menor," and I have written many stories since then; I think now I can objectively analyze the lessons I learned that day with more maturity. I feel less guilt toward Simone and Virginia because I have discovered that, when one tries to write a story (or a poem or novel), stopping to listen to advice, even from those masters whom one most admires, almost always has negative consequences. Today I know from experience that it is no use to write by setting out beforehand to construct exterior realities or to deal with universal and objective themes if one doesn't first create one's own interior reality. It is no use to try to write in a neutral, harmonious, distant way if one doesn't first have the courage to destroy one's own interior reality. When writing about her characters, a writer is always writing about herself, or about possible versions of herself because, as with all human beings, no virtue or vice is alien to her.

By identifying with the strange relative from "La muñeca menor" I had made possible both processes. On the one hand I had reconstructed, in her misfortune, my own amorous misfortune; and on the other hand, by realizing where her weaknesses and failings were—her passivity, her acceptance, her terrifying resignation—I had destroyed her in my name. Although I may also have saved her. In subsequent stories, my heroines have managed to be braver, freer, more energetic and positive, perhaps because they were born from the ashes of "La muñeca menor." Her betrayal was, in any case, what brought about my fall from the frying pan into the fire of literature.

II

How to Rescue Certain Things from the Fire

I have related how I came to write my first story, and now I would like to talk about some of the satisfactions I discover today in that task which at the beginning was so painful for me. Literature is a contradictory art, perhaps the most contradictory of all. On the one hand it is the result of an absolute surrender of energy, intelligence, but, above all, will, to the creative task. On the other hand, will has very little to do with it because the writer never chooses themes, the themes choose the writer. It is between these two poles that literary works flourish, and they generate the writer's satisfactions. In my case, these satisfactions are born of a desire to make myself useful and a desire for pleasure.

The desire to make myself useful is related to my attempt to substitute the utopian world I imagine for the one I must live in. It is a curious desire in that it is a posteriori; my wish to address the problems of women's condition and the other social and political realities which concern me is completely absent when I begin to write a story, despite the clarity with which I perceive its presence when it is finished. It is as impossible for me to intend to be useful to such and such a cause before beginning to write as it is for me to declare my adherence to such and such a religious, political, or social creed. But language as creator is like the powerful current of a river, whose lateral currents ensnare loyalties and convictions, and a writer finds himself or herself swept along by its truth.

My view of the world has inevitably much to do with the inequality that women still suffer from in our modern age. One of the problems that preoccupies me continues to be society's demonstrated inability to resolve effectively our dilemma, the obstacles that society continues to place before us in our struggle to realize ourselves in our private and public lives. I would like to touch briefly here, from among the enormous range of possible topics related to this theme, on the matter of sexually explicit language in women's literature.

Several months ago, I attended a banquet in commemoration of the centenary of Juan Ramón Jiménez. A renowned critic, grey-haired because of his age, approached me. Before a rather large group of people he began to talk to me about my books. Smiling maliciously and winking at me as if we were accomplices, he asked me in a titillating tone of voice charged with insinuation if it was true that I wrote pornographic stories and, if so, would I send them to him so he could read them. I confess that at that moment, perhaps due to my excessive respect for his grey hairs—a respect that seems naive to me in retrospect—I did not have the courage to respectfully call him an SOB, but the incident affected me deeply. I returned home depressed, afraid that the rumor had gotten around among illustrious critics that my stories were nothing more than a more or less artistic transcription of *The Story of O*.

Of course I didn't send my books to the egregious critic, but once the initial disagreeable impression had passed, I told myself that the matter of sexually explicit language in women's literature deserved to be studied more closely. Convinced that the old gentleman was just a specimen of an almost extinct species of openly sexist critics, I decided to forget the matter and turn his petty insult to my advantage and began to read everything that fell into my hands on the theme of obscenity in women's literature.

Today much of the criticism of women's literature is written by women. Their criticism focuses on the problem of women from various angles: Marxist, Freudian, radical feminist, and so on. Despite the diversity of their approaches, women critics—Sandra Gilbert and Susan Gubart in *The Madwoman in the Attic*, Ellen Moers in *Literary Women*, Patricia Meyer Spacks in *The Female Imagination*, Erica Jong in her many essays—all seemed to agree that violence, anger, and a disharmony with their situation had generated much of the energy that made women's narrative possible for several centuries. Beginning with the eighteenth-century Gothic novel, whose most important practitioner was Mrs. Radcliffe; through the Brontës' novels; Mary Shelley's *Frankenstein*; *The Mill on the Floss* by George Elliot; the novels of Jean Rhys, Edith Wharton, and even those of Virginia Woolf—for what is *Mrs. Dalloway* if not a sublimated, poetic, but nonetheless ironic and accusatory interpretation of the frivolous life of the social hostess?—women's narrative had been characterized by an often aggressive, denunciatory language. All had been irate and rebellious though some with perhaps more irony, cleverness, and wisdom than others.

One thing caught my attention about those critics, however: it was their absolute silence about the use of profanity in contemporary women's literature. Not one of them touched on the topic, despite the fact that the use of sexually proscribed language in women's literature seemed to me an inevitable result of a centuries-old current of violence. In 1933, after the prohibitions against *Ulysses* were lifted in the United States, the first women novelists to use profane language were Iris Murdoch, Doris Lessing, and Carson McCullers, all of whom for the first time gave a natural and uninhibited use to the verb "to fuck." Erica Jong had become famous precisely because of the aggressively immodest vocabulary found in her novels, but she never made mention of it in her well-researched and scholarly essays about contemporary women's literature.

It would not serve my purpose to go into depth on this subject, rife as it is with social and political implications. I touch on it merely to give an example of my wish to make myself useful as a writer, a wish that always becomes apparent to me only after the fact. When the distinguished critic approached me at the banquet and referred to my fame as a militant in pornographic literature, I had never asked myself what my purpose was in using sexually explicit language in my stories. When I realized that contemporary women critics were persistently avoiding the touchy subject, my purpose became clear to me. I had wanted to turn the sexually humiliating insult—a weapon society had wielded against us for centuries—against society's own outworn and unacceptable biases.

If profanity had traditionally been used to degrade and humiliate women, I said to myself, it should be doubly effective in redeeming them. If in my story "When Women Love Men" or in "From Your Side to Paradise," for example, profane language has made just one person feel moved when faced with the injustice implied in the sexual exploitation of women, it doesn't matter to me that I may be considered a pornographic writer. I'm content because I know I have been effective.

But my desire to be useful and my constructive and destructive urges are but two sides of a coin held together by a third need, the gleam of the coin's edge, my desire for pleasure. Writing is for me above all a physical knowledge, an irrefutable proof that my human form—individual and collective—exists. But writing is also an intellectual knowledge, the discovery of a form that precedes me. It is only through pleasure that we can encode the testimony of the particular in the experience of the general, as a record of our history and our time.

The fervid condition, in which the writer—woman or man—is absorbed by the pleasure of words, is never achieved on first attempt. The urge is there, but pleasure is skittish and eludes us, slipping through the interstices of words, closing up at the slightest touch like a sentient plant. At first the words seem cold and indifferent to the writer's needs, a situation that inevitably mires the writer in the blackest desperation. But by sculpting and shaping words, loving, and even mistreating them, the writer begins to feel them taking on warmth and movement; they begin to breathe and pulsate under the writer's fingers, until they appropriate her or his own desire. Then the words become tyrants, ruling each syllable, taking over thoughts, occupying every minute of the writer's day and night; they keep the writer from abandoning them until the form that she or he has awakened, the form they also intuit now, becomes flesh. The secret of physical knowledge of the text is found, finally, in the desire for pleasure, and it is that desire that ultimately makes it possible for the author to fulfill other desires: the desire to be effective, for example, or the desire to build or destroy the world.

The immediacy of text and body brings another, more intellectual kind of knowledge: a knowledge born of the incandescence that the desire of the text awakens in me. Any writer or artist, woman or man, has a sixth sense that indicates when the goal has been reached, when what she or he has been molding has acquired the definitive form it must have. Once that point has been reached, one extra word (a single note, a single line) will irreversibly extinguish that spark or state of grace brought about by the loving struggle between the writer and his or her work. That moment is always one of awe and reverence: Marguerite Yourcenar compares it to that mysterious moment when the baker knows it is time to stop kneading the dough; Virginia Woolf defines it as the instant in which she feels the blood flow from end to end through the body of her text. The satisfaction this knowledge gives me, when I finish writing a story, is the most worthwhile thing I have managed to save from the fire of literature.

III

HOW TO STOKE THE FIRE

I would now like to speak a bit about that mysterious combustible element that feeds all literature—imagination. This topic interests me because I often discover, among the general public, a curious skepticism toward the existence of the imagination and because I find that both laypeople and professionals in the literary community tend to overemphasize the biographical details of authors' lives. One of the questions most often asked of me, by strangers as well as friends, is how I was able to write about Isabel la Negra, a famous whore of Ponce, my hometown, without ever having met her. The question always surprises me because it bespeaks a fairly generalized difficulty in establishing boundaries between imagined reality and lived reality, or perhaps the difficulty lies only in understanding the intrinsic nature of literature. It would never have occurred to me to ask Mary Shelley, for example, if, on her walks along the bucolic paths surrounding Lake Geneva, she had ever run into a living-dead monster around ten feet tall. But perhaps this was only because when I first read *Frankenstein* I was only a child, and Mary Shelley had already been dead for well over a hundred years. At first I thought the naive question was understandable in Puerto Rico, among a public little accustomed to reading fiction, but when several critics asked me if I had personally met Isabel la Negra—a woman who had already been dead for several years—or whether I had ever visited her whore-house—a suggestion that would always make me blush violently—I knew that the difficulty in recognizing the existence of the imagination was more widespread than I had thought.

It had always seemed to me that contemporary criticism gave too much importance to the study of writers' lives, but that insistence on the unabashedly autobiographical nature of my stories confirmed my fears. The importance autobiographic studies have achieved today seems to be based on the premise that the lives of writers in some way make their works more easily understood, when in fact it is just the reverse. The writer's work, once completed, acquires absolute independence from its creator, and it is related to the writer only to the degree that it gives deeper meaning to her or his life or deprives it of meaning. But this type of literary exegesis, fairly common today in studies of male literature, is found even more often in studies of women's literature. The number of recently published volumes on the lives of the Brontës, or on the life of Virginia Woolf, for example, surely exceeds the number of novels they wrote. I have a sneaking suspicion that this interest in the biographical facts about women writers comes from the hidden belief that women have less imagination than men and that their works rely more heavily on the unscrupulous plundering of reality than do those by male writers.

There is a social reason for this difficulty in recognizing the existence of the imagination. The imagination is a playing with reality, an irrev-erence toward what exists, a willingness to dare to imagine a possible order of things better than the one we have. Without this playing, there would be no literature. Thus the imagination—like literature—is sub-versive. I agree with Octavio Paz that there is something terribly base in the modern mind's willing acceptance of all kinds of unworthy lies and unspeakable realities while it is unwilling to accept the existence of the fable. This is clear from the way literature is taught in our universities.

There is today, as there has always been, a principally analytical ap-proach to literature. Works are analyzed in dozens of ways: according to structuralist, sociological, stylistic, semiotic, and other methodologies. When the work has been thus analyzed, nothing is left of it except a cloud of disembodied sememes and morphemes. It is as if, in order to dignify the literary work, we must disembowel it like a watch we take apart to study its inner workings, when what really matters is not how it functions but how well it tells time. The teaching of literature in our society seems to be admissible only from the point of view of the critic: to be a specialist, one who disassembles literature, carries status and is remunerated. To be a writer, one who plays with the possibilities of change, however, is a subversive enterprise, which brings neither status nor remuneration. That is why our universities offer so few courses in creative writing and writers find themselves, in most cases, forced to earn their living in other professions, writing literally "for the love of art."

Learning to write (not to do literary criticism) is a magical undertaking, but it is also quite specific. Spells, too, have their formulas, and magicians measure very carefully the amount of charm they put into their caldron of words. The rules on how to write a story, a novel, or a poem are not secret. They are preserved in beakers for eternity by the critics, but they are worth nothing to the writer if she or he doesn't learn to use them.

The first lesson students of literature should learn is not only that imagination exists but that it is also the most powerful combustible element that feeds fiction. It is through the imagination that writers transform the raw material of their experience into the fabric of art.

IV

HOW TO SIMMER THE STEW OVER THE FIRE

I would now like to go straight to the theme that has been simmering at the bottom of my saucepan since the beginning of this essay. The theme is undoubtedly the source of heated debate today, which is why I had not yet dared place it before you at the table. When all is said and done, is there such a thing as women's writing? Does there exist a literature by women, radically different from that of men? Further, shall our writing be passionate and intuitive, based on sensations and sentiments—as Virginia wanted—or shall it be rational and analytical, inspired by historical, social, and political knowledge—as Simone wanted? Are we to be defenders of female values in the traditional sense of the term, cultivating a harmonious, poetic, pure literature, unconditionally realist and even obscene? In sum, shall we be Cordelias or Lady Macbeths? Dorotheas or Medeas?

Virginia Woolf said that a woman's writing was always "feminine," that it couldn't be otherwise, but that the difficulty lay in defining the term. Despite my disagreement with many of her theories, I find myself in complete agreement with her on this. I think women writers of today, before anything else, must write well, and this is achieved only by mastering the techniques of writing. A sonnet has only fourteen lines, a specific number of syllables, and a predetermined rhyme and meter, and is therefore a neutral form—neither female nor male—and a woman is as capable of writing a perfect sonnet as is a man. A perfect novel, as Rilke said, must be a sublime cathedral, constructed brick by brick, with infinite patience, and therefore it too lacks gender and may be written by a woman as well as by a man. Writing well involves a much more arduous struggle for women than for men, however: Flaubert rewrote the chapters of *Madame Bovary* seven times, but Virginia Woolf rewrote *The Waves* fourteen times, doubtless double the number of Flaubert's revisions because she was a woman and knew that the critics would be doubly hard on her.

Perhaps what I'm saying might smack of heresy, a kind of evil brew, but this essay deals, after all, with the writer's kitchen. Despite my metamorphosis from a housewife into a writer, I often confuse writing and cooking, and I discover some surprising parallels between the two. I suspect there does not exist a women's way of writing different from that of men. To insist that it does exist would imply at the same time the existence of a female nature, different from the male, when it seems most logical to insist on their radically different *experiences*. The insistence on a female or a male nature would imply different capacities in women and men, insofar as the achievement of a work of art is concerned, when in fact the capacities of each sex are the same because they are, above all, basically human.

An immutable female nature, a female mind perpetually defined by its gender, would justify the existence of an unchanging female style characterized by specific and easily recognized traits of structure and language in past and present works. Notwithstanding the theories that abound today on the subject, I believe the existence of such traits is debatable. The novels of Jane Austen, for example, were rational, meticulously closed and lucid structures, diametrically opposed to the diabolical, mysterious, and passionate novels of her near contemporary, Emily Brontë. And the novels of both couldn't be more different from the open, fragmented, and psychologically subtle novels of such modern writers as Clarice Lispector or Elena Garro. Style varies profoundly not only from person to person but also from work to work.

Where I do believe women's literature is distinguishable from that of men is in the themes that obsess women. In the past, we women have had a limited access to the worlds of politics, science, or adventure, for example, although today this is changing. Our literature often finds itself determined by an immediate relationship to our bodies: it is we who carry children within us and give birth to them; it is we who nurture them and take charge of their survival. This biological fate curtails our mobility and creates very serious problems for us as we attempt to reconcile our emotional needs with our professional needs, but it also puts us in contact with the mysterious generative forces of life. That is why women's literature has, much more so than men's literature, concerned itself with interior experiences, experiences that have little to do with the historical, the social, or the political. Women's literature is also more subversive than men's because it delves into forbidden zones—areas bordering on the irrational, madness, love, and death—zones that our rational and utilitarian society makes it dangerous to recognize. These themes interest women because they are the patient, varied harvest of their experience, an experience that like that of men, may change, becoming richer and broader.

In summary, I suspect that the endless debate over whether there is or is not a specifically "feminine" literature is vain and insubstantial. What matters is not whether we should write with open structures or closed ones, with poetic language or obscene language, with our heads or with our hearts. The important thing is to apply that fundamental lesson taught to us by our mothers, who were the first to show us how to summon the spirit of the cooking stove. The secret of writing, like the secret of good cooking, has nothing to do with gender. It has to do with the skill with which we mix the ingredients over the fire.

GABRIEL GARCÍA MÁRQUEZ
[1928–]

BORN IN ARACATACA, Colombia—the inspiration for the fictional Macondo of his masterpiece *Cien años de soledad*, 1967 [*One Hundred Years of Solitude*, 1970]—García Márquez worked for more than a decade as a journalist in Latin America and Europe before becoming a novelist and short story writer. Had the Colombian dictator, Rojas Pinilla, not shut down the newspaper, *El Espectador*, García Márquez might not have turned to writing the prize-winning fiction that has won him more fame and fortune than any other Latin American author.

His first published works, the novellas *La hojarasca*, 1955 [translated as *Leaf Storm and Other Stories*, 1972] and *El colonel no tiene quien le escriba*, 1961 [*No One Writes to the Colonel*, 1968], were only translated after the stunning success of *Cien años de soledad*, a book that broke all sales records for publishing in Latin America—though it was written while the author was living on a shoestring in Mexico. García Márquez is recognized as a master storyteller of epic proportions—a latter-day Rabelais and Cervantes with a confessed admiration for Faulkner. Known as "Gabo" to his friends, he found the key to his magical-realist style in the protean qualities of Latin American history and mythology, as the accompanying essay relates.

Other translated works by García Márquez include *El otoño del patriarca*, 1975 [*The Autumn of the Patriarch*, 1976]; *Crónica de una muerte anunciada*, 1981 [*Chronicle of a Death Foretold*, 1982]; *Relato del náufrago*, 1970 [*The Story of a Shipwrecked Sailor,* 1986]; as well as various collections of short stories. His most recent novel is entitled *El amor en los tiempos del cólera*, 1985 ["Love in the Time of the Cholera"].

García Márquez's literary perception of Latin American reality is similar to that of Carpentier, whose concept of the "marvelous real" was also inspired by a fascination with his native Caribbean culture. As García Márquez once said in an interview in the *Paris Review*: "It always amuses me that the biggest praise for my work comes for the imagination while the truth is that there's not a single line in all my work that does not have a basis in reality. The problem is that Caribbean reality resembles the wildest imagination."

In 1982, García Márquez was awarded the Nobel Prize for Literature, the fourth Latin American author so honored, following Gabriela Mistral, Pablo Neruda, and Miguel Angel Asturias. The essay included here was his acceptance speech to the Swedish Academy which was later published in English in *The New York Times* on February 6, 1983.

The Solitude of Latin America

Gabriel García Márquez
Translated by Marina Castañeda

Antonio Pigafetta, a Florentine navigator who went with Magellan on the first voyage around the world, wrote, upon his passage through our southern lands of America, a strictly accurate account that nonetheless resembles a venture into fantasy.

In it he recorded that he had seen hogs with navels on their haunches, clawless birds whose hens laid eggs on the backs of their mates, and others still, resembling tongueless pelicans, with beaks like spoons. He wrote of having seen a misbegotten creature with the head and ears of a mule, a camel's body, the legs of a deer and the whinny of a horse. He described how the first native encountered in Patagonia was confronted with a mirror, whereupon that impassioned giant lost his senses to the terror of his own image.

This short and fascinating book, which even then contained the seeds of our present-day novels, is by no means the most staggering account of our reality in that age.

The Chroniclers of the Indies left us countless others. El Dorado, our so avidly sought and illusory land, appeared on numerous maps for many a long year, shifting its place and form to suit the fantasy of cartographers. In his search for the fountain of eternal youth, the mythical Alvar Núñez Cabeza de Vaca explored the north of Mexico for eight years, in a deluded expedition whose members devoured each other and only five of whom returned, of the 600 who had undertaken it. One of the many unfathomed mysteries of that age is that of the 11,000 mules, each loaded with 100 pounds of gold, that left Cuzco one day to pay the ransom of Atahualpa and never reached their destination. Subsequently, in colonial times, hens were sold in Cartegena de Indias that had been raised on alluvial land and whose gizzards contained tiny lumps of gold. One founder's lust for gold beset us until recently. As late as the last century, a German mission appointed to study the construction of an inter-oceanic railroad across the Isthmus of Panama concluded that the project was feasible on one condition: that the rails not be made of iron, which was scarce in the region, but of gold.

Our independence from Spanish domination did not put us beyond the reach of madness. General Antonio López de Santana, three times dictator of Mexico, held a magnificent funeral for the right leg he had lost in the so-called Pastry War. General Gabriel García Moreno ruled Ecuador for sixteen years as an absolute monarch; at his wake, the corpse was seated on the presidential chair, decked out in full-dress uniform and a protective layer of medals. General Maximiliano Hernández Martínez, the theosophical despot of El Salvador who had 30,000 peasants slaughtered in a savage massacre, invented a pendulum to detect poison in his food, and had street lamps draped in red paper to defeat an epidemic of scarlet fever. The statue to General Francisco Morazán erected in the main square of Tegucigalpa is actually one of Marshal Ney, purchased at a Paris warehouse of second-hand sculptures.

Eleven years ago, the Chilean Pablo Neruda, one of the outstanding poets of our time, enlightened this audience with his words. Since then, the Europeans of good will—and sometimes those of bad, as well—have been struck, with ever greater force, by the unearthly tidings of Latin America, that boundless realm of haunted men and historic women, whose unending obstinacy blurs into legend.

We have not had a moment's rest. A promethean president, entrenched in his burning palace, died fighting an entire army, alone; and two suspicious airplane accidents, yet to be explained, cut short the life of another great-hearted president and that of a democratic soldier who had revived the dignity of his people.

There have been 5 wars and 17 military coups; there emerged a diabolic dictator who is carrying out, in God's name, the first Latin American ethnocide of our time. In the meantime, 20 million Latin American children died before the age of one—more than have been born in Europe since 1970. Those missing because of repression number nearly 120,000, which is as if no one could account for all the inhabitants of Upsala. Numerous women arrested while pregnant have given birth in Argentine prisons, yet nobody knows the whereabouts and identity of their children, who were furtively adopted or sent to an orphanage by order of the military authorities. Because they tried to change this state of things, nearly 200,000 men and women have died throughout the continent, and over 100,000 have lost their lives in three small and ill-fated countries of Central America: Nicaragua, El Salvador, and Guatemala. If this had happened in the United States, the corresponding figure would be that of 1,600,000 violent deaths in four years.

One million people have fled Chile, a country with a tradition of hospitality—that is, 10 percent of its population. Uruguay, a tiny nation of two and a half million inhabitants, which considered itself the continent's most civilized country, has lost to exile one out of every five citizens. Since 1979, the civil war in El Salvador has produced almost one refugee every 20 minutes. The country that could be formed of all the exiles and forced emigrants of Latin America would have a population larger than that of Norway.

I dare to think that it is this outsized reality, and not just its literary expression, that has deserved the attention of the Swedish Academy of Letters. A reality not of paper, but one that lives within us and determines each instant of our countless daily deaths, and that nourishes a source of insatiable creativity, full of sorrow and beauty, of which this roving and nostalgic Colombian is but one cipher more, singled out by fortune. Poets and beggars, musicians and prophets, warriors and scoundrels, all creatures of that unbridled reality, we have had to ask but little of imagination, for our crucial problem has been a lack of conventional means to render our lives believable. This, my friends, is the crux of our solitude.

And if these difficulties, whose essence we share, hinder us, it is understandable that the rational talents on this side of the world, exalted in the contemplation of their own cultures, should have found themselves without a valid means to interpret us. It is only natural that they insist on measuring us with the yardstick that they use for themselves, forgetting that the ravages of life are not the same for all, and that the quest of our own identity is just as arduous and bloody for us as it was for them. The interpretation of our reality through patterns not our own serves only to make us ever more unknown, ever less free, ever more solitary.

Venerable Europe would perhaps be more perceptive if it tried to see us in its own past. If only it recalled that London took 300 years to build its first city wall, and 300 years more to acquire a bishop; that Rome labored in a gloom of uncertainty for 20 centuries, until an Etruscan king anchored it in history; and that the peaceful Swiss of today, who feast us with their mild cheeses and apathetic watches, bloodied Europe as soldiers of fortune as late as the sixteenth century. Even at the height of the Renaissance, 12,000 lansquenets in the pay of the imperial armies sacked and devastated Rome and put 8,000 of its inhabitants to the sword.

I do not mean to embody the illusions of Tonio Kröger, whose dreams of uniting a chaste north to a passionate south were exalted here 53 years ago by Thomas Mann. But I do believe that those clear-sighted Europeans who struggle, here as well, for a more just and humane homeland could help us far better if they reconsidered their way of seeing us. Solidarity with our dreams will not make us feel less alone, as long as it is not translated into concrete acts of legitimate support for all the peoples that assume the illusion of having a life of their own in the distribution of the world.

Latin America neither wants, nor has any reason, to be a pawn without a will of its own; nor is it merely wishful thinking that its quest for independence and originality should become a Western aspiration. However, the navigational advances that have narrowed such distances between our Americas and Europe seem, conversely, to have accentuated our cultural remoteness.

Why is the originality so readily granted us in literature so mistrustfully denied us in our different attempts at social change? Why think that the social justice sought by progressive Europeans for their own countries cannot also be a goal for Latin America, with different methods for dissimilar conditions? No: The immeasurable violence and pain of our history are the result of age-old inequities and untold bitterness, and not a conspiracy plotted 3,000 leagues from our homes. But many European leaders and thinkers have thought so, with the childishness of old-timers who have forgotten the fruitful excesses of their youth as if it were impossible to find another destiny than to live at the mercy of the two great masters of the world. This, my friends, is the very scale of our solitude.

In spite of this, to oppression, plundering and abandonment, we respond with life. Neither floods nor plagues, nor famines nor cataclysms, nor even the eternal wars of century upon century have been able to subdue the persistent advantage of life over death. An advantage that grows and quickens: Every year, there are 74 million more births than deaths, a sufficient number of new lives to multiply, each year, the population of New York sevenfold. Most of these births occur in the countries of least resources—including, of course, those of Latin America. Conversely, the most prosperous countries have succeeded in accumulating powers of destruction such as to annihilate, a hundred times over, not only all the human beings that have existed to this day but also the totality of all living beings that have ever drawn breath on this planet of misfortune.

On a day like today, my master William Faulkner said, "I decline to accept the end of man." I would feel unworthy of standing in this place that was his if I were not fully aware that the colossal tragedy he refused to recognize 32 years ago is now, for the first time since the beginning of humanity, nothing more than a simple scientific possibility. Faced with this awesome reality that must have seemed a mere utopia through all of human time, we, the inventors of tales, who will believe anything, feel entitled to believe that it is not yet too late to engage in the creation of the opposite utopia. A new and sweeping utopia of life, where no one will be able to decide for others how they die, where love will prove true and happiness be possible, and where the races condemned to one hundred years of solitude will have, at last and forever, a second opportunity on earth.

ISABEL ALLENDE
[1942–]

IN ISABEL ALLENDE'S own words,

I was born in Lima just by chance, since I am Chilean. I had a
father like the Count of Satigny, who disappeared without leaving
behind memories. My mother was the guiding light of my
childhood. Perhaps that's why I find it easier to write about
women. She gave me a notebook so I could write about my life at
an age when other girls were playing with dolls, and she also gave
me a wall of my room so I could paint on it the things I wanted.
Later on, she married an extraordinary man who, in time, came to
be the best of fathers to me. He was a diplomat and we traveled
all around the world, which left me for always with a horror of
trips . . .

Isabel Allende, the niece of Chile's president, Salvador Allende,
began work as a journalist at the age of seventeen. After her uncle's
government was overthrown by the military with the aid of the
CIA, she left Chile; she now makes her home in Venezuela with
her husband and two children.

The essay that follows, translated for this collection, was originally a speech given at Montclair State College and published in
the journal *Discurso Literario* in 1984. It chronicles the spiritual
and historical background of her first, now famous, novel *La casa
de los espíritus*, 1982 [*The House of the Spirits*, 1985]. A publishing
success reminiscent of García Márquez's *One Hundred Years of Solitude*—to which it could be compared, indeed, as a family epic
told from a female perspective—Allende's novel is infused with

235

her own experience without being autobiographical per se. The same might be said of her second novel, *De amor y de sombra*, 1984 [*Of Love and Shadows*, 1987], which deals with the atrocities committed by The Pinochet government and the suffering of innocent victims. Her third novel, *Eva Luna*, 1987, is the story of a woman in the Caribbean in the 1950s and 1960s.

In Allende's novels, the heroic characters are females; as she herself has said,

> In Latin America we've seen that in situations of extreme danger the people who take the greatest risks are often women. They are capable of total selflessness, total courage. When the time comes to make a revolution, women are there in the front lines . . . but afterwards, of course, when it is time to divide up the power, they are inevitably left on the sidelines.

In the future—thanks to novels like Allende's and women like the mothers of the Plaza de Mayo—the concept of heroism in Latin America will no longer be defined solely by men.

THE SPIRITS WERE WILLING

Isabel Allende
Translated by Jo Anne Engelbert

Someone has said that books have a guardian angel. The angel doesn't always do its job, but sometimes it does it so well that the book avoids every obstacle in its travels through the world. Born under a lucky star, *The House of the Spirits* has had this good fortune. It was published a few months ago in Spain, and one day I saw it for the first time on a bookstore counter. It was hiding in a corner, timid and frightened. I was afraid for my novel; I knew that it no longer belonged to me, that now there would be nothing I could do to help it. There it was, exposed to the gaze of persons who might judge it without mercy. But as time passed I began to relax, and I now believe that there really is a spirit that watches over it.

They say that every first novel is autobiographical, especially those written by women. That's not exactly true in my case, because I'm not in the book. I am not any of the characters, but I don't deny that I have known many of them and that their passions and suffering have touched me very deeply. Some of the anecdotes in its pages are things I heard from the lips of my mother or grandfather or read in my grandmother's notebooks of daily life. I could say that all together these stories comprise a kind of family tradition.

People often ask me why I chose to write something as vast and complex as a family saga. The answer is that you don't choose a theme, the theme chooses you. Somehow this story began to grow inside me. I carried it in my heart for many years and fed it tirelessly. For this reason, in order to talk about the history of this book I'm going to have to talk about the history of my family and of my country.

My father disappeared from my life when I was very young, leaving so few traces that even if I ransack my memory I cannot even remember his face. My mother went back to her parents' home to live, along with

her children, an event that had a critical impact on my childhood. I think
that this explains why the book gives such importance to the big house
full of spirits where the Truebas live out their lives. Our house was neither so large nor so luxurious as theirs; it didn't have a garden with
singing fountains and Olympian statues nor an army of servants like the
house built by the protagonist of my novel. But to me it seemed enormous, shadowy and drafty, and I was sure it was haunted by ghosts who
rattled the wardrobes and slipped in and out of mirrors. There I grew
up, absorbed in solitary games and excursions to the basement, a mysterious treasure trove of useless junk. That place was my Pandora's box.
It contained the past, captured in old love letters, travel diaries, and
portraits of bishops, maidens, and explorers with one foot on a Bengal
tiger. My fantasy was fed by all that and also by my books. My legacy
from my father was a great stack of books: novels by Jack London, Jules
Verne, Emilio Salgari; the Tesoro de Juventud collection; classic works
of all times. Two eccentric bachelor uncles lived with us, one of whom
had more books than you could even count. No one guided or censored
my reading, so at ten I wept over the tragedies of Shakespeare, tried to
decipher Freud, and became thoroughly confused reading the Marquis
de Sade. I envied people who could write and I filled countless notebooks
with my impossible tales. Thirty years later, when I could not postpone
any longer the decision to write a novel, I took some dreams, experiences,
and fears from that era of my life and concocted a group of characters
who go up in a balloon, invent fabulous machines, travel to India in
search of the 999 names of God, get lost in the jungle looking for treasure, or die in a tenement disguised as the Queen of Austria.

My grandfather was a patriarch, a strong, intolerant man shaken by
uncontrollable passions who died when he was nearly a hundred in full
possession of his faculties, frail and lame, but without a wrinkle, with a
lion's mane of hair and the piercing blue eyes of a boy of twenty. He
was a marvelous character for a book.

I had a magnificent grandmother who died too young but whose
spirit still accompanies me. She was a luminous, transparent being whom
I named Clara in my book. There was little to invent; I took her from
reality, although I did exaggerate a bit. Perhaps it was true that my
grandmother could move a three-legged table with the power of her
thought, that she helped the poor, sheltered poets, and floated above
human frailties with an eternal smile and the most limpid eyes in the
world.

I grew up in my grandparents' house and lived there until my mother
married a diplomat, and we set out on a trip that took us to several
countries. Later I was separated from her for long periods. I am bound

to my mother by a profound, happy, and absolute affection. We developed the habit of writing letters to each other every day, which trained me to be an alert observer of the world, to be aware of people's emotions, to decipher symbols and discover keys, perceiving the hidden side of reality. It also gave me the discipline of writing, something I am grateful for every time I sit down before a blank sheet of paper.

I have no vocation for the nomadic life. All the years I spent wandering about the world I kept yearning to recover the stability of my childhood. That's why when I finally returned to Chile, I took a very deep breath of the air of my country, looked up at its snow-covered peaks and set about putting down roots. "This is where I'm staying; I will live here and be buried here one day under a bough of jasmine," I said.

How can I put into words what I felt then or what I feel even now every time I pronounce the name of Chile? Pablo Neruda described the country as a long petal . . . He wrote poems to its forests, lakes, and volcanoes and to the *cordillera* that accompanies it from north to south, crumbling into a dust of islands before it disappears in the ice of the Antarctic. It is a region of balmy valleys where grapes grow, of lunar deserts, copper mountains, and steep cliffs battered by the waves of the Pacific Ocean. A mad geography inhabited by a hospitable people steeped in poverty and suffering. The Chileans are accustomed to calamity; they live on the crest of catastrophe, waiting for the next earthquake, flood, drought, or political upheaval. It is a land to love with passion and serve with joy, a land to tell about in books.

When I wrote *The House of the Spirits*, my ambition was to paint in broad strokes a fresco of all Latin America. I am aware of the many differences that exist among our countries, but I think that the similarities and affinities are even more striking. I am convinced that a single inexorable and prodigious destiny unites us all and that one day there will be a single country stretching from the Rio Grande to the frozen reaches of the South Pole. In honor of that Utopia I did not place the Trueba family in a particular country. The Truebas could exist anywhere on the continent, and their turbulent passions, their collective, shared suffering, their victories, and their defeats would be identical. This is so much the case that I receive letters from all over South America from readers who tell me that they have identified with the characters and their story, which is similar to their own.

I returned to Chile when I was fifteen years old, beginning to sense my womanhood and to dream about love. I wrote some dreadful poetry, belligerent prose, and the inevitable letters to my mother. I think I already knew then that I wanted to be a writer. Agatha Christie was my ideal because she produced many novels and still had free time for afternoon tea and rose gardening in the English countryside. I had no idea how arduous writing was.

One night at a party a boy asked me to dance. It was the chance I had been waiting for, and after arguing with him for four years, I succeeded in convincing him that we should get married. We have been together ever since. I knew love, had children, and a very full era of my life began. It was the age of the twist, the miniskirt, hippies and marijuana, women's liberation, and the political and social struggles of my country. I worked as a journalist, which is a kind of oblique way of approaching literature. An older colleague gave me my first lessons. He gave me a bit of advice I still heed because it never fails: "Tell the truth. Only the truth can touch your reader's heart."

My life was passionate and active. I was always at the forefront of whatever was going on; nevertheless, a part of me was always looking toward the past.

And so, loving and working and storing up history, I went on living my life. Until one fateful Tuesday—September 11, 1973—when I woke up to a new reality. That day a military coup overthrew the constitutional government of Chile, putting an end to a history of democratic rule that distinguished my country on a continent plagued by dictatorships. What happened in Chile has special characteristics, but it is not very different from what happens in other tyrannies. Outside the country one merely has to read the international press to get information. Inside the dictatorship, on the other hand, information is censored, because control of public opinion is critical to the regime. Thanks to my job as a journalist I knew exactly what was happening in my country; I experienced it firsthand, and those cadavers, torture victims, widows, and orphans left an indelible impression in my memory. The last chapters of *The House of the Spirits* recount those events. I based that account on what I saw with my own eyes and on the direct testimony of people who lived through the brutal experience of the repression.

For those who know and love liberty, it is impossible to adapt to a dictatorship. Many people around us were imprisoned, killed, or forced underground. The time came for me to leave, despite the promise I had made myself to live and die in that country. My husband spread out a map of the world, and we looked for a place to go. That's how we arrived in Venezuela, a hot, green country that took us in together with many other refugees and emigrants. We arrived with our children, with very little luggage, and with sorrow in our hearts.

The enchanted trunks of my uncles were left behind along with the books in the basement, the family portraits, the letters and travel diaries, my grandmother's three-legged table, and her crown of orange blossoms.

My grandfather stayed behind also, sitting in a rocking chair, infinitely desolate and lonely, with a hundred years of memories and no one to share them with.

Far away from my country, I felt like a tree whose roots have been cut off and which is doomed to shrivel and die. Nostalgia, rage, and sadness kept me paralyzed for a long time. Nevertheless, little by little, my emotions were purified, I acquired a larger perspective of reality, and the new country won my heart. Then I felt the necessity of recovering the benevolent spirits of the past, the landscape of my country, the people I knew, the streets of my city, the winter rains, and the peaches of summer. In January of 1981 I woke up one morning with an extravagant idea. I had the thought that if I set down in writing what I wanted to rescue from oblivion, I could reconstruct that lost world, revive the dead, unite the dispersed, capture the memories forever, and make them mine. Then no one could ever take them away from me. I bought paper and sat down to write a story.

When I put the first piece of paper in the typewriter, I didn't know how to accomplish any of this, but I knew I should write. I remembered the words of my old reporter friend: tell the truth. I wanted to talk about the suffering of my people and of other people of that tormented continent so that the truth would touch the hearts of my readers.

It's true that I wrote for the pleasure of writing and because I had waited almost forty years for that moment. But I also did it because of an unavoidable obligation.

Latin America is living a tragic moment of its history. In our lands fifty percent of the population is illiterate and yet writers are listened to and respected. They are the voice of those who suffer in silence. All of us who write and who are fortunate enough to be published should assume the commitment of serving the cause of freedom and justice. We have a mission to accomplish at the front lines. We must combat the obscurantism that oppresses several countries of our continent through the force of our words, with reason, and with hope. We must put letters at the service of mankind. The worst enemy of barbarism is ideas.

I wanted what I wrote to be part of the effort to make our reality known. I wrote the story of a family like mine and like many others, of a country like mine and like any other in Latin America. The story spans almost a century; I started at the beginning, with the things most remote in time, things that had been told to me—transformed, of course, by magic, emotion, and the vagaries of memory. Once I had begun, I kept recounting things in order and without pause straight to the end.

I did not know that this book would change my life. I lacked experience in literature, and I did not imagine the impact that the written word could have.

While the ink was still fresh I had the opportunity to prove that there were spirits that protected my book: its acceptance in Spain was immediate and very warm. That surprised me, since I had thought that Europe was very far from Latin America. Later I learned that this is not so and that human beings are alike all over the world. All that is needed is a little effort for us to understand and accept one another.

Because of the strict censorship in Chile in 1982, I thought that *The House of the Spirits* would not be read in my country. I resigned myself to the idea that my compatriots would never read that story, one that speaks of injustice, fear, and suffering, but also of solidarity, courage, and love as they exist in a country like ours.

I never could have imagined what happened.

The book entered Chile like a pirate, hidden in the suitcases of brave travelers or sent by mail without covers and cut into two or three pieces so that it could not be identified. The few copies that entered the country this way multiplied by magic art. People who had a copy made photocopies that passed from hand to hand. There were lists of people who wanted to read it, and I am told that there were even a few people who rented out copies of it.

Months later the government decided that it was necessary to lift the censorship of books in order to improve its image, although there is still a suffocating muzzle over the mouths of those using the mass media. Along with other books that had been banned for the previous ten years, *The House of the Spirits* entered Chile legally and has headed sales lists since last August.

It moves me to think that the book is being translated into so many languages and that the spirits that live in its pages will be in contact with readers in remote places, offering them a breath of this fabulous continent where I was born. It's hard for me to imagine the Truebas speaking English, German, or Norwegian, but I trust they will get along just fine.

I wrote out of urgent need, as I said in the first line of the book: "to reclaim the past and overcome my terrors." I did not suspect that the benevolent spirit of my grandmother would protect those pages, watching over them in their travels through the world. I like to think about this, to imagine, for example, that Clara, clear, clairvoyant Clara, is here at my side at this moment, wearing her white gown and her woolen gloves, with her false teeth hanging on a chain around her neck.

Yes . . . It's a beautiful idea that books have their own guardian spirit.

MANUEL SCORZA
[1928–1983]

ON NOVEMBER 27, 1983, an Avianca 747 crashed on final approach to Madrid's Barajas Airport killing 183 people, among them the Peruvian writer Manuel Scorza. On the same plane were two other well-known Latin American authors, Angel Rama and Marta Traba, who also lost their lives; all three were on their way to Bogotá to attend a literary conference.

The enormous tragedy of this disaster is underscored by the ironic nature of the essay presented here, which Scorza sent to his literary agent only hours before boarding the jumbo jet in Paris. It was published in Madrid's *El País* on December 5, 1983.

Manuel Scorza was born in Lima, Peru, and was known as a poet, a novelist, and a political activist. As a young man, he became involved in the cause of the Peruvian peasant farmers who sought to reclaim land seized by *latifundistas* and international corporations. Aware that official historians had not recorded the story of these struggles, Scorza created a literary mural of the peasant revolution in his works. His relationship with leftist leaders and his support of Marxist causes brought him over the years a reputation that he pokes fun at in this essay.

Among his early books of poetry are *Los adioses*, 1959 ["The Farewells"]; *Requiem para un gentilhombre*, 1962 ["Requiem for a Gentleman"]; and *El vals de los reptiles*, 1970 ["The Waltz of the Reptiles"]; along with an anthology he edited entitled *Poesía contemporánea del Perú*, 1963. Five of his novels, inspired by the peasant uprising of 1961, are grouped under the title *La querra silenciosa* ["The Silent War"] and they include *Redoble por Rancas*,

1970 [*Drums for Rancas*, 1977]; *Historia de Grambombo el invisible*, 1972 ["Story of Grambombo the Invisible"]; *Cantar de Agapito Robles* ["Song of Agapito Robles"]; *El jinete insomne* ["The Sleepless Rider"]; and *La tumba del relámpago*, 1979 ["The Tomb of the Lightning Bolt"]. Scorza's work has been translated into more than twenty languages.

Manuel Scorza made his home in Paris where he moved after becoming disillusioned with the politics of his native country.

LIST OF ERRATA

Manuel Scorza
Translated by Doris Meyer

Sometimes I think that, in the book of my life, no one was interested in the errata. The department of correction that watches over the book of existence belonging to each one of us took care to point out the disasters in capital letters. And from time to time, in small letters, the delights. But no one bothered to annotate what I considered the most important part of my life: the list of errata. Although now that I think about it, if they had been pointed out in time, I wouldn't be who I am and I wouldn't be writing this article saying that a man who is closer to death than to birth feels an urgency to be happy.

I haven't read my folder at the Peruvian intelligence service, nor the one I probably have at the CIA, but I am sure that they too must be plagued with misunderstandings. No doubt the first one is that I was a conspirator from the time I was eighteen. That was how old I was when the police broke into my house, terrifying some kids who had come to trade marbles with my cousin, and took me away, revolvers in hand. Many of our neighbors in that neighborhood, where a disgrace meant saving face, used to boast about having relatives in jail; some bragged about it and others even invented prison stories. Such a halo of honor wasn't attainable for my family. Injustices of destiny: we didn't have to fantasize. Many of my uncles and cousins had been and were in jail, and for good reason. But my father, always a modest man and not wanting to be considered pretentious, never allowed us to brag. And so we reluctantly endured the boasting of the Toros, or of peg-leg García, or of Willy Zárate, who pretended to have friends or family in the slammer. When the police led me away, under the guise of being a highly dangerous conspirator, the neighbors understood that their days of boasting had come to an end.

But it was an erratum. I wasn't a conspirator or a revolutionary or anything. I was simply in love with Nora Seoane, and I had dedicated a love poem to her which was published in *La Tribuna* on the day that the Aprista party overthrew Bustamante's government. But I was labeled an Aprista, and I stayed in jail, kicked, beaten, and insulted each time I tried to prove my innocence by reciting my poem. I took all this as a down payment on what was my due for the ignominy of being in love and being a writer.

In Mexico, Juanito Chang, Luis de la Puente, Gonzalo Rose, my brother Miguel, and I worked in a laundry. Hunger made us soap, scrub, and iron like dogs for fifteen days. When we went to collect our pay, the owner's boyfriend, an immigration inspector, asked to see our working papers. We didn't have any. We had violated three laws: working without a permit, believing that one could earn money by working, and trusting the proprietors of the Teissy laundry. We deserved their parting words: "Either leave without pay or get out of Mexico."

I was very friendly with Luis de la Puente, and we shared a room at a time when he was preparing his first guerrilla expedition to Peru, the one Gastañeta betrayed. I know that I appear in a photograph in the police files, classified as a dangerous subversive. But that was also an erratum. Luis and I were both asthmatic, and sometimes I suffered a lot from it. So he offered to let me stay in his room so that he could be there, ready to give me the shots I might urgently need for my sickness.

I met my next beloved erratum in Arbenz's Guatemala. Her heart was pure gold, and she gave me twenty-five dollars of her salary to help me get to Mexico; she was beautiful, she was ugly, she was fat, but she didn't seem to mind her body. She fell in love with an Argentine, also asthmatic, and in Mexico they met again: Hilda Gadea and Ernesto "Che" Guevara, who was getting ready to embark on history. But before that, they decided to get married. The poet Juan Gonzalo Rose was a witness at their wedding, and we other Peruvian poets said pretty things and recited love poems at the reception. Obviously, the CIA could only surmise that we constituted a terrorist conclave. But that was another erratum. I wasn't a guerrilla but a poet, a melancholy wanderer.

I returned to Peru. For some reason, I went to Huancayo. Oh, now I remember. Our movement needed to locate an important man who would take charge of its reconstruction. I didn't find him where I expected to, and I don't know why, but I decided to look for him at his brother's house. There he was, and he'd been drunk for fifteen days. A poet too, he was in love with a gorgeous Loretan sister. Desperately in love. Every Sunday he would wait for her at the door of the church, long before mass was over, and one of those Sundays, the girl came out just when he was wiping the sweat from his brow and holding his hat in the other hand. With the charming bad faith that characterizes adored women, she dropped some coins into his hat. Thus, with feminine grace, she branded him a beggar. He never recuperated from the disaster. I found him so distraught that he asked me to take his place at a meeting and later to lead the scheduled protest march. I complied. As always, the police barricaded the streets, attacked us, and dispersed us quickly. I—lyric poet, above all—took the vanguard of those who were escaping from the police, not knowing that one of their most common tactics is to wait for the crowds a few blocks down in order to surprise them and catch them between two ranges of fire. But that time it didn't work. A few streets away, the police appeared with their uniforms, their submachine guns, their bags of tear gas bombs; but we were advancing with such speed that we couldn't stop. There are certain fatal laws of mechanics. One of them says that a body that advances in space without encountering resistance can keep going until it reaches the limits of the universe. I didn't get that far. Despite all efforts, despite my desperate attempt, I couldn't stop myself. And, without meaning to, I fell and knocked down the surprised guards and a disconcerted officer, who imagined that such a charge could only mean the beginning of an insurrection. But it was just another erratum.

At movement headquarters, no one, absolutely no one, wanted to accept the true version of the events. My own boss got furious when he heard it. What was needed at all costs were heroes who could conquer the police. And there was no way to change this erratum.

I imagine that this must be the kind of history that many heroes can't reveal from atop their monuments. This article is also an error: I meant to write an article about a provocative text by Germán Poma de Ayala. But someone who doesn't want me to write those lines gave me a few imperialist bottles of Hungarian wine. How can you reread the *Nueva crónica* after the fifth glass?

ANTONIO SKÁRMETA
[1940–]

ANTONIO SKÁRMETA, BORN in Antofagasta, Chile, studied literature, philosophy, and theater directing at the University of Chile and Columbia University. Until the military coup of 1973, he lived in Chile working as a university professor, journalist, and translator of authors such as Melville, Golding, Mailer, and Kerouac. Since 1975 Skármeta has made his home in West Berlin, teaching drama and film.

His published works include five collections of short stories, three novels (all available in English translation), essays, and radio and screenplays, including his award-winning film *Ardiente paciencia* [*Burning Patience*, 1985], originally a 1983 novel based on the life of Pablo Neruda; it was shown on U.S. public television in 1986 in English translation. Of his works, the best known are the novels *Soñé que la nieve ardía*, 1975 [*I Dreamt the Snow was Burning*, 1985] and *La insurrección*, 1982 [*The Insurrection*, 1983].

Skármeta wrote the essay included in this collection in 1978. In the following statement, written to the editor in 1986, he explains the circumstances and motives behind it:

Angel Rama had organized a colloquium at the Wilson Center in Washington to discuss issues of the new Latin American narrative, and he asked me to write "a personal testimony." This is why the text is a mixture of observations and personal recollections of my beginnings as a writer. It was intended to be subjective. In these pages I described a developing *tendency* in Latin American prose and confirmed by subsequent works; but—in that same rich expressive prose universe—there are many valuable works not definable by the characteristics I mention. I point this out, knowing the categorizing habits of certain academic and journalistic circles to take as *law* what was only put forth as an observation. These pages were published in four or five Latin American magazines, and each one changed the title to its liking, forgetting the intimate and wary one it originally carried: *In the end, the writer's life is the nearest thing he can seize hold of.*

In 1978, the situation in Argentina, Uruguay, and Chile was desolate. By 1986, Uruguay and Argentina had already achieved democracy after the failure of their military governments. In Chile today the opposition to Pinochet has won great spaces for freedom. In all three countries—where circumstances permitted—the writers who stayed in their oppressed homelands managed to create valuable works. They remained independent of the military regimes, and in Chile today, even amidst harsh repression, they are expressing themselves critically.

This version—slightly abbreviated with the author's permission—was published in *Nueva Sociedad* (Costa Rica) and translated for this collection.

A GENERATION ON THE MOVE

Antonio Skármeta
Translated by Lori M. Carlson

My generation of writers is related to the new Latin American narrative, but within a context that makes us sympathetic to some of its aspects and causes us to emphasize others, thereby influencing a change of attitude toward literary creation.

Those of us born around 1940 were the first Latin American writers to confront on a large scale the eloquence of mass communication. Movies in cinerama and technicolor precision immersed us in a new sensuality of the image. Within the distribution monopoly of North American films, fissures opened to admit European cinema, offering a more refined elaboration of the human condition, and, more important for writers, original concepts of montage.

The spectacular advancement in transportation stripped overseas journeys of their epic grandeur and relegated to the past farewell rites that used to be lavished on travelers. For weeks travelers were showered with an affection paralleling that of reverential mourning, then walked to the door and rendered soaked-handkerchief good-byes, which left lovers disconsolate and encouraged false oaths of tenderness, resulting in complications worthy of a comedy of entanglements brought on by distance and the perfect indolence of the mails. Now telecommunication links individuals with rare efficiency and urgency: epistolary tortures are avoided by the use of digital telephones that establish communication with the most distantly located friend, out-of-the-way lover, or unattainable boss, so excuses can be invented for not returning to work on the appointed day. The music industry has made the universe of sound intimately perceptible, surpassing forever the monophonic screech of the Gardelian needle. High fidelity and stereophonic equipment enthusiastically spread not only the gospel of rock music—which to this day is the ash cross on the foreheads of my generation of writers—but they

250

also enliven the expressive possibilities of folksongs, which hitherto had been relegated to the guitar's narrow, clichéd waist. Folk music can be embellished with a fantasy and understanding akin to that of a jazz combo improvising on a traditional theme. Television brings contemporary history to our bedroom, bothering our silent walls of meditation and reflection with the irresistible dizziness of its images and familiarizing us with unforgettable faces from Vietnam to Peor es nada (a small village in northern Chile). Industrial mass production and the open consumer market make owning a car no longer a privilege of the rich and, thus, we travel the world more quickly, more intensely, and less profoundly.

Mobility increased our sensual horizons and pierced the darkness of intimate obsessions. From an early age our heroes moved on wheels. In Chile we were the pioneers of the motorscooter—the Lambretta or Vespa—travelers of the highway heading for the ocean or the mountains, accompanied by girls with long hair blowing in the breeze and arms wrapped around our, then, slim waists. Our generation was the first to benefit from the Pill, simply by placing a couple of bills on a local drugstore counter. The Pill has displaced both illegal abortion and pharmaceutical preventatives which apart from their dubious efficacy, required such manipulation that, at the moment of our deepest feelings, we missed the pleasant moisture that typifies the tropics as much as the higher dignity that our love's intensity deserved. Sexuality and its exercise will be remembered as my generation's anthem: having done away with the causes for trauma, we have submitted to an unrestrained exploration of eroticism. Finally, sex has been deprived of its tragicomedic platitudes. The "surrender"—permit me this nostalgic homage to erotic archaeology—assumes no more commitment than the act. Forget obsessive ecclesiastical literature, the trauma of the adolescent who looks through peepholes at amorous couples nourished on the deepfelt pages written by writers educated in Catholic schools. Now we have delicious promiscuity, the product of an increasingly free and easy world. The collective intimacy of the hippy 1960s qualitatively and quantitatively changed our existence. By the same token, pot—in Chile the San Felipe kind is best—popularized surrealist imagery which had previously been reserved for eponymous bards. In lesser proportions, "Lucy-in-the-Sky-with-Diamonds" caused forgotten experiences to jump to our astonished consciousnesses, revealing films we didn't know had been filmed in our minds and creating various kinds of anxiety. It made us think about atavistic fixations, not in the jungle or in the monastery, but at the neighborhood fair with the kids on the block and with Beatles records; it plugged us into the world in a radically unconventional way. Portable tape recorders with built-in microphones and cassettes replaced magnetic bands, denying the journalist and James Bond the exclusivity of recording someone's voice. This development favored the rendering of colloquial turns of phrase, the investigation of street slang, and testimonial literature.

Technology's presence is a major theme in several works by young writers. And to put an end to this list, the photocopier permits us to reproduce the written page. It's possible not only to protect our fingers from a scandalous carbon but also to obtain neat copies of pages that editors have just finished reading and that judges have finished evaluating. I think that only since the invention of the copy machine have judges of literary contests become interested in reading, and it has considerably improved their judgment. Before the copier's accessibility, adjudicators dealt with an ensemble of marks, and prizes were awarded according to speculation about the contents instead of appreciation for the words of a work of literature.

THE DISCOVERY OF LATIN AMERICA

The development of events was even more interesting on the sociopolitical level: the progressive democratization of education generalized the use of reason among students of the middle and working classes. Labor organizations overcame repressive laws. Through reform measures, an effort was made to postpone revolution (many Latin American novels, short stories, and plays have treated this theme from the bourgeois point of view). There were liberation movements in the Third World, Che died in Bolivia (his portrait hung in every teenager's bedroom across the continent), socialist countries lent their power and influence, Cuba carried forth its revolutionary program drawing the world's attention to Latin America (and its literature), our continent questioned its image as a passive provider of raw materials for industrial nations, and above all, this questioning served to detonate young peoples' consciousness of reality, teaching them to see Latin America and not just stubborn national borders. It was a time for hope, for activism. We no longer lived our everyday life in a reiterated, skeptical, and sleepy landscape that typified the middle class, but as history, tension, and future.

Some writers turned up their noses at this precocious confusion and concentrated on the intimacies of their psyches and families. But our generation participated fully in society, and in numerous cases it did so in the more explicit form of ideological militancy. Under these circumstances, an interest grew in learning about Latin American literature. In addition, the *Casa de las Américas* in Cuba, with its yearly literature prize and its publications, was responsible for much of the new communication. Winning the prize didn't mean one's books would be stocked in bookstores throughout Latin America—because the commercial blockade made these small details its business too—but it did permit the prize-winning book to reach the hands of interested critics, journalists, writers, and professors. Thousands of books flew through the mails constituting a kind of clandestine map of the continent's new narrative and poetry, which began to establish names and styles.

This is the context within which my generation would read, write, and act in different stages. But now I must stress that our connection to the earlier stage of Latin American narrative—coinciding with Cuba's revolutionary success and with the publication of Vargas Llosa's *La ciudad y los perros* [The Time of the Hero], preceded by the clamorous publicity of the Seix-Barral prize and the Hopscotchization of the universe by the publishing house of Sudamericana—was practically non-existent. When those works arrived—and others by writers of various ages under the sonorous Boom effect—we had already advanced in a direction that, in some cases, was related to their work and in others deviated from it. But in the beginning, our treatment of literature, with respect to narrative, took a very non–Latin American route. In fact, we fled in another direction. Attracted to the richness of the aforementioned context, we found no interpretation of our uneasiness from chronically hoarse literature professors with their yellowed *segundo sombras*, jungled *vorágines* and *doña bárbaras*, fainted *amelias*, and gutted *echeverrías*—polarizations consigned even today to civilization and barbarism, culture and nature—punctilious regionalists who, for twenty pages, footsied around a tomato without eating it. Everything said, moreover, in a tone existing only in those dusty manors of college books with their proper archival odor and words dressed up like operatic tenors. The pompous metaphors, the exaggerated anguish, the trauma or the delights of adultery, the spleen, impossible loves, the forlorn pathos or cynical paternalism in describing the proletariat made us benevolently smile and prudently yawn. We didn't read literature in those days in a studious manner; neither did we read it as *fiction*. We read it for its distillation of experience, its signs of life, fantasies that swept away the prejudice and convention poisoning the young life of our metropolis. Years later, our polished instincts and our experience in the *sui generis* job of professor would lead us to perceive the merits of those works we belittled. The fact is that, for us, they offered no bridge to our story: that of boys living in cities scarcely described in literature up to that time.

This is where our literature starts out: the Latin American city—no longer the village, the pampa, the jungle, or the province—a chaotic, turbulent, contradictory place plagued by low lifes, by masses of poor who have left the rural areas to find work. The city full of people who hunger for life, love, adventure, and a chance to change the world, to

make a utopia. We felt more comfortable with Camus' existential literature than we did with Mallea's Argentine novels. The serene and dramatic language of *L'Etranger*, monastical in comparison to the empty
exuberance of local texts, opened our eyes to a way of saying *natural*.
The explosive combination of religious visions and adventures, which
Kerouac breathlessly narrated, alerted us to the possibilities of a prose
that would generate life and more life in its communicative fever. And
speaking of "breathless" words, Godard, whose ready camera provided
breathing, insolent film, interpreted our cheerful imaginings of the middle-class prison. The imaginative composition of images, a mixture of
audacity and creative triviality, turned out to be an interesting propo-
sition for structuring our texts. The impudence of Lazlo Kovacs (the
Belmondo character)—the self-irony and inclemency with which he observed his own life—seemed to capture the "mood" of our own plans
for living. One single line by Camus, "Youth is the physical terror of
death to the animal that loves the sun" was a center tackle capable of
running through all the asphyxiating zones of old rambling houses abundant in our literature. So, from existentialism we not only gleaned the
anguish but also the affirmation of life facing its limitations. Sisyphus.
The texts we thought of as contemporary were written—even though
critically—in cities that exercised their massive influence through a massive communications network extending from Europe to Latin America.
It is fitting to mention here that, contrary to the cackling of the most
schematic leftists in each of our countries, the fascination for the "alien-
ating" offer of imperialism didn't align young artists with the reaction-
aries or neutralize them. Quite the contrary. In Chile, the generation of
younger artists actively supported the progressive movements that culminated in Allende's election. This is our generation's trait in Chile: distrust for everything that might hinder spontaneity. When one enters political life, one does so totally, without reservation or taboo. This also
explains the creation of various parties of young leftists and the read-
justment of the most traditional groups to the new attitude of the young.
A big leap from the 1950s when even the student who studied in Paris
or New York was placed in parentheses by the Marxists. Several of them
would later die defending democracy in the face of Fascist rifles.

PROSE AND POETRY

North American literature, with its rhythms and lyrics of rock music and
its various offshoots, its trenchant imagery in film and intensive focus
on daily life, began to feed our prose. In these expressions, we found
words that were as right in their context as trains on a track, oranges on

a tree, cars on a street. There was no intention in them to rise to dignified, ornamental, or alchemic levels. Colloquialisms were absorbed without hesitation. And this attitude toward language brought with it something more important: the acceptance of daily events as a point of departure for fantasy. Literature turned away from the meticulous reproduction of the naturalists (so unnatural), the flaccid creolist picturesqueness, the psychological treatises explaining personal behavior. Popular slang became the stepping stone for poetic exploration. We teenagers of the street were as immersed in pop music as the heroes of the movies we loved were in soundtrack; were attracted to mass events such as sports (which we didn't think of as a vulgarity), dance, political action; were fascinated with the tactile possibilities of helping to plant democracy; were smitten by television images; were made worldly by travel; and found in colloquial language the appropriate tool to sculpt reality. With a language open to the streets, the literary act was becoming democratized. Our language grew amidst the perspectives of a society pressured toward progress by its most oppressed, and it treated the country like a family. The harmonic growth of all these factors, between 1970 and 1973, is recorded by the national publishing house Quimantú. Before its establishment, a national writer who was able to sell three thousand copies of his novel was considered fortunate. During Salvador Allende's government, the printing runs of Chilean and foreign authors reached fifty thousand copies.

A decade earlier, the situation was practically sordid. Latin American reality was swept out of sight by information sources. The sale of pioneering books was limited to the erudite. We didn't even know what was happening on our own continent. To the few writers conferences came young writers from Peru, Argentina, and Bolivia carrying overnight bags and their first published books—printed on brown wrapping paper and published by martyr presses—whose errata usually exceeded the text. Only during these gatherings did we put ourselves to the test with readings and discussions about similar experiences. Otherwise the only way for a Mexican writer to find out what a Chilean writer was doing would be through private correspondence. Our publishing houses didn't benefit from middle-class investments and they lacked sufficient faith and audacity to approach the larger markets. Except for the literature of Argentina and Mexico—also insular in its local market—fiction usually remained unpublished. A writer who espoused the many renovating facets of Chilean prose, such as Carlos Droguett, lived ignored by national critics for years, accumulating many unpublished manuscripts in his desk drawers. Only in the 1960s did he attract attention in Chile, and thanks to "Eloy," an award for his book in Barcelona. In effect, Europe has created a public awareness of Latin American writing. It's not at all a trivial fact that Carpentier, Asturias, Vargas Llosa, García Márquez, and so many others began their careers there, where the publishing industry was most expedient and professional in attending to their talent. These same names would later raise the fallen finances of the Latin American houses, which only published essays and academic texts, skeptical and whiny in their attitude toward creative possibilities.

Another factor would influence our attitude toward literature: the intuition that lyric rather than narrative recourses were better suited to our expressive intentions. I believe this is a common denominator among narrators who characterize the sixties and those who announce the seventies. Angel Rama pointed out that a decisive element in the formation of the new narrative was the fusion in the twenties and thirties of the great American lyric writers and narrators of the vanguard. At that time, under the influence of Vicente Huidobro, López Velarde, César Vallejo, and later Borges and Neruda, an autonomous, poetic, liberated language, absolutely specific to literature, was employed in narrative writing. This language eluded considerations of logic and lexicography to create, instead, a syntax of tension in which the most secret and insinuating values of words would come to the surface. Now it seems a proven fact that the programmatic elevation of this freedom is a factor in the success of today's narrative—from its metaphysical raptures to its playful abuses.

The ground in Chile was fertile for the development of this tendency. Many poets form an obligatory reference on our expressive horizon, but Neruda is the dominating figure. From his most complicated works in *Residencia en la tierra* to the transparent rusticality of his odes or the amorous sonnets and the epic *Canto general* he points us toward the concept of creative work as a sociobiological growth. His is a model of markedly historical and participatory poetry. Neruda's unbridled enthusiasm for his surroundings and for his people inspires him to sing not only their traditions, their courageous groping for a better world, their jobs and faces, but also leads him to the celebration of an onion or a liver. From Whitman he learned the lesson that all is tellable, all is singable. The world is infinitely expressable for the rhapsodist who, in a poet's guise, travels with and among mortals. Later, Parra's antipoetry provoked an ironic variation of attitude toward poetry; through his terse work using the commonplace he created a dramatic, playfully prosaic voice, which strove to reorder the world and articulate it from the "average man's" point of view.

With those two poets and that style, we started the most stimulating dialogue. From there, more than from anywhere else, we arrived at a poetic colloquialism during the years in which we began to read the new Latin American novelists. When they came forth triumphant, brilliant, and marketable, some would follow in their direction. Others would affirm their own originality, within the context already described, trying to cultivate a personal style.

A BANAL TIME

A quick observation concerning Cortázar, Carpentier, Donoso, García Márquez, and Droguett might touch upon the differences between their generation and ours. A novel as exciting as *Rayuela*, which discusses the themes of rationality/magic, schematization/complexity, linear narration/ multiple narration, formal discourse/deconstructed discourse, transcendence/trivialization (pardon this salad of dichotomies, Don Julio), is a touchstone, I think, for a momentary definition of terms. The dramatic and engaging search for transcendence in Cortázar's writing, based on irony and a simultaneous "unreading" of the text through its reading, becomes in younger writers an unproblematic acceptance of simple, everyday existence as a self-sufficient source of life and inspiration. It doesn't matter how experimental the structure or language. Reality ends, in the final analysis, at the tip of our noses.

I believe that our generation is characterized by complete coexistence with reality and by a refusal to disintegrate reality in order to reformulate it with a surreal meaning. This occurs via infrarealism, pop art, active contact with Latin American political reality, and the universalization of village life through mass communication. In this sense, our primordial attitude is nontranscendent. For example, making absolute an allegorical system where the grotesque degrades reality, as in Donoso, would never occur to us, nor would the underscoring of history as in the mythic hyperbole of García Márquez, nor the refounding of Latin American literature as in the "magical realism" of Carpentier. To the contrary, while they distance themselves in order to see, we get closer to daily life with a greater intensity.

Their protagonists are exceptional beings who feed on incontrollable obsessions. The intensity of Johnny or Oliveira places each on the periphery of history. The Aurelianos, José Arcadios, and Ursulas are beings trapped in great and surprising events that unfold in an expanded time which, in turn, determines their unusual actions.

The grotesque reality that Donoso creates conforms to an autonomous world frenetically alien to what we normally see from day to day. It is the exceptional, the strange or outrageous, the mythical or the historic distorted by abundant fantasy that defines the attitudes and techniques of these writers, whether it be through the gracefulness of García Márquez, the telling irony of Cortázar or the gripping pathos of Droguett when he urges on his child with dog paws. Rulfo—perhaps the author with the most influence on the colloquial work of young writers, the first great Latin American known to us in the fifties—also projects this attitude, but in a dramatically different way. The superreality encountered by his wandering characters seems more like an infrareality as demeaning as that of everyday existence. The terrible emptiness found in the tension between the one and the other, described with humorous popular imagery, has the rare quality of impressing us as drama, not just as a startling display of imagination. In any case, what these works have in common is their intentional grounding in abnormality, their questioning or interpretation of reality from a distance, and their global reference to reality through parable and myth. In the best sense of the word, it is a *pretentious* literature, and fortunately, its achievements are equal to the intensity of its efforts.

Younger narrative prose, despite the stridency of its complex verbal apparatus, is unpretentious in practice, anticultural in orientation (that is, for culture with a small "c"), and sensitive to everyday life. Its heroes are passersby recruited from the Latin American city rather than privileged gazers of the commonplace around them. Even though it shares with the preceding literary generation a powerful conception of language as a spectacle that should stand out for its signifying function, its speech corresponds to a chaotic and segmental treatment of reality without trying to represent all of it. I am thinking of works by José Agustín, Gustavo Sainz, Aguilar Mora, Luis Rafael Sánchez, Manuel Puig, Reinaldo Arenas, Gudiño Kieffer, Miguel Barnet, Oscar Collazos, Sergio Ramírez, Osvaldo Soriano, Manlio Argueta, Luis Britto García, Cristina Peri Rossi, Alfredo Bryce, Ariel Dorfman, Ivan Egüer, Mempo Giardinelli, Poli Délano, Eduardo Galeano, Ana Lydia Vega, Elena Poniatowska, Luisa Valenzuela—to name only a few among the most internationally known.

Inebriation provoked by the lyric explosion of colloquial language (before in Rulfo, in perfect equilibrium) leads young narrators, especially Mexican writers, to sanctify the jargon of their age. Vocabulary is charged with a slang that is the standard by which a generation studies itself. From their wealthy ghetto—cars, Acapulco, boutiques, Europe, bars, hotels, rock music—they scornfully look out at the adult world. Adults speak pompously, but they cynically and skillfully manage society to suit themselves. If there is something that youth learned from them, it is the strategy of cynicism. Voluntarily marginated from adult life and disaffected by the middle class, they use irony to describe it; it doesn't occur to them that it's susceptible to change. Rather than prove and unveil a society's mediocrity and scandal, as Carlos Fuentes has done in his urban novels, this young clan of writers chooses to squeeze out the nectar of their time. The gamut of characters that traverse their pages lack special relevance. Frequently resembling the "nowhere man" of the Beatles "thinking nothing about nobody," they tend toward triviality. Their texts live not so much by the slim dimension of their adventures or the interest of their heroes as by the exciting attraction of a literature of a heretofore unknown urban group with its relaxed language that rejoices in itself. These works abound in a naturalness that was lacking before and that years later would be expressed in a peculiar rhetoric: allusions and reflections about film, radio, television, quotes from rock ballads or advertising jingles, a text weaned from everything that conventional society deemed proper. Sexual play is the most popular sport and the most expedient human interaction. And so they pass their days, entertained in their hormonal games, without worrying much, taking into account their respective countries' inactivity, pulling the dead weight of a middle-class society that sickens them and makes everything meaningless. The intensity, the flavor of life is the discotheque. And a good number of these cosmopolitan works aspire to being as rhythmic, ephemeral, and compulsive as the records of the day.

As the new writing made itself known in this process—which could be characterized as infrareal in theme and characterization, pop in its attitude, and realist-lyric in its language—from Europe via the *nouveau roman* (and the massive critical apparatus that accompanied it) came a current that distrusts narrative possibilities, repudiates anecdotes as trivia, freezes emotion, and makes a protagonist of the remaining text itself. This aseptic approximation to narrative art emphasized the colloquial language that some Latin American writers were already developing in an autochthonous way, and it became the password for an even more radical experimentation, supported now by the prestige of semiotics, renovated structuralism, and the "agony" of writing. This tendency took hold in Argentina more than in other countries, and, fueled by its believers, who were usually narrators as well as critics, it achieved a certain ephemeral, yet not insignificant importance.

EXPRESSION AND POLITICS

At this juncture emphasis should be given to the importance of a writer's context in understanding the way his work is received. The obvious difference one notes in the use of different expressive devices obliges one to be attentive to the unique aspects of writing in each country. This isn't dependent on national idiosyncrasies but on the decisive influence that dissimilar historic climates have on us. Thus, it is very different to be a young writer in Mexico where the rhythm of change and perspectives has been mitigated by an institutionalized revolution, than in Cuba where the Marxist revolution has upset old structures in a radical way, or in Chile where one lives convulsed in the explicit alternatives that the 1960s and 1970s offered: revolution or reform or fascism. It could be said somewhat superficially that in those societies where progressive forces are not strong enough to threaten the status quo and involve the populace, the writer—unless he has a very developed political conscience—resorts to the solitary job of placing reality, solitary skepticism, and the celebration of marginal heroes in parentheses. Or he simply makes literature from literature.

I would like now to refer specifically to Chile and succumb to the abusive first person to tell about the "effect that the new novel had on my work and its characteristics."

In 1963, after a decade of overly explicit failures, I decided that the errors of a story called "La cenicienta en San Francisco" weren't so obvious, and I was inspired to prepare a collection of my short stories. I had already formulated the basis of my esthetics. Coinciding with the sensibility of those days and with the attitude that the new novel would have, it seemed to me that society was surrounded by a thick rhetorical language through which was imposed upon it the bourgeois vision of existence and community. Insensitive in those years to the gestative movement of political reform, which was very treacherous and costly for anyone who wasn't involved with it, I began a violent search for the most basic human elements and narcissistic impulses within me. The awful routine of a young society, prematurely conventionalized and bureaucratized, encouraged me to cultivate the most natural forces of my temperament. It seemed frightful to have lost the sense to perceive existence as something replete with mystery, futurity, and sensuality. In this mercantilist scheme of things, the ability to be surprised, to appreciate the very act of breathing, to fantasize uncensored conduct, and be troubled, awed, and perplexed was too rare. Poetic thought and anarchic adventure attracted me. Challenging an entrenched literature that moved hopelessly within this social framework, my work sprang to existence in the most ingenuous, free-spirited, and spontaneous way, as a celebration of life. Of the I—moved by the immense and inexplicable animal fact of existing among other men, and thank God, women. My style and attitude was defined by rapture. All of the sensual and cultural aspects of the world incited me to think, to feel, to fantasize.

LYRICISM AND MORE LYRICISM

And here my basic temperament is linked with another, which I have already mentioned as common to the new narrative: lyricism. The feeling of amazement inspired me to read other writers who were amazed. Not only was I surprised again at the diverse ways in which the enterprise of living (delirium, anguish, love, despair, happiness) culminated in their works, but also at the vigorous styles used to express these major emotions.

Another aspect of the new narrative that seems, to me, to be generalized: those works didn't claim to be true or false, neither ontological nor mythical models, but poetic exercises. Out of skepticism toward democracy, not only did I smile at Borges' idea that philosophy was a branch of fantastic literature, I agreed with emphatic gusto! This way of thinking led to antidogmatism: each one of us got by as best he could and told his story. Literature was an act of coexistence with the world and not an interpretive lesson about it. The "truths" discovered along the way were radically provisional, however enthusiastically proclaimed. This relativistic attitude, which respected a problematic reality and rejected conventional genres and schema for approaching it, was another point in common with the expressive devices of the new novel. In order to be faithful to its origins, it multiplied its narrative points of view, allowed protagonists to be more than psychologically pedestrian, and broke the spatial–temporal coordinates with the poetic certainty that each moment is pregnant with history and potency. It reduced the importance of logic in order to concentrate on the color and emotion of events. On all accounts, it was neither a thesis nor a moral message. Just poetry.

The institutions of lyricism and its painstaking work with language fared better with the richness of the world and our experience in it. This was the key to the luminous simplicity of the lyric poets in the south of Chile, in the pointed prose of antipoetry, in the epic gushing of the followers of Saint John Perse or Whitman. The use of lyric devices liberated the act of storytelling from structural responsibilities with its action-plot-characters complex.

With this basic attitude—generationally and progressively alert to the simple conduct of people who organized themselves to overcome the injustices of the system—my literature was a result of a tension that still feeds my prose: on the one hand, unleashed emotion, experimentation, breathless excess in order to render the weight, color, and emotion of an object or a person; and on the other hand, a profound respect, love, and interest for everyday appearances, for the sweet trivia of the street, for the people and their stories, for the youth sectors of the middle class— to which I belong—and for the concrete vitality of proletariat. So, it's not strange that from my first book, *El entusiasmo* [*Enthusiasm*], to my novel *Soñé que la nieve ardía* [*I Dreamt the Snow was Burning*], my rebellious expression has encompassed experimentation and reality in its most urgent contingency. . . . But I always made sure that reality itself would determine the narrative center of gravity.

This criterion had seduced me ever since my first stories. It seemed that I had to activate prose in a way that would seduce the reader and distract him from thinking of the time being robbed from him, time better used in other ways. I conceived of the act of literature as the following scene: I knock, open the door, leave the story in the reader's hands, turn around and leave, returning only to spy through a crack at the final effect. Cortázar, in his interesting essay, "Some Aspects of the Short Story," explained his technique. The story would have to win by a knockout. If I had to define my intentions in boxing terms, too, I'd have to say that I aspire to a draw or even a loss like the Chilean soccer team—but honorably. The knack: with common language and familiar situations, place the reader in a type of "story." Once this is achieved with the greatest economy possible, the aesthetic aim is to develop the story as a search for itself in which both my reader and I have the sensation of not knowing where we're going. In this respect, not much usually happens in them. More than by an accumulation of facts, the stories are characterized by a massive scrutinizing of each instant, relentlessly urging it to "let loose" its "Truth. . . ." The preoccupation with images—a sacred criterion—should be at the service of an event's truth and not merely ornamental. This is the key difference between a narrator who is nourished by lyricism and a poet who bows to prose. Therefore, my stories, which stem from daily life, take off from it, fly at various altitudes to see it better and to communicate its emotion, and humbly return to their point of departure with humor, pain, irony, and sadness, according to how they've fared in their travels. They are—to parody myself before somebody else does—airplane stories: they take off, fly, and land.

Permanent and Fleeting Experiences

The ideal effect of my narrative could perhaps be summarized thus: the reader and I share a fleeting experience in an ephemeral, accelerated, and sadly violent world. In this brief moment, the whole phenomenon of literature is available to me.

This is my world, my attitude, my concept of creation and its eventual achievement. This was also the sphere of my innocence. Now I want to express this information from the point of view of a writer who abandoned his country five years ago—due to conditions imposed on Chile by the military government of Pinochet—and headed for countries that still had the will to exist in the contemporary world, not like my country, studying cave-dwelling ancestors.

I indulge in this marginal note because a part of the literary production of at least three Latin American countries has been generated for some years now in exile; such is the case for Argentina, Chile, and Uruguay. I want to explain how the institutional break in Chile affects our profession as writers in such a radical way that it leads us to reformulate ourselves as individuals and as artists.

To talk, to communicate, is an historical phenomenon, a way people can understand themselves, a cultural tradition. For writers, professionally imbued with the universe of language, a violent alteration of context reveals that the identity of its speech is not only rendered in local slang, but in the collective way society has of conceiving existence, cradled in tradition and language, which in turn determines the true quality of its imagery.

I make this observation because until September 1973, the date of the coup overthrowing Allende, I lived in a country in which the exercise of free speech suffered no limits. Freedom was a given. Something so natural that it was a birthright, as normal as breathing or using our hands. Its presence was so transparent that, more than a privilege won in history, it seemed a gift of nature. This explicit reality determined the way society saw itself and conditioned the interrelation between societal levels. Language was buttressed by something that guaranteed the exercise of democracy and is understood in every culture: the security of life. In a lawful state, laws assure and regulate public life, but they also provide for something much more elemental: the protection of survival. Biological life is guaranteed by those who govern on behalf of those they represent. In Chile, the offensive triumph of the military essentially alters this second natural state, which is the culture of a country—that is to say, its identity. Once arbitrary violence assaults legitimate power, death and repression become a constant on society's horizon. To live and survive are one and the same. A generalized feeling of the fragility of existence takes over and strongly affects our trust of one another. Insecurity and suspicion are determining criteria for survival: a girlfriend disappears, a friend is assassinated, the newspaper is shut down, books are burned, officials and poets are buried under bayonets, fathers stay unemployed, brothers go into exile. Daily life in its entirety is dynamited by uncertainty. Seen in literary terms: it is unread and unspoken. This culture can no longer be one of innocence: It must forever deal with risk and the enemies of humanity. This is a geographical, biological, and metaphysical upheaval. Existence assumes a frightful character. Everything that once was known is now questionable.

The consolation of survival in exile cannot mitigate the amputation from the climate and cultural identity of one's country. Far from allowing oneself to be fooled by the sparkles of cosmopolitanism, the abrupt act of exile shows the author how attached he is to his country and how this country is the natural territory for his work. Now one can see in a film, a book, a painting, or a song that the inchoate quality in each—that is, the composition of its parts that conjures up and epiphanizes the unnamed—provides the richest significance. In a torrential or stingy narrator, in one who is conventional or gutsy, the element that makes a book more than a group of beautiful pages, gives it influence, and mobilizes life—if only by way of consciousness and not in praxis—is that it refers back to the world of its origin. Exile reveals to me the small transcendence of a book, which is a *sui generis* sign that demands from its context the activation of its meaning. Out of its context, it presents an incomplete world, and that unfinished-ness, however brilliant it is, is the *entire* book. What before would have been enough for me no longer suffices, after the trauma my country has experienced.

A book read in the country of its origin, in the tradition where it burst forth with new life, is a ceremony of cultural identity where our faces, failures, streets, deaths, and hopes appear in the prestige of the written word and where our verbal winks and ticks define the truth of the text, its degree of sobriety or irony. In this way, the vocation of writing is a call to rescue or recover the country. A book read by the people whom it describes is a community act. Identity is confirmed, the aspiration of dreams and ideals is consciously maintained, and the greatness of daily acts under risk is valued. Through a book one can imagine better and understand not only the difficult reality of a fabled world but also the difficult reality in which the book is read.

Many of the Latin American artists of the 1970s cannot give their works to spectators and readers among whom they would grow and become emotion, conscience, and dialogue. The condition of exile will mark their work. Their artistry will have to survive with the wound of absence and postpone the meeting with their compatriots until the history that prevents it can be honorably modified. It would be very strange if these compatriots weren't present in their works. The way I see it—now that Latin America is struggling between humanity and barbarism with penetrating lucidity—it is inevitable that the youngest writers are going to become more and more responsive to the continent's convulsions and changes. This is the material that will form their lives. And after all, his own life is the nearest thing a writer can seize hold of.

LYGIA FAGUNDES TELLES
[1923–]

LYGIA FAGUNDES TELLES was born in São Paulo, Brazil, and educated there and in Rio de Janeiro. She was still in her teens when she published her first collection of short stories, *Poroẽs e sobrados*, 1938 ["Above and Below Stairs"], which attracted the attention of several influential critics. A second book, *Praia viva*, 1944 ["Living Beach"], was published while she was in law school, and she soon decided to abandon the legal profession and devote herself to creative writing. A period of intense literary activity followed, and in the late 1940s, Fagundes Telles began to contribute to a number of important newspapers and journals, including *Letras e Artes*.

Her individual prose style began to crystallize in the stories of *O cacto vermelho*, 1949 ["The Red Cactus"]; from the 1950s onward she traveled widely and took part in literary congresses at home and abroad. Novels such as *Ciranda de pedra*, 1954 [translated as *The Marble Dance*, 1986]; *Verão no aquário*, 1961 ["Summer in the Aquarium"]; and *As meninas*, 1973 [*The Girl in the Photograph*, 1982], and collections of short stories such as *Historias do desencontro*, 1958 ["Stories of Missed Encounters"]; *Antes do baile verde*, 1970 ["Before the Green Dance"]; *Seminário dos ratos*, 1977 [*Tigrela and Other Stories*, 1986]; and *Filhos pródigos*, 1978 ["Prodigal Sons"] have made her one of Brazil's most popular and commercially successful women writers, as well as the recipient of most of its major literary prizes.

Among her preferred themes is the conflict experienced by females between society's expectations and a personal need for self-fulfillment. In a book of notes entitled *Disciplina do amor*, 1980 ["Discipline of Love"], Fagundes Telles testifies to the prejudice women have had to contend with in the literary world:

> A literary critic of the nineteenth century, irritated with the work of a poetess who dared to suggest political desires in her poems, wrote "It is distressing when one hears the delicate voice of a lady advocating revolution. As for myself, I would always desire that the poetess be in colloquy with the flowers, with springtime, with God." Rummaging in old files in the (vain) attempt to organize them, I ran into the clipping of a short review published in 1944. It deals with a little book of stories I published when I was in law school: "This young woman has pages that, in spite of being well-penned, would have been better had they come from a man's hand."

Lygia Fagundes Telles was recently elected to the Brazilian Academy of Letters. The essay included here was especially written and translated for this collection.

THE TRUTH OF INVENTION

Lygia Fagundes Telles
Translated by Giovanni Pontiero

I began to write as soon as I learned how to write—at the age of seven or eight perhaps? And if I speak of that wild, impetuous period of my life, it is because I attach enormous importance to the territory of child-hood which I trod barefooted, listening to the stories of other children. They were terrifying stories (because fear was an essential ingredient) about skulls that spoke in low-pitched voices, about beheaded mules, galloping women who had slept with the priest and given birth to normal children until their seventh, which inevitably turned out to be a werewolf. I would listen. But the night when I, too, began to invent stories, I discovered that as I was telling them, my fears gradually subsided. It was no longer I who trembled but my audience as they sat huddled on the stone steps at the entrance to my house. This discovery made me feel strong and powerful. I found it truly amazing that by transferring my fear to others (that fear that handicaps and shames me), I was able to free myself. I spread my wings with confidence. I felt secure. And so I communicated my fears to my playmates. And everything else. But it was still too soon to speak of a transference or catharsis. In that golden age, it was merely instinct leading me along the path of innocent, creative happiness.

The more successful of my stories were repeated because children adore repetition: a weakness shared by children and old people. But such was my excitement that I finished up fusing episodes, interchanging the names of my characters, and altering the beginning of the story. Or its ending. "But it didn't end like that!" some more attentive listener would protest, for my audience always consisted of the same playmates. The solution was to write down the stories as soon as I was able to write, on the back pages of my school notebooks, in bold, round handwriting and with a colored illustration at the top of each page. I started to unfold (or weave) my stories, setting down the main plot without forgetting the embellishments. Heavens! the impact made by that detail about threads of red wool caught between the gaps in the woodcutter's teeth: when he smiled, his terrified wife recognized the threads from the red smock that had swathed her little son who had been devoured in his cradle by a black mastiff on the last night of the full moon.

How I longed to write down these fantasies so as to ensure their permanence. How I longed to store up words the way I stored fireflies in a soap box—only to release them almost immediately; but for those few seconds it was nice to imagine them there in the box under my control, a hidden green light within my reach. Just as within my reach there were pomegranates and mangoes which were also gathered when green and stored in a hiding place unknown to everyone except me, an unused kiln at the bottom of the back garden: in the deep grotto of bricks and ashes, the fruits matured in silence. In darkness. There was born the age-long instinct to endure by means of the written word—a challenge to death. An obsession with the infinite in our finite state: for to endure is the main preoccupation of every creative writer.

My birth sign is that of Aries (nineteenth of April) which is the dwelling place of the planet Mars. The color of Aries is red, but I also wager on green. My standard (were I to possess such a thing) would be partly green and partly red, the colors of hope and passion but not without a tinge of wrath, for I am a Third World writer. Without wishing to sound pessimistic, it is worth bearing in mind that forty percent of the Brazilian population lives in a state of abject misery. Without forgetting the high percentage of illiterates, who do not live in a state of misery but who simply cannot read nor write. Greater still is the number of people who can read but who are not in the habit of opening a book. Or if they are, they prefer the rubbish imported from the United States which floods the Brazilian market by means of the media. Despite everything, I still wager on green like my father, who was addicted to gambling and tried his luck at cards. Or, to be more precise, at roulette. I gamble with words. I gamble without partners or onlookers and I play a somewhat difficult game. Have I lost?

"Tomorrow we win," my father would say, feeling his pockets, which a short time before had been bulging with chips and were now empty. I feel my pockets, which are bulging with words: *Les jeux sont faits!* cautions the pale man with the face of destiny. Not yet, I reply, and I carry on with my quest which is a joyous quest because I am fulfilling my vocation, which is also my passion. The rewards? Now then, what are the rewards? We Brazilian writers are not even read in Latin America. Who knows about us in Venezuela? In Chile? In Colombia? I recently attended a congress of contemporary Latin American writers in Cali, having been invited to speak about the role of women in Brazilian literature. And I ended up explaining to an audience of Latin American writers what language we speak and how we live—describing our customs and traditions to fellow writers from neighboring countries who only have the vaguest ideas about Brazil which have been distorted by folklore.

Gerald and Sara Murphy, a dramatic and at the same time lively couple, who formed part of the Scott Fitzgerald group in the twenties, wrote a book of memoirs: *Living Well is the Best Revenge*! In view of our present situation, we Brazilian writers could say something similar. Yes, we attract all too few readers and are ignored both at home and abroad. Censored. So what? It does not matter: our revenge is to write.

For we do write well, although few people seem to be aware of the fact. And we have a sense of humor. I honestly believe that Brazil is the best-humored nation in the world: humor masks our despair. "And what about humor?" the poet inquires. In humor there is salvation. In humor and in God who tortures us and goads us into keeping our balance on the high trapeze.

I am a writer and a woman—a profession and a condition which are both difficult to sustain, especially when I recall how my environment (namely, the Brazilian mentality) hampered my development as a professional writer. I was timid by nature and the deeply rooted prejudices against women writers caused me endless anguish and frustration. Liberation has eventually come with the extraordinary changes that have taken place in Brazil since my own adolescence. The real moment of progress came in the aftermath of the excitement that ripped the country when the military dictator Getúlio Vargas committed suicide in August 1954.

I was brought up and educated in São Paulo. In the midforties, I was studying law at university when I took part in a student demonstration with a handkerchief tied round my face. To this day I can still hear the sound of horses' hooves on the cobblestones. As we flew from the mounted police, one of my fellow students fell in the middle of the road, the blood spurting from his chest. No, Castro Alves, no, my beloved poet! It was not "the budding of genius," but the spurting of blood. That I should have become more liberated than Brazil itself can be attributed to the fact that individual freedom is much easier to achieve. One day, the nation will reap the rewards of those historic events.

"You were courageous to assume two male professions, that of writer and the other of lawyer," someone once said to me at some gathering or other at the Brazilian Academy of Letters. I can now reply: the people who really showed courage were our first women writers, those wretched creatures who stepped out of their corsets and stood with bared breasts on the frontline. Today, everything has become much easier and there is much less distrust of women writers. The old prejudices have been effectively eroded. Even the jokes about literary women have worn thin. Nevertheless, a certain critic recently attacked the narcissism of the woman writer. He accused her of being much too preoccupied with herself and engaged in a constant search of her own identity: "In what mirror have I lost my face?" Her eyes fixed on her own navel. The critic in question forgot to consider the historical reasons that set the seeds of this intimate note in feminine literature. "In the old days, it was men who told women what they were like," one of my characters comments in the novel *As meninas*. There, you have it! A woman discovering herself: what world could she possibly wish to describe except her own?

A great deal has been said and written about the modernization of culture and, in the same context, about the evaluation of woman as writer. I myself believe that, in the twentieth century, modernization in general has only modernized the bourgeoisie—that is also the view of Paulo Emilio Salles Gomes, and it strikes me as being very sound. As a member of a fraternity that needs to find other means of subsistence, beyond the relatively modest earnings gained from writing, I see myself (and other profesional women writers) demanding wider recognition and esteem. No easy thing to achieve. As for those women who truly belong to the bourgeoisie, they have never been in need of any form of protection.

Do we choose to become writers, or were we chosen? Chosen, with the option of renunciation. But we have no intention of renouncing. On the contrary, we shall go on struggling. Holding out. We know (because we are ever on our guard) that there are three candidates for extinction: the tree, the Indian, and the writer.

But we hold out against extinction. When I traveled across Africa, one of the men from UNESCO told me: "Every time an elderly African dies, a library goes up in flames." Is it possible that, before we finally manage to resolve the indigenous question, we shall succeed in capturing something of African literature and life, wherein the sacred and the beautiful merge, so that we might nourish our own culture and remorse?

We hold out, as witnesses of this world. Witnesses of this society and all that is good about it. And bad. And there is a good deal that is bad. Yet at the same time, there is no lack of goodwill and inspiration.

I have just used a word that has gone out of fashion, but which seems to me to be irreplaceable in the vocabulary of any creative activity: inspiration. Some of my narratives are *inspired* by a simple image—an object, a house, or a painting. The idea might have been born in the brief reflection of a landscape as seen through a window or from a moving train. Other stories originate from some phrase I might have said or heard, and which I have remembered. Then one day, for no apparent reason (how? why?) my memory resuscitates the phrase, which multiplies itself as in the miracle of the loaves. There are also certain narratives that emerge from dreams—a flood of symbols. Metaphors in the depths of the unconscious which has suddenly flung open its doors—everyone out! Mass escape! But it is necessary to be selective. To interpret. But the majority of my narratives have secret origins, which I myself cannot explain simply because they are beyond explanation.

In several written testimonies, I have tried to bring my readers closer to some understanding of the mystery. Only to end up grafting fiction onto fiction. Sorcery? Magic? Unattainable mystery with its grain of uncertainty and madness. I know that fiction will become reality. Just as reality will become fiction. And if I have invented this testimony, that invention has now become the truth.

Augusto Roa Bastos
[1917–]

PARAGUAY'S MOST GIFTED and respected author, Augusto Roa Bastos was born in the village of Iturbe. He attended schools in the capital, Asunción, and began writing as a child. At seventeen, he was conscripted to fight in the Chaco War between Paraguay and Bolivia, after which he worked for several years in bank, and later on the editorial staff of the paper *El País*. With the aid of a grant, he then traveled to Europe, spending nine months in England. World War II took him away from Paraguay again, when he served as a newspaper correspondent in Europe and North Africa.

In 1946, he was named Paraguay's cultural attaché in Buenos Aires, but a civil war at home ended his diplomatic post. Roa Bastos stayed on in Buenos Aires, working primarily as a journalist, but also writing poetry, short stories, novels, and screenplays. Because of his opposition to the dictatorship of Alfredo Stroessner, who has ruled Paraguay for over forty years, Roa Bastos made his home in Argentina and, most recently, in France.

Among his published works are volumes of poetry in both Spanish and Guaraní, the language of the native Indians of Paraguay, and seven collections of short stories portraying the problems of his country and its indigenous population. In 1959 he published the novel *Hijo de hombre* [Son of Man], a monumental work depicting the dramatic history of Paraguay, which won several international prizes. His most recently translated work is another major novel, *Yo el supremo*, 1974 [*I the Supreme*, 1986], based on the life of the nineteenth-century Paraguayan dictator

Doctor Francia; it is a masterful exposé of the subjectivity of all historical texts, using parody to contrast the dictator's version of events with that of various historical texts and to point to the limitations of all written language as an instrument for communication.

The essay that follows was originally written for *El País* in Madrid and published on July 8, 1985. It is published here in English for the first time. In this essay, Roa Bastos speaks for himself and his compatriots on the subject of exile, which has many levels of interpretation for Paraguayans.

Writing: A Metaphor for Exile

Augusto Roa Bastos
Translated by Helen Lane

The political, social, and cultural picture presented by Paraguay under the dictatorship of longest standing on the Latin American continent dramatically reveals the devastating effect that the latter has had on the creative sources of society in their various manifestations. In this backward society endlessly playing out, as a sort of punishment, the "ongoing hallucination of its history"—the culmination of a century of intermittent, endemic dictatorships resembling tropical fevers—the phenomenon of exile, through this perversion of history, forms part of its nature and its destiny.

Exile, first of all, of the country itself within its landlocked prison, marked by territorial segregations, by migrations and emigrations, by mass exoduses: among them, that of its native peoples, the first at the time of the expulsion of the Jesuits (1767), which in turn represented the first banishment of foreigners in colonial Paraguay. This nonetheless did not prevent the country, once it had become independent, from attaining the status of the most advanced nation, materially and culturally, in Hispanic America. Under the rule of the famous Dr. Francia, founder of the Republic and builder of the nation-state in accordance with the principles of the Enlightenment and the French Revolution, there took place in Paraguay the first successful experiment in autonomous government and independence in the history of Latin America: something that the liberators of the continent themselves were not able to achieve after the battles for emancipation. The economic interests—the penetration and domination of the British Empire in that part of the world—could not permit the utopia of self-determination to prosper in this little isolated, landlocked country and thus set a dangerous example. At the instigation of the British and with their aid, the financial centers of the Brazilian Empire and the oligarchies of the Río de la Plata, who were dependent on England, contrived to bring about the so-called War of the Triple Alliance. Lasting for five years (1865–1870), this war devastated Paraguay, exterminated two-thirds of its population, and stripped it of more than half its territory. Paraguay was thus reduced to ruins. All that was left of this unfortunate nation was a "great catastrophe of memories" and in its midst a raving mad reality blowing tremendous gusts of their history into the faces of the survivors, in the words of the Spaniard Rafael Barret, writing at the beginning of this century.

The emptiness of the past, its isolation, its lack of communication, its harassment by neocolonialist interest kept even the echoes of cultural currents that were transforming the ideas, the arts, the literatures of Latin America from reaching this enclave, withdrawn into itself and brooding upon its national calamities. To all of this there must be added the double barrier of its bilingual culture: Paraguay is the only totally bilingual country in Latin America; the native oral language, Guaraní, is the real national language of the people. This is the space of mestizo culture, where more than four centuries of purely oral expression has turned writing into an absent text: the root metaphor of exile.

This cultural and linguistic exile hence aggravates, from within, all the other forms of alienation that inner exile implies, since it means the destruction of the last freedom by fear: fear installed as public conscience in a country crushed by the system of totalitarian repression that holds that country in contempt.

The fragmentation of Paraguayan culture, the imbalance of the forces of production, the overwhelming fear that has taken over the functions of a conscience at once public and secret, individual and collective, have profoundly affected the creative powers of a society that lives, as a sort of ironic punishment, on the shores of one of the most beautiful rivers in the world, that river that gave its mythic name to the country: *Paragua'y*: *plumed-water* or *river-of-crowns*.

Brutality and terror have dammed those sources that nourish the works of writers and artists and project the originality of a people. It is evident that this expressive process can take place only when such works fuse the social energy of the collectivity and the essence of its life, its reality, its history, its cultural, social, and national myths that fecundate the creative subjectivity of poets, novelists, artists. The greatest alienation of that collectivity is to live torn between reality as it ought to be and reality as it is: between the plenitude of life that has been stolen from it and the monstrosity of the vegetative life that causes foreign to its historical and social nature have imposed upon it.

The writer cannot comport himself like an ethnologist. Passivity, keeping his distance, are not his forte. Paraguayan writers, authors of fiction, poets belong to a culture whose internal structure continues to be oral, stubbornly resistant to the signs of *cultivated* writing, which stands for artificiality and domination. Imagination thus remains a prisoner of this twofold alienation: that of language, in expressing a reality that overwhelms it; and that of a reality that is polyphonic sound, a reality that manifests itself only through orality, the inflections and modulations of verbal expression. And as we are well aware, it is not good intentions that make a literary work; it is, rather, the meanings of its internal structure, the instinctive force that emanates from it, the mediation of "an art that is undoubtedly conscious, yet in search of a form not conscious of itself," an art that is not ideological yet cannot escape ideology.

In the inventory of the forms of exile of the Paraguayan writer (outward exile and inner, dispossession of life not lived, deprivation of work not yet done, segregation from his reality, lack of communication with his national public among those scattered in the diaspora, lack of communication with those suffering from inner exile), linguistic exile is their paradigm, the true metaphor of reality transformed into unreality.

The problem of the Castilian–Guaraní polarity may be the key sign of this sort of linguistic schizophrenia. In which of the two languages is the Paraguayan writer to write? If literature is fundamentally a matter of language, and hence of communication, the choice should be or would seem to be inevitable: Castilian or Spanish.* But on writing in Castilian, the writer, and the author of fiction in particular, feels that he is suffering his most intimate alienation, that of linguistic exile. To what desperate straits might he be driven if he thus keeps at a distance that portion of reality and collective life that is expressed in Guaraní, of Paraguayan culture bearing the indelible mark of its oral nature, of original mythic thought? As he sits writing in Castilian he feels he is engaged in making only a partial translation of a linguistic context that is split in two. And as he does so, he splits himself in two. He will always have something left that has not been expressed. This brings the Paraguayan writer face-to-face with the need to *make* a literature that as yet has no place in literature; to speak against the word, to write against writing, to invent stories that are the transgression of official history, to undermine, with subversive, demystifying writing, the language loaded with the ideology of domination. In this sense, the new generations of fiction writers and poets find themselves committed to the task of advancing this *literature without a past* that comes from a past without literature, of expressing it in their own language.

The Guaraní cosmogony conceived of human language as the foundation of the cosmos and the original nature of man. The nucleus of this

---

*Castilian is standard literary Spanish. [*Trans.*]

myth of origin is the esoteric and untranslatable *ayvú rapytá* or *ñe'eng mbyte râ* as the very essence of the soul-word: the *ayvú* of the beginning of time. Noise or sound impregnated with the wisdom of nature and of the cosmos engendering itself through the austere and melodious Father of the beginning and the end; originator of the word that founds. A secret word that is never uttered in the presence of strangers, and the one that forms, along with *tataendy* (flame-of-the-sacred-fire) and *tatachiná* (mist-of-the-creative-power), the trinity of prime elements in the cosmogony of the ancient Guaranís. Their primordial divinities did not fulminate punitive laws against one who aspired to wisdom. They brought about the communion between knowing and doing, between unity and plurality, between life and death. Every man was God on the way to purification, and God—or the many gods of that theogony—was both the first man and the last. They did not impose exile, but the pilgrimage of the *multitude-person* to the *land-without-evil* that each one bore within and amid all.

In present-day Paraguayan society, thrown out of balance by oppressive power, the ancestral voice—that last language in which a threatened and persecuted people takes refuge—has also been confiscated. A language without writing that in another time contained within itself the very essence of the soul-word—seed of the human and the sacred—it is today trying to find its space as a word, the irradiation of reality through the unreality of signs.

Contemporary Paraguayan writers are aware that they find themselves at an extreme point of a historic succession. This makes them abnormally conscious not only of the problems of their society but also of their artistic task. For those writers subjected to internal exile, as for those forced to scatter in the diaspora, the work of literature once again means the imperative need to embody a destiny, to find their place once more in the vital reality of a collectivity, their own, in order to nourish themselves in its profoundest essences and aspirations, and from there go on to embrace the universality of humankind.

These narrators understand that achievements of this sort, by their very nature, can be realized only on the aesthetic plane, on the plane of the word and of writing, through the very conception of the art of narration, which is not only, as is commonly thought, the art of describing reality in words but also the art of making the word itself real.

This commitment tends to penetrate beneath the skin of human destiny as deeply as possible; to bring into being, in short, the most complete image possible of the individual and of society, the most intimate image possible of the vital and spiritual experience of the human person of our time. It is in this way that, allying personal subjectivity with historical and social conscience, creative imagination with moral passion,

Paraguayan writers can overcome their dramatic lack of communication and isolation of today and become an integral part of the whole of the literature whose language is Hispanic.

PABLO ANTONIO CUADRA
[1912–]

BORN IN MANAGUA, the poet and journalist Pablo Antonio Cuadra spent most of his early life in his family's home city, Granada, on Lake Nicaragua. Cuadra was deeply influenced by the life of the native peoples around the lake, whose culture and folklore have nourished his poetry.

Cuadra was one of the founders of the post–Rubén Darío, or Vanguard, movement in Nicaraguan poetry in the 1930s, and his early publications of poetry and prose date from that period. He is the author of more than twenty books. Cuadra had also been active as a journalist since directing the review *Vanguardia* (from 1930 to 1932) and later other journals; the culmination of this aspect of his writing career occurred when he was asked to codirect the country's most important newspaper, *La Prensa*—first the literary supplement, later the newspaper itself—in Managua.

Among his many published works are *Poemas nicaragüenses*, 1934 ["Nicaraguan Poems"]; *Poemas con un crepúsculo a cuestas*, 1949 ["Poems Bearing a Twilight"]; *El jaguar y la luna*, 1959 [*The Jaguar and the Moon*, 1974, translated by Thomas Merton]; *Poesía, 1929–1962*, 1964; *Tierra que habla*, 1974 ["Talking Land"]; and *Cantos de Cifar y del mar dulce*, 1979 [*Songs of Cifar and the Sweet Sea*, 1979].

When Somoza's forces assassinated Cuadro's colleague, *La Prensa*'s director, Pedro Joaquín Chamorro in 1978, popular opposition to the dictator increased dramatically. In 1979, the revolution inspired by Sandino's rebellion in the late 1920s was accomplished. Although Cuadra was in favor of the ideals of the revolution, he felt that the Marxist government of Daniel Ortega betrayed those ideals. For six years, *La Prensa* survived amid increased tension, hostility, and censorship, concluding in the "indefinite suspension" of publication by the Sandinista government in July of 1986.*

It is sadly ironic that Nicaragua's two major poets, Pablo Antonio Cuadra and Ernesto Cardenal, who once shared the same goals, are now divided by the revolution they promoted. As has happened so often in Latin America, the close relationship between politics and literature has created a rift that threatens the cultural integrity of the country.

Cuadra wrote this essay expressly for this collection in 1986, shortly before the closing of *La Prensa*. Confined to "interior exile" while he is in Nicaragua, Cuadra now chooses to spend most of his time with his family in Austin, Texas, where he teaches Central American poetry at the University of Texas.

La Prensa was allowed to begin publishing again in October, 1987, in partial compliance with the provisions of the Central American peace plan signed in August 1987. As this book goes to press, the final outcome of this accord is uncertain. [Ed.]

POETRY AND THE TEMPTATIONS OF POWER
"the swan's confusion among the puddles"
RUBÉN DARÍO

Pablo Antonio Cuadra
Translated by Steven White

Although I was born in Managua, Nicaragua's capital, in 1912, my father's family is from Granada. From the time I was four to the age of forty-six, I lived in this city-port on the shores of the "freshwater sea," as Nicaragua's Great Lake has been called. There, I went to a Jesuit high school and later began my studies of law, which I quit during the final exams because I thought that being a lawyer would not be compatible with being a writer. Next to that Great Lake, my brother Carlos and I established a farm (stealing it from the jungle) that had cattle, various crops, and a sawmill. Because of this work, I was always navigating the lake, living with the people who sailed its waters. My poetry takes its sustenance from that life as well as from my knowledge of the Nicaraguan people. But I also devoted many years of my free time to investigating our history, our culture and folklore, and to the study of our indigenous cultures and their languages.

I offer this biographical information as background because the writer gives shape to the material that is part of his world—he forms his works from the mud of his land. He will inevitably perceive in the mud the problems of his land, and these problems will affect his creation.

The beginning of my literary life coincided with a group of young people (who knows what attractions and gatherings produce these generational blossomings!) and we founded the Vanguard movement. We were still almost children, but if one reads the controversial writings and manifestos from those years (the movement began in 1929) one can clearly see our two main goals: (1) a break with the recent "modernist" past so that we could open ourselves to assimilate the new currents in international literature of the vanguard and (2) a search for and an affirmation of our Nicaraguan identity. The first objective (even though we didn't realize it at the time) was part of Rubén Darío's legacy to us: we

281

continued his work, rejecting what was provincial and striving for the universal. The second was necessary for a young country, but became imperative for our generation, because in those years, Nicaragua was the victim of foreign intervention. The movement of the Nicaraguan Vanguard was, in short, a search for two things—what was "new" and our ancient roots. But my poetry (because of the horizon of my work, my life, and my history), when compared to that of other poets of my generation, was more affected by the agony between the vernacular and the ecumenical.

Our initial reaction to the luxurious baggage of Rubén Darío and, above all, his disciples, was similar to that of Santa Teresa in sixteenth-century Spain when she rejected the courtly language and literature that preceded her. We wanted "to write the way people spoke" ("with neither finery nor cosmetic touches"), but without losing a certain universal quality. In other words, we wanted "a deeply artistic spontaneity," a new artifice capable of recovering the natural.

The enterprise of finding our roots had complementary dynamics—upwards and outwards like a tree that sinks it roots as it grows toward the sky. But in this operation our universalism came up against the historical fact of intervention and the remarkable feat of Sandino's protest, which radicalized our nationalism. It was difficult to resist succumbing to the idea of a closed and angry *we*. But poetry possesses great powers as an antidote. We didn't fall into the traps of "telluricism," or folkloric nativism. Nor were we confined by national aesthetic concerns.

Elsewhere, I have written a definition of our movement of the Vanguard by using the formula: PICASSO + LA COATLICUE. Picasso: the invention of the future; Coatlicue (the Nahuatl goddess of the earth): the discovery of the past. We created a balance between the temptation of the cavern and the invitation of distance. In my work, however, the peasant's eye prevails and my poetry is a rural vision of the world or, to paraphrase T. S. Eliot, the rediscovery of the Occident through the eyes of the Indian.

Looking back on my life and on my itinerary as a writer, now that I have reached the age of seventy-three, I realize that the biggest and most frequent obstacle that rose before me and my work was Politics or Power. Rubén Darío speaks in a poem about "the pain of not being what I might have been." A wound like that never stops bleeding! Nevertheless, I think that without those scars of opposition I wouldn't be the person I am. Don't limitations and frustrations define a human being?

Power (or politics), that twentieth-century demon, tempted me in three stages and in three disguises: *first* in my early youth as totalitarianism; *second* as the hostility of a right-wing dictatorship; and *third* as the deceit and hostility, too, of a left-wing dictatorship.

1

The totalitarian temptation had its basis in our literacy cult of "the new."
In the mythic ambience of change, in that contradictory joining of the
Apocalypse and Genesis that saturated the world of our between-wars
generation, the critical situation of our country pushed us to break with
the past and to invent a *new* politics. We believed, and not without reason, that the disputes of our political parties had caused the foreign
intervention, underdevelopment, and other defects in Nicaragua. This is
why we rejected democracy and proposed such solemn dilemmas as "Order versus chaos," "Decadence of the Occident versus New Age," "Rome
versus Babylon," etc. We dreamed of a new order that would strengthen
the nation and alleviate social injustice through power. But, influenced
by victorious totalitarianisms, we believed that our cause had to be
backed by violence and domination.

We left history behind to enter the territory of utopia, and once we
took that step everything made us bolder: Spengler or Bardiaeff, the
good Don Ramiro de Maeztú or Maurras, or Primo de Rivera, or Con-
fucius, or Machiavelli, or Ezra Pound, or Pessoa. . . . I don't know what
kind of ideological synthesis or aberration it might eventually have come
to (I do know that those years of fanaticism were lost ones for poetry).
But Somoza, the dictator who emerged at that time in Nicaragua and
whom we had initially supported, put me in jail, accused me of being a
supporter of Sandino, and made me feel in my own flesh the effects of
the kind of politics that denies freedom and creates a cult of charismatic,
absolute power.

Shortly thereafter, World War II erupted and with it, the "grand
words" that showed their emptiness. For me, it was a difficult process
that, among other things, allowed me to sharpen my critical sensibility,
even of myself. How could I advance and rectify my mistakes? It seemed
to me that underlying the fanaticisms and what presumptuously are called
"convictions" was emptiness, a vast "wasteland."

I also found an angular stone cast aside by others. A sturdy column
among ruins. Christ.

2

My process was slow. A young man doesn't abandon his myths, or the
ruins of his myths, so quickly. Around me, I saw a literature rise, a system
of politics decline. The same phenomenon occurred throughout Hispanic

America. At that time I was studying Rubén Darío, and his example (an island of culture surrounded by savagery) seemed to symbolize that contradiction between two principles. In our Indian past, our best civilizations always limped along—they were always incomplete. The Mayas, Toltecs, and Incas reached cultural heights, while in other aspects their cultures were paleolithic. I asked myself if that would always be our destiny—to be part of a culture that reached universal heights with a political system sunk in the most shameful depths.

At the end of the 1940s, I fled the dictator and exiled myself to Mexico where I lived for three years and had two transforming experiences. The first was the Indian with his sense of religion and time; the second was the magic touch of his past (*my* past). The Indian grandmother still speaks to us from the top of the pyramids! Since then, I have adopted the firm ideal of joining the legacies of Athens and Tula.

When I returned to Nicaragua in 1954, Pedro Joaquín Chamorro asked me to be copublisher, with him, of the newspaper, *La Prensa*. After thinking about it for a long time, I accepted. Pedro Joaquín's proposal forced me to confront two challenges: the journalist versus the poet, and political commitment versus creative freedom.

Time, for the journalist, is linear and demands, like public speaking, an ability to improvise. It is antagonistic in its relation to the poet's conception of time, which is circular because the poem repeatedly returns to its text that will never be finished. The poem demands "to go beyond." "To go beyond," says Lao-tse, "means *to return*." Working as a journalist tore me apart and made me two different people. The difference was manifested in the tools I used: for journalism, I used a typewriter; I write my poetry by hand.

The other challenge affected my life more deeply. To direct *La Prensa* meant, at that time, putting myself on the firing line of the struggle against the dictatorship. It forced me into the difficult task of preparing my nerves for fear and tumult. But in terms of literature, the very risks of that struggle taught me, paradoxically, never to confuse the poet's personal commitment with that of his work. It was precisely because I wanted to strike at the heart of the tyranny that I was very cautious. I was a radical in the defense and nurturing of creative freedom. Furthermore, this was when *engagé* poetry in Spanish reached its level of greatest prestige. The dramatic downfalls of a poet as great as Neruda (or the rapid aging process of the most intelligent examples of "committed" poetry in Spain and throughout Latin America) alerted me to the dangers of substituting political for aesthetic criteria. This is true for all forms of criticism, including my own self-criticism.

I can state with pride (though pride usually ends in sadness) that from those years until 1979, by establishing and directing publications, encouraging artistic life and new values, publishing works and finding publishers for works other than my own, I was able to promote a cultural movement—united in friendship and freedom—whose ranks were filled with almost all the writers and artists in Nicaragua. This movement was one of the principal sources of the revolution against the dictatorship. We produced politicized art, but it was an art that was expressed with freedom, even when it could have cost us our lives. Its belligerence was born of freedom—freedom engaged in the struggle. Freedom also gave birth to its authenticity. As we shall see later, this authenticity, which gave Nicaraguan literature a high standing in Latin America, did not know how to sustain itself in the hour of triumph—when the Revolution was confiscated and the right-wing dictatorship of Somoza was deceitfully and treacherously replaced with a dictatorship of the left.

And what about my experience as a journalist? The story of *La Prensa* is one of the most dramatic chapters in Nicaraguan history. Pedro Joaquín Chamorro and I wanted to turn *La Prensa* into a new, revolutionary newspaper, a creator of culture, a voice of the people, and an element of change. But the brutal pressure of the right-wing dictatorship (the dynasty of the three Somozas) frustrated our best efforts and forced us to change our strategy. We struggled for survival and for the most basic rights. One of Ulysses' tricks to survive against Polyphemus was calling himself "Nobody." Frequently, the best defense against the police is stupidity.

During intervals of freedom, we raised our standards in terms of trained personnel, as well as the structures and forms of journalism. We were even able to turn the supplement, *La Prensa Literaria*, into the main cultural voice of all Central America. But once again censorship, exile, and imprisonment beset us and so we had to go back somewhat to the law of the jungle, refining our five senses by thinking of ways to get a message (however ironic) past the censorship of the police.

While I cannot, in this essay, go into the long, unequal struggle between a dictatorship and a "republic of paper," one moment was particularly poignant. On January 10, 1978, a friend telephoned me: Pedro Joaquín Chamorro had suffered an accident. It was 8:00 in the morning. Several minutes later, the people at *La Prensa* called with more information. It was no accident. It was murder. I found Pedro lifeless: more than thirty bullets had perforated his noble chest. Then I went to *La Prensa*, fearing that I would find the offices occupied by Somoza's National Guard. But as I got closer, I saw all the people who were running to defend the newspaper. That same night, at the wake, the popular insurrection began.

Those were very difficult months. Urban guerrilla warfare. National strikes. Battles in the streets. Tense journalism: one had to attack, but calculate each word. We were in the sights of the rifles.

In July of 1979, the dictator sensed that he could no longer halt his downfall, so he sent planes to bomb *La Prensa*. Then his troops doused the offices with gasoline and burned them.

3

Poetry had emerged victorious against a right-wing dictatorship. By struggling for freedom, poetry had remained free. Nevertheless, during the last year of struggle, the tyrant's unbearable oppression had taken us to that dangerous moment (we were to pay for it later) in which we said, "Anything is better than this monster!" In Nicaragua, there was a slogan people shouted: "*¡Cualquier cosa es mejor que Somoza!*" ("Anything is better than Somoza!"). At the moment when the most care ought to have been taken in terms of making alliances (one of the most difficult political situations in a power vacuum), desperation made us ally ourselves with the devil. And Mephistopheles charges dearly! A few months after the triumph, the new dictatorship demanded, in the name of the people's liberty and as a revolutionary pledge, our newly earned freedom as a tribute. And so began the struggle of an ideology against a culture. But that ideology has had to impose itself, little by little, through a strange kind of costume ball. Never declaring the truth, always denying or disguising it.

If we have learned anything in Nicaragua, it is that communism advances insofar as it hides itself. But that negation of humanity and that advancing by means of deceit is deeply sterilizing. Duplicity and hypocrisy can create "slogans" but not poems, propaganda but not life. There are no roots and no realities with which to nourish creation. This explains why, after six years of the Revolution, literary creation in Nicaragua has been so poor. And this Revolution is supposed to be the outpouring of an entire, formidable revolutionary literary movement that captured the world's attention.

It is painful to recount the disillusion. I remember the symposium we organized in Managua in November of 1979 (four months after the triumph). The theme was "The Writer and the Revolution." Ernesto Cardenal, Minister of Culture, presided and Julio Cortázar was the guest of honor. People from all the different literary generations in Nicaragua participated. Cortázar proposed the terms of the point of departure: "A double commitment," he said. The commitment to the people (from the true depths of one's being/*ser*) and the commitment to one's literary works (from the authenticity of doing/*hacer*). But Xavier Argüello, the youngest and last to speak at the roundtable discussion, defined the terms of the point of arrival: "There is no longer any commitment," he said. "Commitment has been surpassed. We are freedom itself. We are the people themselves." As the Augustinian said, "Love and do what you wish." The large audience loudly applauded that rainbow in the sky of a new revolution proclaiming freedom as the essence of commitment. Two Cuban poets who were invited to the conference expressed to me something that went beyond happiness—their enthusiasm for the kind of resolutions concerning creative freedom, pluralism, and intellectual independence that, according to them, would "inevitably exercise an influence on the Cuban process."

But the honeymoon was short-lived. The commanders of the Revolution and some intellectuals soon began to set certain limitations and to decree prohibitions. In answer to our cry (the same one that was heard in Paris two decades ago) "It is forbidden to forbid!", the magazine *Ventana* (the cultural supplement to the Sandinista newspaper *Barricada*) printed the old Mussolini-like speech by Fidel Castro—"Everything within the context of the Revolution, nothing against the Revolution"— whose political interpretations (as well as those made by the police) have resulted in a surprisingly high number of imprisoned and exiled Cuban writers and artists: the highest number in the history of this dark half-century.

In a parallel manner, there was a growing pollution in the moral atmosphere of the Revolution. Because the Nicaraguan Revolution was a "clean revolution." I am referring to the Christian spirit of the people, the Christian background of the majority of the young combatants, the kind of pluralistic unity open to dialogue that was formed in the struggle against the dictatorship, and the high moral category of some of the revolutionary leaders. All of these elements, among others, helped to create an atmosphere of generosity, fraternity, and humanism during the struggle and after the triumph as well. Our Revolution, more than any other, received the world's admiration and sympathy. But then the Sandinista command began to unmask its ideology, trample the sacred commitments of blood, and unilaterally impose its own political party. They began to use dirty methods and to accumulate, layer upon layer, the imported detritus of other revolutions and terrorist organizations thereby contaminating the clean record of our Nicaraguan Revolution. Thus:

—the hatred (the ideological kind that gratuitously turns into the *compañero's* adversary) and the social hatred, the hatred between social classes that had never been seized on by the people except by the most fanatical,
—the homicidal, slanderous language,

—the systematic lies,

—the spirit of reprisals and vengeance (that the people never accepted either, only the so-called popular tribunals),

—the profanity,

—the trampling of rights,

—the demeaning obligation to spy and to denounce,

—the use of mobs, or groups of assailants, who are protected by the powers that be in their aggressions,

—the looting and confiscation of goods as revenge or political sanction,

—religious persecution,

—and, to top it all off, our beautiful Revolution in the name of freedom has given us censorship.

This is what censorship means regarding *La Prensa*: constant pressures; the impossibility of writing a single editorial for up to three months at a time; threats and beatings of distributors, typesetters, journalists, and collaborators. They send mobs to assault us, they imprison us, withhold our passports, open our mail, tap our phones, slander us with no recourse, and systematically censor information and writings. But the censorship doesn't stop there. It also affects radio and television stations; publishing houses; historical, literary, and religious magazines—even the homilies of the priests at mass. The inoffensive Academia de la Lengua must inform the Ministry of Justice (seventy-two hours in advance) when it plans to have a meeting of its members. Because of such measures, I believe that Nicaragua's cultural process will atrophy more and more with each passing day.

Furthermore, it would be difficult for even the most egotistical soul to lock himself in some closet and not become tainted by this chaotic filth. I saw how many of my intellectual friends became hardened (as all bodies do when they live in mire). I've seen the extraordinary and irrational resistance of their fanaticism. My own religious faith suffered when faced with this blind political or ideological faith. I went through a kind of self-examination or temptation. I've had to hold fast to the Christ of failure, the one who gives life but who doesn't ask for lives when faced with that overpowering, cruel, inquisition-like sense of certainty that characterizes the builders of paradises. As a poet, I've felt the need to introduce a new light into my conscience—a light that, however weak and human, signals the difference between faith and fanaticism.

Many mistakes have been cast upon humanity's heart by leftist dictatorships. The poet, because of his sympathy for the poor and those who suffer, initially believes that Marxism-Leninism opts for the needy

and the poor. But in just a short time he realizes that Marxism, in practice, opts for a state of immense power, control, and coldness—"the cold-
est of the cold monsters." What emerges from its pious commiseration
with those who are exploited is a merciless boss who imposes a new
slavery in the name of freedom. And after it is too late, the proleteriat
realizes what a high price it paid for bread that it still may not be able
to get. This is why I believe that poetry and art don't suffer a similar
fate under a leftist dictatorship. Several of my friends who flaunted their
independence in front of the right-wing dictatorship have happily bent
over backwards to all the demands of the revolutionary leaders ("*Comandantes*, give us our orders!" is the obligatory cry). In unthinking op-
portunism, they quickly replaced their aesthetic judgment with political
judgment, instantly lowering the quality of what they produced: instead
of creation, propaganda.

Those who resisted losing their creative freedom, those who did not
believe that power gives the *comandantes* some sort of divine inspiration
to guide culture, arts, and letters—these people had to go into exile.
Those, like myself, who have refused to lose their country, have known
an interior exile. It reminds me of T. S. Eliot's opportune prayer from
"The Rock":

preserve me from the enemy who has something to gain: and from the
friend who has something to lose.

A short time ago, Carlos Drummond de Andrade dedicated a letter
and a beautiful poem to me to console me in my exile and to encourage
me to continue

the hard occupation
of harvesting deception

Because I have lost friends (which is like losing part of the heart's
territory) and have seen my dreams fall time after time. I don't consider
the fallen stones rubble, but rather the materials of experience to one day
build a humble, humanistic Republic (not a paradise), a place where
people can live and converse together (not a utopia), where a poet can
see his vehement dreams of justice and his radical need for freedom satisfied (though always in need of further perfection), where he can retain
his human solidarity as well as his personal dignity.

LUISA VALENZUELA
[1938–]

BORN IN BUENOS Aires into a family where literature
was part of her upbringing—her mother is Luisa Mercedes Lev-
inson, a well-known Argentine author—Luisa Valenzuela began
her own literary career writing for local magazines and working
on the editorial staff of *La Nación*.

While residing for several years in France, she wrote her first
novel, *Hay que sonreír* (1966), later translated into English and
published with some of her short stories as *Clara* (1976). This
book was well received in the States, establishing Valenzuela as
one of the few Latin American women writers to be known in
this country—even among devotees of Latin American literature.
Since then, her publications include *Aquí pasan cosas raras*, 1976
[*Strange Things Happen Here*, 1979], minimalist stories filled with
satire and black humor and inspired by Valenzuela's horror at the
cold-blooded atrocities committed in her country under the military regimes of the late 1970s; also the novel *Cola de largartija*,
1983 [*The Lizard's Tail*, 1983], a fictional parody of the career of
López Rega, demoniacal adviser to Isabel Perón; and *Cambio de
armas*, 1982 [*Other Weapons*, 1985], a collection of stories about
power and the male/female relationship. A recent issue of the *Review of Contemporary Fiction* was dedicated to her work.

Valenzuela's fiction can be linked to the tradition of magical
realism in Latin America, with an element of the absurd and surreal. Her defiance of the limits of traditional discourse and her
bold choice of themes—eroticism, death, and violence, for example—have earned her a reputation for being aggressive and in-

novative. Her writing clearly shows that female authors in Latin America are breaking taboos and charting new courses of expression.

In 1969, Valenzuela came to the United States under a Fulbright Fellowship and, after traveling in Europe and Latin America, she made her residence in New York in the late 1970s, visiting Argentina periodically but devoting her professional time to writing and teaching in the States.

The essay included here was originally published in *The New York Times Book Review* on March 16, 1986.

A Legacy of Poets and Cannibals: Literature Revives in Argentina

Luisa Valenzuela
Translated by Lori M. Carlson

I am afraid that my country from the moment of its discovery has been faithful to a literary tradition that has promoted misrepresentation and fantasy. In 1516 Juan Díaz de Solís, sailing from Spain, knew he had reached the new continent and not the East Indies, so he began to search for a passageway to the other ocean. He thought he had found it to the far south, entering what he called the Freshwater Sea, now known as the Río de la Plata, on the Atlantic coast of southern South America. (Four centuries later Jorge Luis Borges would dub it the river of "dreamery" and mud.) To its discoverers it appeared only as a vast body of water with swampy shores. On its west bank a handful of men were left to establish a settlement. Poetry was already lurking: on board with Solís was Martin del Barco Centenera, who wrote an ode titled "The Argentina," thus giving a name to the new lands. A misnomer, since there was practically no *argentum*, no silver, there. The ode bestowed on the newly named Argentina tritons, sirens and other European mythical creatures. It was written while the first settlers, surrounded by Indians, were forced to eat their dead.

That is why I believe we are descendants of poets and cannibals. And every so often the cannibals get hold of power, and silence and kill the poets. This happened during the 10 years that followed the death of Juan Domingo Perón in 1974, years that saw a military dictatorship lasting from 1976 until the end of 1983.

Now, with the return of democracy, the poets' turn has come, the turn of all those who, as Martin Buber once said, discover while writing. That's why we're coming back, in every way possible. Many writers who were in exile are coming back, some literally, others through their books. Even those who were killed during the military dictatorship are now being recalled and republished.

After 10 years of bloody censorship, does a nation remember how to write? Do people remember their own names when next-door neighbors had "disappeared" and could not be mentioned again? How do people recognize the truth when what is now known as the complicity of silence has stifled them?

Memory was to be recovered gradually, painfully. One of Argentina's greatest writers, Ernesto Sábato, was chosen by President Raúl Alfonsín to head the Argentine National Commission on the Disappeared (Conadep), which, after grueling research, compiled a book titled "Nunca Más" ["Nevermore," 1986] providing case histories of the former government's victims and locating the military's clandestine torture centers.

In his house in the quiet suburban neighborhood of Santos Lugares, now free from the threats he received while gathering the material for Conadep, Mr. Sábato says, "I haven't been reading or writing for over five years now because of an eye ailment. So I have gone back to my other old love, painting. But I am witnessing Buenos Aires' extraordinary revival. Everybody is now working as in a feast, thanks to democracy."

Argentine writers today must fight the dark legacy of the military dictatorship's manipulation of language—such as the idea of a "divided literature," which in a subtle way invalidated the writing of those who published outside the country. "What will they do, how will they write, those who can't hear the voices of their people or breathe their sorrows and solace?" Luis Gregorich, a prominent literary critic who, although not sympathetic to the military, was caught in their semantic trap, asked rhetorically. His reply was dismal: their books "will end submerged in insignificance and doubt." Facts proved differently. Some of the most vital Argentine writing of the period was produced abroad by writers who had left the country and were free to speak out: the persecuted David Viñas, for example, whose novel, "Cuerpo a Cuerpo" ("Face to Face"), an epic of courage and machismo, appeared in Mexico in 1979.

Argentines often bloom best in alien ground—just think of Julio Cortázar, who, having lived in Paris for 30 years, was the most Argentine of Argentine writers. On the other hand, for the writers who remained during the dictatorship, a pervasive censorship was successful in silencing many. Some were even silenced to death.

Having spent five years in New York, I returned for a visit at the end of 1983 to celebrate President Alfonsín's inauguration and the publication of my novel "The Lizard's Tail," which had appeared in English in the United States in 1982. Because the novel offered a mythicized and damning version of recent Argentine history, it could not have been published there during the military dictatorship. Although no government official admitted then that there was censorship of any kind, the danger to writers and publishers was evident. Some writers suddenly disappeared; many were threatened by the paramilitary forces. Publishers' offices were bombed, and thousands of books were destroyed. The threat became so intense that in 1977, when I completed the novella "Other Weapons," which spoke about the torture and oppression so common at the time, I didn't even dare to show it around.

There could be no humor in "Other Weapons," but later, in "The Lizard's Tail," I felt freer to allow language to play its own games. Perhaps I needed the perspective of exile to unlock my imagination, to regain the feeling I had in 1975, when in one month I wrote the stories collected in "Strange Things Happen Here." Those were violent times too, but somehow the violence seemed out in the open then. We knew where the enemy was and felt there was a possibility of fighting back. To write those stories, I would go to cafés every day and pick up phrases or moods that would trigger them, and I used humor, the absurd, the grotesque, to break through the barrier of censorship. But as the violence became more and more perverse, I realized I could not fight back, could not speak out. I sensed I could not write anymore. I left in 1979.

It is true that the best-known writers remained in Argentina during the military dictatorship, among them Mr. Borges, Mr. Sábato, Adolfo Bioy Casares, Silvina Ocampo, Manuel Mujica Lainez, Beatrice Guido. In addition to many reprints of celebrated books by these writers, some of the new fiction published then in Argentina included Beatrice Guido's "La Invitación" ("The Invitation"), a tense novel of terror and oppression that takes place on the Patagonian ranch of a weapons dealer, and Manuel Mujica Lainez's last novel, "El Escarabajo" ("The Scarab"), the baroque history of a cursed ring from the time of the Pharaohs to our day.

I returned to Buenos Aires again last June and stayed four months. More and more valuable fiction by Argentine authors was being published. Some took the form of new editions of forbidden books, which rekindled the memory of those who had been murdered by the military. "Operación Masacre" ("Operation Massacre") was one of those. Its author, Rodolfo Walsh, had written some of the most dazzling short stories in the Spanish language. His love for literature killed him. He had created what he called "the polemic letters." In 1977, he wrote the last one, but it never reached the newspapers. Walsh was murdered as he was delivering it. The letter maintained that the Triple A, the name of the murderous Anti-Communist Association of Argentina, actually stood for the three branches of the armed forces.

Now the voices of those who were silenced come back stronger than ever. A new edition of the exceptional novel "Mascaró, el Cazador Americano" ("Mascaró, the American Hunter") by Haroldo Conti is finally being read *and understood* for its political metaphor. The protagonist, Oreste, joins a circus that awakens the spirits of the people living in small coastal towns. The circus is forced to dismantle, and Oreste is caught and tortured.

Torture in Argentina was once a daily occurrence, and Conti was one of its victims. He disappeared in 1977, never to return. The military was successful in dismantling the "circus." They destroyed the economy to such an extent that now, when there is freedom of speech and a hunger to read, books have become luxury items.

In a highly literate country of some 30 million people, "a book is a best seller today when it sells only 3,000 copies," says Daniel Divinski, the owner of the publishing house Ediciones de la Flor, who has returned from exile in Venezuela. Like him, many Argentine intellectuals have returned, despite their success in other countries, to confront the rotten economy. "Nobody is born a foreigner," they say, reinstalled in the very traditional café life of Buenos Aires. There the mood has changed, for those who are back—mainly from Mexico and Spain—tend to join together and reminisce. Of my peers, my two favorite writers have remained abroad. Sara Gallardo, who now lives in Italy, has depicted moving and memorable characters from the Argentine countryside. And in Paris, Alicia Dujovne Ortíz has just published her first book written in French. But there is nothing to fear: the book, "Buenos Aires," is a very personal and nostalgic song to her city.

New or re-established publishing houses are struggling to reinstate Argentina as the leader in the Latin American publishing world. In 1983 Bruguera Argentina was one of the first to bring out the works of a large number of Argentine writers, mostly documentary novels about Argentina's recent past. Some publishers, like Celtia, have even had the courage to specialize in short-story collections, ranging in subject from the fantastic to the political.

Since a good-quality paperback can cost as much as 10 pounds of sirloin steak, or up to 10 percent of a worker's monthly wage, some say the high price of books is equivalent to censorship. But books are published nevertheless. Since the major newspapers have good cultural supplements, talented writers who have emerged in the last few years are in the public eye, even though very few literary magazines have survived in the troubled economy. And in Buenos Aires, people can browse in bookstores that are open all night. I know a man who reads entire novels by going down Corrientes Avenue from bookstore to bookstore, reading a chapter in each.

In a posher part of the downtown area, the Clásica y Moderna bookstore has become a lively rendezvous for writers. When they get together, they often discuss the new awareness of Argentine literature. I see three main trends in this. One is the writing about the experience of departure and exile. Hector Tizón, back in his lovely northwestern province, Jujuy, in his house facing the mountains, recalls writing his poetic novel "La Casa del Viento" ("The House of the Wind"), in which the protagonist, moving toward the frontier, encounters all manner of loners. "I wrote it in Madrid in order to say goodbye to my land, my dogs and my characters," he says. "I thought I would never be able to come back."

The second current theme among Argentine writers is a combination of the picaresque and the utopian—using the very Argentine "grotesque" and passions perhaps built up during censorship to create novels full of dark reality and the joy of words, compensating for the previous impossibility of utterance.

The third is writing about history. Many recent novels have feasted on the country's history, very freely fictionalized. These novels not only work as antidotes for the official history texts—so manicured and antiseptic—but also as tools for understanding what has happened.

Argentina's social reality has given a political tint to its literature. Even our great Mr. Borges, who once said he was the only Argentine who didn't have a solution for the ills of his country, has finally accepted its political reality. Not only did he publish an emblematic short short story ("Juan López and Juan Ward") about a war between the Argentines and the British over two "now too famous islands," he made manifest his new political awareness while attending the recent trials of Argentine military leaders. Entering the Palace of Justice, he told reporters he approved of some form of amnesty. On his way out, he vented a very different opinion: "If just a tenth of what I've heard today is true, and I am sure it is, there should be no pity for the military."

Reporters follow Mr. Borges' every footstep; tourists drop by to visit him; he has become a national monument. "I don't know why they pay attention to me," he complains. "I am a simple man who enjoys simple pleasures, like discussing with my lifelong friend Adolfo Bioy Casares the works of Bustos Domecq. We like his books so much that I am afraid we actually write them."

More than any other reading material, the transcripts of the military trials, published in the daily newspapers and in a special weekly, allowed Argentines to recover their words, to acknowledge the pain and the panic that had muffled them for years. And with this reading came a need to write, to express themselves. Literary workshops—both private and government-sponsored—are now amazingly popular. People, young and old and from all walks of life, attend, and the government sends writers into poor neighborhoods to run the workshops. For the people of Argentina, writing has become a form of catharsis, "a way of erasing the guilt and shame of all that went unsaid," according to Hebe Solves, a poet and a pioneer in conducting literary workshops. There seems to be a public awareness that only by naming the terror can we avoid being terrorized again.

Perhaps my country was not misnamed after all. Its voice is coming back, and it rings with a silvery sound.

Isaac Goldemberg
[1945–]

THE CHRONOLOGICAL OUTLINES of Goldemberg's life to the present are documented in the pages that follow. Like many Latin Americans, he inherited several cultures through his mixed bloodline: Indian and Catholic Spanish on his mother's side and Russian Jewish on his father's. It was the awareness of his Jewish heritage in particular—and the claims it made on his emotions, politics, and psyche—that brought Goldemberg to experience a feeling of alienation in his native country, Peru. It is also at the heart of all his writing, from his early poetry, *Tiempo de silencio*, 1970 ["Time of Silence,"], and *De Chepén a la Habana*, 1973 ["From Chepén to Havana"], to his novels, *La vida fragmentaria de Don Jacobo Lerner*, 1976 [*The Fragmented Life of Don Jacobo Lerner*, 1977]—"a tragic and heroic parody of the legend of the Wandering Jew"—and most recently the bilingual edition of *Hombre de paso/Just Passing Through*, 1981, and *Tiempo al tiempo*, 1984 [*Play by Play*, 1985]. Like his countryman Vargas Llosa, Goldemberg only barely disguises his autobiographical self in his latest novel, which he also casts in the framework of popular culture—here, a soccer match—providing an apt metaphor for the clash of cultures within the adolescent protagonist. The battle between the New World and the Old—between his mother's and his father's legacies—is played out in his mind like a match narrated by an aggressively vivid broadcaster.

If it can be said that Latin Americans feel estranged from the rest of the world by virtue of their geography and culture, then Jews in Latin America risk being doubly estranged. Through literature, Goldemberg has found a way to mitigate his alienation by artistically externalizing, if not resolving, his cultural conflict.

Goldemberg has lived in New York City since 1964. After receiving a degree from City College, he began teaching at New York University in 1968. He is the coordinator of the Latin American Book Fair held annually in New York City.

These autobiographical pages, translated expressly for this collection, were originally published in the literary journal *Hispanamérica* in 1985.

On Being a Writer in Peru and Other Places

Isaac Goldemberg
Translated by David Unger

1945: Born in Chepén, a small village in northern Peru, about an hour and a half from Trujillo. My memory of the town and nearby landscape is rather hazy, made more so by the fact that time, distance, and my imagination have transformed it little by little. I think of it now as a lush area hemmed in by the desert, the ocean, and the Andes. What's certain is that Chepén wasn't on the coast, although it wasn't far from the sea. Our sea was the railroad tracks. And I'm also sure that the town was flanked by tropical vegetation. If it weren't, there'd be no way to explain the sweltering heat, the vast amounts of fruits, and those downpours that were like fists beating upon us. And the Andes? Cajamarca wasn't too far off; moreover, the Andes crisscross the whole of Peru both physically and spiritually.

I was born, yes, in Chepén in the bosom of the family that was questionably Catholic. From my maternal grandfather I inherited a bloodline whose roots were unclear: there was talk of English, Italian, and Basque ancestors who came to Peru in the middle of the nineteenth century, amassed a great fortune for the better part of fifty years, only to find themselves bankrupt by the twentieth century. As a result, my great-grandfather, Felipe Bay Zumarraga, ended his life by putting a bullet in his head. From my grandmother, a native of the Andean town of Cajamarca and a folk healer by trade, I inherited a stream of blood no less confused: Andalusian on one side, Indian on the other. From my father, a Russian Jew who immigrated to Peru in the thirties, I only inherited—at least for the first eight years of my life—the weight of his shadow.

Here's one fact that may be of interest: my birth date, November 15, and the town where my mother was born share a curious connection. According to history, on that very date four centuries earlier, the Spanish priest Valverde entered Cajamarca's main square, where the Spaniards and the Incas had gathered, and gave the Inca king the Bible saying: "Here's the word of God." Atahualpa took the book, put it to his ear, frowned, and tossed it into the air shouting: "I don't hear a thing." At that moment the Spaniards opened fire, scattering the Indians in all directions, and captured Atahualpa who, after he was granted the privilege of baptism, was condemned to the garrote.

1946: My family gives in to the parish priest's missionary zeal and has me baptized. Years later I would discover that, though my grandparents had ten children, my baptism was the only one my family ever celebrated. From then on, the parish priest becomes my father and the church a second home.

1948: One day an old man comes to the house claiming to have been sent from Lima by my father. He brings me a pile of gifts as if he were one of the Magi. One gift catches my eye: a six-pointed gold star. The old man ceremoniously places it around my neck while he says in a voice choked with emotion: "Don't ever take it off. You are one of us now." A few days later the star ends up at the bottom of a river. I weep over it all afternoon, and I remember being plagued night after night by awful nightmares in which an old gypsy, eyes ablaze, comes into my room and asks to know what happened to the star.

1950: I learn to read from two sources that, at first glance, seem contradictory: the Catholic missal and Hollywood movies. That's how I become the priest's helper during mass and the cinematographic reader of the family. Practically illiterate, my aunts and uncles take me to the movies so that I can read the Spanish subtitles to them. A youthful conflict develops: I'm not sure if I want to be a priest or an actor when I grow up.

1951: I read my very first book, *The New Testament*, and I also learn to write. I write my first book: I copy the Gospels word for word, letter for letter. My favorite is the Gospel according to John which starts off: "In the beginning was the Word."

1953: First exile: I leave my village for Lima. My father awaits me there and 5700 years of Judaism fall on me like a ton of bricks. My father takes me to his house and I submerge myself in it thinking my true home isn't here, but in the town that I've left behind. Soon I discover that my father is a Jew and that his world stretches beyond the borders of Peru. I begin to ask myself who am I, what am I. I hunt around for mirrors to see if I can recognize myself. No luck. I'm alone confronting my own fragmented image. I've got to be someone else, I tell myself, and that someone is my father. I must become what he is: a Jew. But to be a Jew I must erase my past. Thus, my second exile; from myself. I have to stop being in order to be.

1954: I begin attending León Pinelo, a Jewish school. It's the first day of school for me. I know no one, and in comes the teacher. He picks up a piece of chalk, scribbles some very weird symbols on the blackboard from right to left. Then he turns around and pronounces a few totally incomprehensible words. What's worse, the class then begins to repeat the teacher's words in a kind of litany. I sit there nailed to my chair wondering if I am going crazy. After four months of playing an invisible role in the class, I finally realize that they've been speaking Hebrew all along. That year I write my second book: an exact copy of a book of stories from the Hebrew Bible.

1955: I join the *Betar*, a club of young Zionists linked ideologically to Israel's Herut Party which advocated a Jewish homeland on both sides of the Jordan. Little by little Peru starts receding into the background: we study Peru's history, geography, and customs in school, but it's as if we were studying a foreign country. The Jewish community resembles a small Israeli ghetto nailed to the heart of Lima and, at the same time, it's also like a small Jewish village in Eastern Europe. For the first time I suffer an identity conflict when both my Jewish as well as my Peruvian friends ask me: "If Peru and Israel went to war, who would you fight for?" I tell my Jewish friends for Israel and my gentile Peruvian friends for Peru. That year I write my first original book, a lengthy narrative poem that tells a story of love and abandonment. The autobiographical link is clearly there: an Inca king conquers a foreign land, falls in love with a princess, and then returns to his kingdom not knowing that the princess is carrying his child.

1957: My father and I move into a new house that belonged to a friend of my father's who had emigrated with his family to Israel. It has an unbelievably huge library, full of books by French, Russian, and American authors. Peruvian writers stand out by their very absence; there are, however, an abundance of books by classical Jewish writers, especially those written by Sholem Aleichem.

1958: I'm now a writer. I begin to write a novel entitled *The Miser*. Set in my hometown, it is based upon my maternal grandfather. And yet, the landscape I describe is Russian, not Peruvian, and Chepén is a pretty faithful copy of Kasrilevke, the mythical town created by Sholem Aleichem. I can't get beyond chapter three. That same year I discover Cesar Vallejo's *Trilce* and Ciro Alegría's *El mundo es ancho y ajeno* [*The World is Far and Wide*], books written by writers born in La Libertad, my native province. I am particularly moved by those poems in *Trilce* that speak of family and home life. In Vallejo I find a familiar voice, a voice filled with echoes of my hometown. It is a voice—obviously I wouldn't discover this until years later—that not only reveals the poet's innermost conflicts but actually extends to the very roots of the thoughts and feelings of his *mestizo* race. I'm also deeply influenced by one of the central themes of Ciro Alegría's book: the world is a huge place, there are many areas to explore, but it will always be a foreign land for the Indians. Couldn't the same have been said about the Jews of the Diaspora?

1959: My bar mitzvah is celebrated early one Thursday morning. No more than twelve very old, wrinkled, and somber men show up at the synagogue. The ceremony lasts fives minutes, just enough time for me to stammar through the two prayers I had memorized. In April of that year, my father takes me out of the León Pinelo School and puts me in the Leoncio Prado Military Academy. I'm the only Jew in the whole school and, for the first time in my life, I come face-to-face with anti-Semitism. There's no point in behaving like a good Peruvian Catholic from Chepén. My first and last name give me away, and I find myself forced to defend my Jewishness with my fists.

1960: I read for the first time José María Arguedas' novel *Los ríos profundos* [Deep Rivers]. It's the story of a boy in search of his identity or, actually, in search of a way to reconcile his Western with his Indian roots. The boy wanders through a not very clearly defined world, caught between two cultures that clash not only on the surface but in the very heart of every Peruvian. This book by Arguedas would be vitally important to me and would spur me to examine a similar problem in my own writings: the cultural and racial crossbreeding in Peru, incorporating history and myth.

1962: Third exile: I finish high school and my father sends me to Israel to study agronomy. As I get off the boat in Haifa, I'm astonished to find that the dockworkers as well as all the people swarming around the piers are Jewish. An understandable reaction, if you consider that I was part of a community of barely five thousand Jews among 15 million Peruvians. I live in a kibbutz for a year, and then I spend another six months in a Haifa boarding house run by an Argentine lady. That's where I discover Borges and Kafka.

1963: I leave for Barcelona to study medicine. A month later I receive word of my father's death in Peru. I give up my medical studies, become an insurance salesman, and go back to work on the novel I had abandoned when I was twelve. It's still called *The Miser*, but now the book in set in Peru. Again, I get nowhere and I put it aside after writing three or four chapters. Twelve years later I would finally realize that if I wanted to write the book, I would have to make my father's world part of it.

1964: I return to Peru. All ties with my family, on both sides, have been broken. I'm married by now and my wife, a girl from New York that I had met in Israel, is about to give birth. I'm unable to get any work, and I feel estranged from my native land. Our first child is born, and our financial situation grows worse each day. Fourth exile: my wife convinces me that we should go live in New York. A month after our arrival, I enroll in college and, from 1964 until 1969, all I do is work and study. I do find time, however, to write two books of poetry. The first dies a quiet death at the bottom of a drawer. The second book, *Tiempo de silencio* [*Time of Silence*], is published in 1970 by a small press; the title is perfect, given the response it receives: not a word is written about it.

1973: My second book of poems, *De Chepén a la Habana* [*From Chepén to Havana*], is published in New York. I treat personal experiences in this book and I begin to explore Jewish themes for the first time. A few critics review the book, one of whom discovers a strange, exotic voice in my poetry. "The poems in this book," he said, "comprise a kind of journey in search of a traveler: the father. The poet is the prototypical uprooted man, traveling against the current of history as he searches for his roots." Already in this book of poems was the seed that four years later would give fruit to my first novel.

1977: My novel, *The Fragmented Life of Don Jacobo Lerner*, is published in an English translation. Using autobiographical material, it brings together the most important experiences of my childhood: my early Catholic upbringing, the experience of exile, the clash between Jewish and Peruvian culture. On the one hand, the novel establishes a sort of counterpoint between the short history of the Peruvian Jewish community and the much broader national experience. Yet, this reality plays against a much larger world: the four thousand or so years of Jewish history. To a large degree, the story of the novel—Jewish immigration to Peru in the 1920s, the life of Jacobo Lerner, etc.—is only a backdrop for the re-creation of an experience that is at once historical and mythical: the Jewish exile.

1981. Hombre de Paso/Just Passing Through, my third book of poems, is published in a bilingual Spanish/English edition. It includes several poems from *From Chepén to Havana* and is a kind of poetic autobiography: the attempt to create an "I" through the process of self-examination. The poetic "I" undertakes a journey that embraces a complex history, with many roots, times, and spaces. "The protagonist is 'passing through' at many levels: as someone subject to the world at large; as a victim of exile; and as the product of a process attempting to integrate his various cultural roots." Also, with this book, Peruvian critics began to notice the "Peruvian" quality of my writing, a discovery that forces them to reevaluate my first novel. "Goldemberg's novel," one of them suggests, "represents the start of a Judeo-Peruvian literary crossbreeding of special significance." With these words, I finally deserve Peruvian citizenship as a writer.

1984: My second novel, *Play by Play* is published; it reintroduces several themes that were developed in my earlier books. Underneath the plot line, this novel is a meditation on what it means or what it could mean to be Peruvian and/or Jewish. Throughout the whole book, characters and readers run up against the same question: what does it mean to be a Jew and/or a Peruvian? The novel offers, in a parodic style, the following answers:

> Let's see: To be Jewish and/or Peruvian is:
> *Ser*:
> *Estar*:
> A lucky star:
> It's to be from a country of sharp contrasts:
> It's to let the country go down the drain fast:
> It's to have a Hebe Mame:
> Or a screwed-up Mom:
> It's to warn a Jewish Mother:
> It's to belong to a race:
> To pray for belongings:
> To look for spiritual guidance:
> Or be a misguided spirit:
> It's a people:
> Not a steeple:
> A religion:
> It's to populate a region:
> A confluence of races:
> A race against integration:
> It's Zionism:
> Cynicism:
> Nonism:
> It's crazy:
> A destiny:
> A necessity:
> Something foolish:
> History:
> Hysteria:
> What is it?:

The novel suggests that you mark with a Cross (or a Star) the answer you—character or reader—think is correct.

CLARIBEL ALEGRÍA
[1924–]

CLARIBEL ALEGRÍA was only nine months old when her father, an antiinterventionist during the U.S. Marine occupation of Nicaragua, was forced into political exile. Thus, the Nicaraguan-born Alegría spent most of her early years in El Salvador. The year following her family's exile Augusto César Sandino began a guerrilla movement to protest foreign invasion and the puppet rule of the Somoza family; Alegría did not return to her native country until the victory of the FSLN (Sandinista Front for National Liberation) in 1979.

Alegría came to the United States in 1943 and earned a bachelor's degree from George Washington University. In 1947 she married Darwin J. Flakoll, with whom she has collaborated on a number of books in Spanish and English including *New Voices of Hispanic America: An Anthology*, 1962, and *Nicaragua: La revolución sandinista*, 1982 ["Nicaragua: The Sandinista Revolution"]. She has lived in Mexico, Chile, Uruguay, Mallorca, and most recently, in Nicaragua where she has been active in the Sandinista revolutionary cause. Alegría calls her poetry and prose "letras de emergencia" (emergency or crisis writing), an expression that captures the double meaning of the urgency and emerging spirit of her work.

Her writing has a strong testimonial quality, such as, for example, the novel *No me agarren vive: La mujer salvadoreña en lucha*, 1983 ["Don't Take Me Alive: The Salvadoran Woman in Combat"], in which the female protagonist becomes radicalized and joins the guerrilla forces. Alegría's political commitment to Sandinista Nicaragua is matched by her active concern for the status of women in Latin America and the need to address the entrenched prejudices of the social structure.

Her published works include novels, *Cenizas de Izalco*, 1966 ["Ashes of Izalco"] and *Albúm familiar*, 1982 ["Family Album"], as well as books of poetry, *Vía única*, 1965 ["One Way"]; *Sobrevivo*, 1978 ["I Survive"], which won the prestigious Casa de las Américas Prize; and the bilingual edition, *Flores del volcán/Flowers from the Volcano*, 1982, in which she evokes the terrible toll of war in her native and adopted countries. In the Preface to this last collection, the translator, Carolyn Forché, quotes Alegría as saying: "I have no *fusil* [rifle] in my hand, but only my testimony."

The accompanying essay was provided by the author in English. An earlier version of this essay appeared in 1984 in the journal *Fiction International* in an authors' forum on "Writing and Politics."

THE WRITER'S COMMITMENT

Claribel Alegría

Political commitment, in my view, is seldom a calculated intellectual strategy. It seems to me more like a contagious disease—athlete's foot, let's say, or typhoid fever—and if you happen to live in a plague area, the chances are excellent that you will come down with it. Commitment is a visceral reaction to the corner of the world we live in and what it has done to us and to the people we know. Albert Camus penned a phrase in "The Myth of Sisyphus" that impressed me profoundly. "If a man believes something to be true yet does not live in accordance with that truth," he said, "that man is a hypocrite."

Each of us writers, I have found, is obsessed with the personal equation and, however successfully he or she camouflages it, is surreptitiously pushing a world view.

"What am I doing here? Where am I going?"

These are the eternal existential—and profoundly political—questions, and the creative writer dedicates his life to communicating the answers he has stumbled across while negotiating the booby traps and barbed wire barricades of this twentieth-century obstacle course.

Let me be unashamedly personal, then. I spent the greater part of my life writing poetry, without the slightest notion that I had an obligation to commit myself literarily or politically to what was happening in my country—El Salvador—or my region—Central America.

There were political antecedents that marked me, of course. Thirty thousand peasants were slaughtered in El Salvador when I was seven years old. I remember with hard-edged clarity when groups of them, their crossed thumbs tied behind their backs, were herded into the National Guard fortress just across the street from my house, and I remember the *coup de grace* shots startling me awake at night. Two years later, I remember just as clearly my father, a Nicaraguan exile, telling me how

Anastasio Somoza, with the benediction of the Yankee minister, had assassinated Sandino the night before.

I left El Salvador to attend a U.S. University; I married, had children,
and wrote poetry, convinced that Central American dictators—Martínez,
Ubico, Carías, Somoza—were as inevitable and irremediable as the earth-
quakes and electrical storms that scourge my homeland.

The Cuban revolution demonstrated that social and political change
was possible in Latin America, but surely the Yankees with their helicopter gunships and Green Berets would never permit such a thing to
happen again. Nevertheless Fidel and Che sensitized me to the currents
of militant unrest just below the surface of the American *mare nostrum*
in the Caribbean. We watched the eddies and whirlpools from Paris and
later from Mallorca while I nourished my growing burden of middle-
class guilt. What was I doing sitting on the sidelines while my people
silently suffered the implacable repression of the Somoza dynasty in Nicaragua and the rotating colonel-presidents in El Salvador? Some of my
poems took on an edge of protest, and my husband and I wrote a novel
about my childhood nightmare: the 1932 peasant massacre.

I caught the political sickness from the Sandinista revolution. Shortly
after Somoza's overthrow in 1979, my husband and I went to Nicaragua
for six months to research a book about the historical epic of Sandino
and his successors of the FSLN. We were in Paris, on our way home to
Mallorca, when we heard of the assassination of Archbishop Oscar Ar-
nulfo Romero, the only Salvadoran figure of international prestige who
had served as the voice of the millions of voiceless in my country. In
response to that brutal and tragic event, all but two or three of El Salvador's artists and intellectuals made the quiet decision, without so much
as consulting each other, to do what we could to try to fill the enormous
vacuum left by his death.

Since then, I have found myself writing more and more poems and
prose texts that reflect the misery, the injustice, and the repression that
reign in my country. I am fully aware of the pitfalls of attempting to
defend a transient political cause in what presumes to be a literary work,
and I have tried to resolve that dilemma in a roughshod way by dividing
my writing into two compartments: the "literary-poetic," if you will, and
what I have come to think of as my "crisis journalism."

Political concerns do have a way of creeping into my poetry, however—simply because the Central American political situation is my major obsession, and I have always written poetry under obsession's spur.
When I think back, though, I can truly say that my "commitment" to
literature has always been, and remains, a simple attempt to make my
next poem less imperfect than the last.

But there is something further: in Central America today, crude reality inundates and submerges the ivory tower of "art for art's sake." What avant-garde novelist would dare write a work of imagination in which the Salvadoran people, in supposedly free elections, could only choose between Robert D'Aubuisson, the intellectual author of Monseigneur Romero's assassination and the recognized mentor of the infamous "Squadrons of Death" and José Napoleón Duarte, who, as the nation's highest authority for the greater part of the last four years, has systematically failed to bring the known perpetrators and executors of that sacrilegious deed to justice?

What Hollywood writer four short years ago could have envisioned a script in which all the horrors of Vietnam are being reenacted on the Central American isthmus?

America, America, God shed his grace on thee,
and crowned thy good with brotherhood,
from sea to shining sea.

Can this be the America that sends Huey helicopter gunships, A-37 Dragonflies, and "Puff, the magic dragon" to rain napalm and high explosives on the women, children, and old people in El Salvador's liberated zones, to convert the village of Tenancingo among others into a second Guernica? Is this the nation that christens Somoza's former assassins of the National Guard as "freedom fighters" and "the moral equivalent of the Founding Fathers" and sends them across the Nicaraguan border night after night to spread their message of democracy by slaughtering peasants, raping their women, and mowing down defenseless children while blowing up the cooperatives and health clinics and schools the Nicaraguans have so painfully constructed over the past six years?

How has America become entrapped in this morass of blood and death?

An American President, John F. Kennedy, made a prophetic statement twenty-five years ago. His words were: "Those who make peaceful evolution impossible, make violent revolution inevitable."

Anastasio Somoza, Jr., made peaceful evolution impossible in Nicaragua, so the Nicaraguan people had no choice but to overthrow him. Again today, as it has so often in the past, the U.S. government has allied itself with the forces in El Salvador who make peaceful evolution impossible: the forces that have put an abrupt end to the limping agrarian reform program, have encouraged a recrudescence of the Squadrons of Death—and have forced a suspension of peace negotiations with the FMLN-FDR.

The burning question for all of us today is: how will America find its way out of this bloody swamp?

Central American reality is incandescent, and if there be no place there for "pure art" and "pure literature" today, then I say so much the worse for pure art and pure literature. I do not know a single Central American writer who is so careful of his literary image that he sidesteps political commitment at this crucial moment in our history, and were I to meet one, I would refuse to shake his hand.

It matters little whether our efforts are admitted into the sacrosanct precincts of literature. Call them newspapering, call them pamphleteering, call them a shrill cry of defiance. My people, sixty percent of whom earn less than eleven dollars per month, know that only through their efforts today will it be possible for their children and grandchildren to eventually have equal opportunity to learn the alphabet and thus gain access to the great literature of the world: a basic human right that has been denied most of their elders.

Selected Bibliography

The following bibliography contains works of literary history and criticism which may be useful to those interested in learning more about the authors and issues presented in this volume. I have limited the list to easily accessible works published in English since 1960; for those fluent in Spanish or Portuguese, further bibliographies in both languages can be found in many of them.

Baceresse, Salvador. *Contemporary Latin American Fiction*. Edinburgh: Scottish Academic Press, 1980.

Brotherston, Gordon. *The Emergence of the Latin American Novel*. New York: Cambridge University Press, 1977.

Brushwood, John S. *The Spanish-American Novel: A Twentieth Century Survey*. Austin: University of Texas Press, 1975.

Chevigny, Beu Gale, and Gari LaGuardia, eds. *Reinventing the Americas: Comparative Studies of Literature of the United States and Spanish America*. Cambridge: Cambridge University Press, 1986.

Coutinho, Afrânio. *An Introduction to Literature in Brazil*. New York: Columbia University Press, 1969.

Donoso, José. *The Boom in Spanish American Literature: A Personal History*. Trans. Gregory Kolovakos. New York: Columbia University Press in association with the Center for Inter-American Relations, 1977.

Foster, David W. *The Twentieth Century Spanish-American Novel: A Bibliographic Guide*. Metuchen, NJ: Scarecrow Press, 1975.

Foster, Merlin H., ed. *Tradition and Renewal: Essays on Twentieth Century Latin American Literature and Culture*. Urbana: University of Illinois Press, 1975. (See Luis Leal, "Native and Foreign Influences in Contemporary Mexican Fiction," pp. 102–128.)

Franco, Jean. *The Modern Culture of Latin America: Society and the Artist*. New York: Praeger, 1967.

Fuentes, Carlos. *Latin America at War with the Past*. Toronto: CBC Enterprises, 1985.

314   SELECTED BIBLIOGRAPHY

González Echevarría, Roberto. *The Voice of the Masters: Writing and Authority in Modern Latin American Literature*. Austin: University of Texas Press, 1985.

Harss, Luis, and Barbara Dohmann. *Into the Mainstream: Conversations with Latin-American Writers*. New York: Harper & Row, 1967.

Jacobson, Richard L. *Black Writers in Latin America*. Albuquerque: University of New Mexico Press, 1979. (See part 3.)

MacAdam, Alfred. *Modern Latin American Narratives: Dreams of Reason*. Chicago: University of Chicago Press, 1977.

Magnarelli, Sharon. *The Lost Rib: Female Characters in the Spanish-American Novel*. Lewisburg, PA: Bucknell University Press, 1985.

Menton, Seymour. *Prose Fiction of the Cuban Revolution*. Austin: University of Texas Press, 1975. (See part 2: "Literature and Revolution.")

Meyer, Doris, and Margarite Fernandez Olmos, *Contemporary Women Authors of Latin America: Introductory Essays*. Brooklyn, NY: Brooklyn College Press, 1983.

Miller, Beth, ed. *Women in Hispanic Literature: Icons and Fallen Idols*. Berkeley, Los Angeles, London: University of California Press, 1983.

Muñoz, Braulio. *Sons of the Wind: The Search for Identity in Spanish-American Indian Literature*. New Brunswick, NJ: Rutgers University Press, 1982. (See chapters 8 and 9.)

"On Literature and Exile." (Special section) *Review 30* (September–December 1981): 10–23. (A publication of the Center for Inter-American Relations, *Review* is a primary source of information about English-language translations of Latin American literature. This section includes essays in English by Angel Rama, Augusto Roa Bastos, Julio Cortázar, and Fernando Alegría.)

Schulman, Ivan, ed. *Latin America in Its Literature*. Trans. Mary G. Berg. New York: Holmes & Meier, 1980. (See E. Rodríguez Monegal, "Tradition and Renewal," pp. 87–114.)

Schwartz, Ronald. *Nomads, Exiles and Emigrés: The Rebirth of the Latin American Narrative, 1960–1980*. Metuchen, NJ: Scarecrow, 1980.

Stabb, Martin S. *In Quest of Identity: Patterns in the Spanish American Essay of Ideas, 1890–1960*. Chapel Hill: University of North Carolina Press, 1967.

"The Latin American Novel Today." (Special issue) *Books Abroad* (Winter 1970): 7–50. (Published since 1978 under the new title *World Literature Today*, this journal is also a significant English-language source of information about Latin American literature. Special issues have been devoted to García Márquez, Summer 1973; Vargas Llosa, Winter 1978; Octavio Paz, Autumn 1982; and Carlos Fuentes, Autumn 1983.)

Tittler, Jonathan. *Narrative Irony in the Contemporary Spanish-American Novel*. Ithaca, NY: Cornell University Press, 1984.

Designer: Linda M. Robertson
Compositor: Auto-Graphics, Inc.
Text: 10/12 Galliard
Display: Galliard